Selections from
Friedrich Schleiermacher's
Christian Ethics

LIBRARY OF THEOLOGICAL ETHICS

Basic Christian Ethics, by Paul Ramsey
Christ and the Moral Life, by James M. Gustafson
Christianity and the Social Crisis, by Walter Rauschenbusch
Conscience and Its Problems, by Kenneth E. Kirk
Economic Justice: Selections from "Distributive Justice" and "A Living Wage," by John A. Ryan, edited by Harlan Ray Beckley
Ethics in a Christian Context, by Paul L. Lehmann
Feminist Theological Ethics: A Reader, edited by Lois K. Daly
Georgia Harkness: The Remaking of a Liberal Theologian, edited by Rebekah Miles
The Holy Spirit and the Christian Life: The Theological Basis of Ethics, by Karl Barth
Love and Justice: Selections from the Shorter Writings of Reinhold Niebuhr, edited by D. B. Robertson
The Meaning of Revelation, by H. Richard Niebuhr
Moral Discernment in the Christian Life, by James M. Gustafson
Moral Man and Immoral Society, by Reinhold Niebuhr
Morality and Beyond, by Paul Tillich
The Nature and Destiny of Man: A Christian Interpretation (2 vols.), by Reinhold Niebuhr
Radical Monotheism and Western Culture: With Supplementary Essays, by H. Richard Niebuhr
Reconstructing Christian Ethics: Selected Writings, by F. D. Maurice, edited by Ellen K. Wondra
Religious Liberty: Catholic Struggles with Pluralism, by John Courtney Murray, edited by J. Leon Hooper
The Responsible Self: An Essay in Christian Moral Philosophy, by H. Richard Niebuhr
Situation Ethics: The New Morality, by Joseph Fletcher
The Social Teaching of the Christian Churches (2 vols.), by Ernst Troeltsch
The Structure of Christian Ethics, by Joseph Sittler
The Ten Commandments: The Reciprocity of Faithfulness, edited by William P. Brown
A Theology for the Social Gospel, by Walter Rauschenbusch
Treasure in Earthen Vessels: The Church as a Human Community, by James M. Gustafson
War in the Twentieth Century: Sources in Theological Ethics, edited by Richard B. Miller

Selections from Friedrich Schleiermacher's *Christian Ethics*

FRIEDRICH SCHLEIERMACHER

Edited and Translated by
James M. Brandt

WESTMINSTER
JOHN KNOX PRESS
LOUISVILLE • KENTUCKY

© 2011 Westminster John Knox Press

First edition
Published by Westminster John Knox Press
Louisville, Kentucky

11 12 13 14 15 16 17 18 19 20—10 9 8 7 6 5 4 3 2 1

Selections from *Die christliche Sitte nach den Grundsätzen der evangelishcen Kirche im zusammenhänge dargestellt*, originally published in *Sämmtliche Werke* div. 1, vol. 12 edited by Ludwig Jonas (Berlin: G. Reimer, 1843).

Scripture quotations are translated from Luther's *Bibel.*

Book design by Sharon Adams
Cover design by Lisa Buckley

Library of Congress Cataloging-in-Publication Data

Schleiermacher, Friedrich, 1768–1834.
  [Christliche Sittenlehre. English. Selections]
  Selections from Friedrich Schleiermacher's Christian Ethics / Friedrich Schleiermacher ; edited and translated by James M. Brandt.
    p. cm.—(Library of theological ethics)
  Includes index.
  ISBN 978-0-664-22611-4 (alk. paper)
  1. Christian ethics. I. Brandt, James M., 1952– II. Title.
  BJ1253.S3213 2011
241—dc22

2010033599

PRINTED IN THE UNITED STATES OF AMERICA

Westminster John Knox Press advocates the responsible use of our natural resources. The text paper of this book is made from 30% postconsumer waste.

For my parents,

Irene E. Brandt
and
Victor L. Brandt,

and for my students and colleagues of
Saint Paul School of Theology

Contents

*Phrases within brackets are supplied subheads. Subheads not in brackets are translated from *Christliche Sittenlehre* (see © page). Chapter numbers have been added, and "A" and "B" have been deleted from original subheads.

PART ONE: EFFICACIOUS ACTION

DIVISION I: RESTORING OR PURIFYING ACTION

DIVISION II: BROADENING ACTION

Library of Theological Ethics
General Editors' Introduction

The field of theological ethics possesses in its literature an abundant inheritance concerning religious convictions and the moral life, critical issues, methods, and moral problems. The Library of Theological Ethics is designed to present a selection of important texts that would otherwise be unavailable for scholarly purposes and classroom use. The series engages the question of what it means to think theologically and ethically. It is offered in the conviction that sustained dialogue with our predecessors serves the interests of responsible contemporary reflection. Our more immediate aim in offering it, however, is to enable scholars and teachers to make more extensive use of classic texts as they train new generations of theologians, ethicists, and ministers.

The volumes included in the Library comprise a variety of types. Some make available English-language texts and translations that have fallen out of print; others present new translations of texts previously unavailable in English. Still others offer anthologies or collections of significant statements about problems and themes of special importance. We hope that each volume will encourage contemporary theological ethicists to remain in conversation with the rich and diverse heritage of their discipline.

ROBIN W. LOVIN
DOUGLAS F. OTTATI
WILLIAM SCHWEIKER

Preface and Acknowledgments

My scholarly work in historical theology has never wandered far from Friedrich Schleiermacher's *Christliche Sittenlehre*, or *Christian Ethics*. I was first directed to this often-overlooked work by my adviser at the University of Chicago, B. A. Gerrish. In the 1980s, when denominational identity retained much more force than it has today, Gerrish urged his graduate students to write dissertations on figures who were not from the student's denomination. As I understand it, this had been Gerrish's own experience under Wilhelm Pauck: Gerrish, a Presbyterian, wrote on Luther (his magnificent study on Luther and Reason).[1] For me, lifelong Lutheran that I am, the Reformed Schleiermacher fit the bill. Because of my interest in matters of faith and culture and because of the need for a new study of the *Christian Ethics*, I was drawn to this text.

As part of the research for my dissertation, I produced a rough translation of the whole of the Jonas edition of the *Christian Ethics*—over seven hundred pages in length. Eventually my dissertation was revised and published.[2] Shortly thereafter I approached Westminster John Knox about a translation of the *Ethics*, thinking that the rough translation needed only some polishing. I had forgotten how maddeningly complex Schleiermacher's German can be. I have been through the selections that appear in this volume at least four times and, though I am confident enough to publish them here, I know that I, for one, could labor much longer on any number of passages and still have hesitations.

I am pleased that this work has found a home in the Library of Theological Ethics, a fitting place for it, alongside other treasures from the tradition of Christian ethical thinking. I am grateful for the encouragement of editor Jana Riess. Her keen eye has improved the work in numerous ways. Thanks to William Schweiker for reading the "Translator's Introduction" and making helpful suggestions.

For over twenty years now I have been privileged to teach at Saint Paul School of Theology. I am indebted to many in that school for the experience of community where rigorous thought is pursued in service of faith and ecclesial life, always with commitment to matters of peace and justice. In gratitude I dedicate this book to all the students and colleagues who have been partners in the enterprise of theological reflection. Thanks to student John Slattery for reviewing portions of the text with me. I am grateful to Harold Washington for suggestions about translation of Latin phrases and Israel Kamudzandu for Greek. To Jeanne Hoeft, with whom I have the honor of leading students to Guatemala and who read and commented on early drafts of the translation, I say "Gracias."

My parents, Irene and Victor Brandt, have supported me through good times and bad. As a small token of my gratitude and love, I also dedicate this book to them.

Over the years I have received innumerable helpful suggestions about difficult texts in Schleiermacher from Edwina Lawler and Terence Tice. They are both excellent colleagues. And then, for a week each summer for the years 2004–2009, Terry and his spouse, Catherine Kelsey (a fine Schleiermacher scholar in her own right), opened their home to me. I stayed as their guest. All day long, often into the evening, Terry and I pored over the *Christian Ethics*. We rejoiced each time a challenging passage was rendered into coherent English. Terry and Cathy are wonderful hosts and scholars. It was a joy to share Schleiermacher and life with them. This translation is so much the better for their contributions. Any and all imperfections that remain are to be called to my account.

I am grateful that my three sons, Matthias, Jesse, and Micah, bore with me over the long haul of this translation project. No better reward for us all than to canoe together (with Tray) in the BWCA. Also, Kathryn Fuger has been by my side for much of the time I've labored on this project. I am blessed and humbled by her love and encouragement and hope that I return them in some measure.

James M. Brandt
Kansas City, MO
Eastertide 2010

Translator's Introduction

By James M. Brandt

The work of Friedrich Schleiermacher (1768–1834) represents a crucial turn-
ing point in the history of Christian theology. This is variously identified as
the beginning of modern or liberal Protestant theology or of the "New Protestantism" as contrasted with the Reformation movement launched by Luther
and Calvin. Schleiermacher's theological magnum opus, the *Christian Faith*
(or *Glaubenslehre*), is regularly classed with the *Summa theologiae* of Thomas
Aquinas, Calvin's *Institutes of the Christian Religion*, and Barth's *Church Dogmatics* as among the great systematic expressions of Christian theology. However,
Schleiermacher's work in theological ethics is as overlooked as the *Christian
Faith* is celebrated, an oversight that must be addressed.

The *Christian Faith* represents work in dogmatic theology that is genuinely
new, providing a paradigmatic shift in theological self-understanding after the
insights and ravages of Enlightenment developments; likewise, the *Christian
Ethics* provides a renewal of ethics that is distinctively Christian and Protestant, engaging and transcending the intellectual currents of its own time, with
potential to speak to Christian ethical thinking in the present. Published posthumously in 1843, Schleiermacher's *Christian Ethics* describes the actions that
flow from Christian self-consciousness or piety, actions that are oriented to the
reign of God on earth as the highest good, actions that constitute life in Christian community and Christian participation in the civil society. Schleiermacher
achieves a comprehensive vision that includes all areas of human life: aspects of
ecclesial life include education/formation, discipline and reform, public worship
and witness in daily life; in the "outer sphere," attention is given to aspects of
social life, including economic and educational life, life in the family, governmental structures, criminal justice and warfare, artistic expression and "free sociality." The *Christian Ethics* can be characterized as combining an ecclesial ethics
of piety and a transformative theology of culture.

1

In Schleiermacher's distinctive vision, ethics attends to human historical life; it describes the processes by which reason or spirit forms nature to be its agent and organ. Reason's ongoing formation of nature is the moral task common to all humanity. Christian ethics appropriates this task and addresses it from its own point of view. It takes up all cultural life for itself, giving the whole process a new telos: the glory of God. This marks Schleiermacher's ethical project as at once humanistic in attending to the moral task common to all humanity, distinctively Christian in that all Christian activity is grounded in the higher consciousness given in Christ, and theocentric in letting the Christian vision orient all human good to the highest good of the reign of God. At the same time, the *Christian Ethics* exhibits historical consciousness that recognizes and embraces the historical, contextual, and embedded character of all theological construction, including Christian ethics itself: there can be no final statement of Christian ethics because it must always be appropriate to a particular sociohistorical context. This is also an ecclesial ethics: Christian community is the living body of Christ and is the sine qua non of the Christian life. This *Ethics* has the church as its ground and goal, and it operates with a polar opposition between the individual and the universal. Above all, this means recognition that the individual cannot exist apart from the community or whole. Still, Schleiermacher affirms the uniqueness of individual persons and communities and recognizes that Christian spirit manifests itself uniquely in different individuals. Individual difference is to be valorized and respected.

These themes indicate something of the complex character of Schleiermacher's project in Christian ethics. His ethical theory emerges out of deep engagement with the intellectual and cultural currents of his time. Schleiermacher reappropriates elements from his own heritage in the Protestant Reformation, the Pietist tradition in which he was formed, the critical spirit of the Enlightenment— above all Kant, and the developing romantic movement. Taking elements from each of these sources, he fashions his *Ethics* out of this material and creates something genuinely new. Making these selections from the *Christian Ethics* available in English translation will enable more direct engagement with the depth and detail of Schleiermacher's thought and add his voice to the conversation about Christian ethics among English-speaking scholars and students.[1]

CULTURAL, INTELLECTUAL, AND THEOLOGICAL CONTEXT

Schleiermacher's philosophical and theological project, including his *Christian Ethics*, responded to and was shaped by the cultural and intellectual movements of the day. Above all, it engaged the Enlightenment project that culminated in many ways in Kant's philosophy and the romantic movement that was coming to flower during Schleiermacher's first stay in Berlin (1796–1803). The religious and theological currents of the time—Protestant Orthodoxy, Pietism, and the "natural religion" of rationalist thinkers—were also influential elements in the context that shaped Schleiermacher as a person and thinker. He forged his project by engaging these diverse movements and currents, taking up elements from each and reacting against other elements. It was his genius to envision human life—particularly its religious and ethical dimensions—in a way that transcended what had gone before. In what follows, we will briefly sketch Schleiermacher's relation with his context.

The Enlightenment of the seventeenth and eighteenth centuries marks the birth of the modern world in the West. Working at a high level of generalization that does not do justice to the diversity among Enlightenment figures, we can characterize the movement as being manifest above all in modern scientific and political thinking that develops along with the philosophical turn to reason, experience, and utility. Isaac Newton was the hero of the age. Philosophers developed great confidence in the powers of human reason and faith that a mathematical model of deduction could deliver certainty and universal truth in all realms of human endeavor: scientific, political, religious, and moral. Enlightenment thinkers saw education as the key to progress in all these realms. They possessed a spirit of critical inquiry and subjected all claims to critique. Reason and critique were brought to bear against traditional authorities in church and state. Wearied by the religious warfare that ravaged Europe in the century and a half following the Reformation, Enlightenment thinkers challenged dogmatism and intolerance. Aesthetic expression in this period stressed order and form. The straight neoclassical lines in architecture and exquisite form of Mozart's music come to mind. The German expression of enlightenment (*Aufklärung*) focused on religious and philosophical issues and was kept away from the explicitly political reflection of its French and British counterparts by the tight rein that German princes exercised over intellectuals. Schleiermacher appropriated the Enlightenment's critical spirit and brought it to bear in his theological work, including his *Christian Ethics*. Critical appropriation of the inherited tradition of Christian ethics was a hallmark of this work, not least in its turn away from an imperative ethics of duty in favor of description of the Christian life as oriented toward the highest good.

Romanticism resists definition even more than does the Enlightenment movement to which it responds. Romanticism turned toward artistic expression—especially poetry and the novel—and the imagination in contrast to the Enlighteners' emphasis on reason, logic, and science. There was also a related turn toward history, particularity, and individual uniqueness against the Enlightenment's stress on atemporal, universal truths. The passion of Brahms's music and the fairy tales collected by the brothers Grimm exemplify the romantic sensibility. For the romantics, the infinite was present in the finite and revealed itself in the unfolding of history—especially in art, in individuals of genius, and in the distinctive cultural and social life of peoples and nations. Schleiermacher was a member of the romantic circle in Berlin in the late 1790s, a circle that included the Schlegel brothers (Friedrich and A. W.) and the poets Novalis, Ludwig Tieck,

Friedrich Hölderlin, and Jean Paul. At the insistence of his roommate Friedrich Schlegel, Schleiermacher published his first great work, *On Religion: Speeches to Its Cultured Despisers*. This work is imbued with a romantic spirit, particularly in its understanding of religion as "sensibility and taste for the infinite," a "holy soul stirred by the universe," and "love [of the] world spirit."[2] This turn, to focus on the character of religion as feeling of the infinite, is appropriately identified as the founding of modern, or liberal, Protestant theology.

Taken together with recognition of the historically mediated, dynamic character of religious traditions, Schleiermacher strikes a balance between subjectivity and the corporate character of tradition where authentic religiosity is found. This balance marks all of Schleiermacher's theological work, including his *Christian Ethics*. The *Ethics* is grounded in Christian self-consciousness or piety that exists only in the context of tradition-formed community moving within the flux of history. These characteristics, consistent with romantic sensibility, shape the *Ethics* in prominent ways.

In seeking to assess where Schleiermacher stands in relation to the Enlightenment and to romanticism, it is probably best to join Richard Crouter in acknowledging that he combines themes from both movements in a distinctive way. "For Schleiermacher the artistry of poetic insight, the desire to clarify categories, and dialectical turns of reason prominent in early German Romanticism combine to feed his Enlightenment rationality."[3] The *Christian Ethics* is enlivened by a critical rationality and historical consciousness that affirm individual uniqueness and subjectivity, freedom from coercion, historic forms of social relationships (family, church, state) in which equality and mutuality are normative. A strong case can be made that this ethical vision is infused with a commitment to Enlightenment rationality modified by concerns characteristic of early German romanticism.

We can also detect the influence of Moravian Pietism on Schleiermacher's life and thought. Friedrich's father, Gottlieb Schleiermacher, experienced a Pietist awakening under the influence of the Moravians in 1778. Friedrich was subsequently schooled by the Moravians for four formative years, first at their school in Niesky in 1783–85 and then at their seminary in Barby in 1785–87. Despite his later break with the Moravians, Schleiermacher carried with him something of their stress on personal conviction, their deep sense of mystic communion with the Savior, and their emphasis on formation in faith by means of pious practices. After his critical turn, Schleiermacher refers to himself as a "Moravian of a higher order." There are ways in which the *Christian Ethics* reflects a Pietist sensibility: ethics grounded in pious self-consciousness, emphasis on the importance of personal relationships within the Christian community, and appeal to practices such as care for the poor and sick that function as a form of repentance or restoration of one's spirit.

Schleiermacher never had the kind of intimate connection with Protestant Orthodoxy that he had with Pietism, but he knew the systematic theologies of Orthodox thinkers, with their concerns to protect and defend their own

Lutheran or Reformed confessional tradition. It is noteworthy that "in form, if not always in substance, the *Christian Faith* preserved connection with the great dogmatic systems of Protestant Orthodoxy."[4] Schleiermacher also reports that the first time he lectured on dogmatic theology, he consulted the theological systems of Johannes Andreas Quenstedt (1617–88) and Johann Gerhard (1582–1637), both orthodox Lutheran theologians, and cites both of them in the *Christian Faith*.[5] In his *Ethics* as in his dogmatics, Schleiermacher gives central place to redemption in Christ; this is a prime example of a way in which Schleiermacher "preserves connection" with orthodoxy. Closer comparison with the ethical work of orthodox theologians reveals significant differences in conception and approach. Where the orthodox theologians understand ethics in terms of obedience to the command of God and appeal to the Decalogue, the Sermon on the Mount, or other biblical injunctions, Schleiermacher proposes a descriptive ethics that lays out the "distinguishing characteristics of the Christian life"[6] as they are appropriate in the current context. He asserts that the actions of Christians are "actually continuations of the action of Christ himself." The actions of Christ "established the reign of God, at which all Christian action aims, and indicated its characteristics, so that all action of the Christian church is nothing but the realization of these characteristics."[7] Thus Schleiermacher departs from orthodoxy and its imperative, biblical ethics; instead he lays out a descriptive ethics that is focused on the continuing action of Christ in and through the church.

Given this grounding of ethics in redemption by Christ and the way it is lived out in the Christian community, Schleiermacher stands closer to orthodoxy and Pietism than he does to Enlightenment rationalism, with its appeal to "natural religion." German rationalism amounted to a reduction of religion to morality, which reaches its pinnacle in Kant. The creed of natural religion can be fairly characterized as belief in the existence of a Supreme Being who is worthy of worship. Since God is perfectly happy in Godself, the only worship that has meaning is moral action that tends to human fulfillment. Added to this is the belief that good will be rewarded and evil punished, in this life or the next. So this German rationalist credo is often summarized as belief in God, morality, and immortality. Kant's thinking in his second critique, the *Critique of Practical Reason*,[8] represents a heightening of this moralization of religion such that "rationally permissible belief structure now explicitly rests on the self-certifying moral experience."[9]

Several features of the second critique deserve mention. Kant begins with the human sense of moral obligation: the sense of "ought" that confronts us as duty. Since "ought" implies "can," the moral sense leads to the postulation of human freedom as the necessary ground for the possibility of moral experience. And since, in the end, there must be unity of virtue and happiness, of duty and desire, God and human immortality must also be postulated in order that this unity may be obtained. Notice here that Kant begins with moral sense and then moves to postulate "religious" claims about God and immortality. Materially,

Kant's ethics is deontological, an ethics of duty. He distinguishes between the Categorical Imperative, which on the one hand defines the moral duty to which we are obligated simply because it is right, and hypothetical imperatives, which on the other hand are teleological: we perform certain actions in order to attain certain ends. For Kant, there is a deep chasm between the noumenal realm of freedom, duty, and motive, which is the moral realm governed by the Categorical Imperative—and the phenomenal realm of determinism, goals, and inclination, which is the realm of nature governed by hypothetical imperatives. This also represents a dualistic view of the human self in which there is a gap between reason/morality and body, a gap between intention and action. One result is that it is not possible to judge the "objective" morality of any action since morality resides with intention, with the motive behind the action.

As we noted above, Schleiermacher had drunk deeply at the well of Enlightenment critique. Kant's first critique, with its clear sense of reason's limits and its rejection of reason's ability to make metaphysical claims, shaped Schleiermacher's early thinking and stayed with him throughout his intellectual career. On the other hand, the conception of religion as feeling or intuition in the *Speeches* represents a strong reaction against Enlightenment identification of religion as knowledge or morality, a strong preference for the positive religions as places where religious sensibility can be cultivated, and a corresponding rejection of natural religion. This rationalistic conception falls short of the living reality of pious feeling because it fails to grasp the kernel of religion, its inward subjective feeling. Instead it satisfies itself with dogmas and opinions—the husks, which provide no nourishment. Schleiermacher never wavers from these commitments first articulated in the *Speeches*. The *Christian Ethics'* grounding in piety from which flow thought and action continues this emphasis on the subjective character of religion.

The *Christian Ethics* also reverses Kant's second critique by making the theological moment precede and ground the ethical moment. Although Kant begins with the sense of moral obligation and moves to postulate freedom, God, and immortality, for Schleiermacher Christian ethics

> must be a presentation of communion with God as determined by communion with Christ, the Redeemer, inasmuch as this is the motivation for all Christian action. It can be nothing other than a description of those ways of acting which arise from the dominion of Christianly determined religious self-consciousness.[10]

So, not only does Schleiermacher begin with the pious moment of communion with God; this also grounds his descriptive approach. Instead of Kant's imperative ethics of duty, Schleiermacher develops a descriptive approach to an ethics of the highest good. The *Ethics* provides a kind of phenomenological description of the Christian life. Finally, and very importantly, Schleiermacher's conception of the human agent, the ethical self, differs from that of Kant. For Kant, at least in the first two critiques, there is a gap between the noumenal realm of freedom, reason, and duty on the one hand, and the phenomenal realm of determinism, nature, and goals on the other hand; but for Schleiermacher the "original unity of mind and body, subject and object, thinking and being, percept and perceiver" is presupposed by human experience.[11] Thus Schleiermacher asserts an "organic self—the embodied self,"[12] which means that the ethical task is reason's appropriation of nature. In the *Christian Ethics* this is described as the process by which Christian spirit and flesh are united: flesh comes to be the organ of spirit, spirit the agent of flesh. In this way, ethics is conceived as a process that involves formation of the embodied self over time and finds expression through particular practices that constitute the Christian life. All this is directed toward the highest good of the reign of God and is based in the experience of redemption, an experience of (relative) blessedness. So Schleiermacher begins with a theologically defined moment—the experience of blessedness in redemption—and sees this as grounding the ethical moment as it initiates a process that is expressed by means of action and that drives toward a goal—the reign of God. In these ways Schleiermacher's theological, descriptive, and teleological ethics, based in a sense of human embodiment, stands in stark contrast to Kant's ethical vision.

THE *CHRISTIAN ETHICS* IN SCHLEIERMACHER'S PHILOSOPHICAL SYSTEM

The *Christian Ethics* occupies a particular place within Schleiermacher's overall philosophical-theological system, and it will be helpful to indicate that place with some precision. In his *Dialektik*, Schleiermacher puts forward his comprehensive view of all human knowledge. Schleiermacher does not claim that *Dialektik* generates all knowledge; rather it presupposes all the processes of human knowledge already in place and seeks to bring that knowledge to self-consciousness or transparency by naming its tasks, presuppositions, limits, and structures.[13] Thus *Dialektik* remains at a purely formal level, but it also identifies the two "real" sciences: physics and ethics. Physics deals with nature, while ethics concerns itself with reason as manifest in human history. Both of these realms of knowledge include a speculative and empirical side, based on two different ways of knowing. Speculative knowledge seeks to identify the essence of particular areas of knowledge and names the concepts necessary to understand that area. Empirical knowledge concerns things in their existence and makes judgments about forms of knowledge manifest in history. Empirical knowledge depends upon the concepts identified by speculative knowledge while also testing the adequacy of these concepts. All of these disciplines have a descriptive character.[14]

In addition to his *Christian Ethics* (which is empirical, attending to the manifestation of reason or spirit in the Christian tradition), Schleiermacher produced a *Philosophical Ethics*. This complex work, based on lecture notes that Schleiermacher revised, was published posthumously. We note only those aspects of the work that are most germane to our purposes. The task of philosophical ethics is speculative: to identify the basic concepts, structures, and rules operative in human historical-cultural life. Thus we might think of the *Philosophical Ethics* as a "phenomenology of the activity of moral reason in history,"[15] identifying the concepts necessary to understand cultural life.[16] Schleiermacher intends his *Philosophical Ethics* to be comprehensive of all aspects of culture: the task is to describe the products of reason in various spheres of life. What reason produces is connected to what Schleiermacher identifies as the four great forms of human community in cultural life: the state, "free sociality," school and academy, and the church. These four communities correspond to the four basic products of human reason. Schleiermacher asserts that reason can have either a symbolizing or an organizing function. Reason organizes nature and shapes it for its own ends.

Nature becomes the organ of reason when, for example, agricultural work shapes the natural world for human ends or when a group of friends come together to celebrate a birthday. The farm and the party are concrete examples of nature becoming the organ of reason so that human spirit is manifest in a productive way. The farm and the party differ from each other because agriculture embodies a form of reason that is predominantly "identical": the rules governing agricultural production have an objective character to them. On the other hand, the party embodies a form of reason that is predominantly "individual," in that there is much more freedom for ways in which the party might be shaped—much more room for individual differences in expression, all of which could be equally reasonable. Agriculture, like all economic activity (and the political activity that oversees and governs it), falls under the rubric of the state, while a party is an instance of free sociality. In contrast to reason's organizing function is its symbolizing function. In this case nature becomes the symbol of reason making human communication possible through a system of signs and symbols.

Nature becomes the symbol of reason, for example, when individuals gather for an academic conference or when people come together for religious worship or in a musical organization. The academic conference represents the "identical" side of reason since the objective and identical pole dominates here. On the other hand, worship or a chorus manifests the predominantly "individual" side of reason for in these cases there is great diversity in the ways that reason can be expressed. The academic conference falls under the form of academy (and school) because the focus is on knowledge, while worship falls under the church or religious community. The chorus as a form of artistic expression has no specific community to which it refers (corresponding to church in the realm of religion), but art, like religion, expresses the "individual" side of symbolizing reason.

The differences among these four manifestations of reason and corresponding forms of human community are relative, and Schleiermacher asserts that actual human life most often includes aspects of two or more of these manifestations. This can be seen in the fact that both the family as the most basic form of human community and the highest good (conceived as the perfection and interpenetration of all four areas and communities in and for all persons) comprehend all four elements in themselves. Even more, the perfection of any of the four distinct communities would include the other three communities within itself and would represent the whole.[17] Thus an important aspect of the *Philosophical Ethics* is how, in a formal way, it lays out the drive of reason toward the highest good, defined as the complete fulfillment of all manifestations of reason and encompassing all persons.

Forms of Reason and Forms of Human Community in Schleiermacher's Philosophical Ethics

	Reason that is predominantly identical	*Reason that is predominantly individual*
Organizing function of reason (Nature as organ of reason, productive of goods)	Economic life—the state (e.g., the farm)	Social life—free sociality (e.g., the party)
Symbolizing function of reason (Nature as symbol of reason, representative of knowledge, meaning and value)	Intellectual life —the academy and schools (e.g., an academic conference)	Religious and artistic life —the church (e.g., a worship service or a concert)

THE *CHRISTIAN ETHICS* IN SCHLEIERMACHER'S THEOLOGICAL SYSTEM

Whereas the *Philosophical Ethics* is speculative, identifying the concepts necessary for understanding human culture, the *Christian Ethics* is empirical—drawing on the concepts generated by its philosophical counterpart and offering judgments about a specific historical tradition. Thus we can name where the *Christian Ethics* fits within the philosophical scheme, but where does it fall in the theological system? To answer this question we must attend to Schleiermacher's classic 1811 work *Brief Outline on the Study of Theology*.[18] Here Schleiermacher conceives of theology as combining the highest levels of ecclesial and scientific interest. Theology is done in service of the church, and its goal is to inform leadership for the ecclesial community. At the same time theology must meet the most rigorous standards of scholarship; by the depth of its reflection, it must prove that it belongs among academic disciplines. The *Brief Outline* conceives of theology as comprising three moments: philosophical, historical, and practical. The philosophical moment borrows concepts from philosophical ethics that will be needed to understand Christianity's historical development. It also seeks to identify the essence of Christianity in a preliminary way. The second "moment"—the work of historical theology—includes biblical study, history of the church, and description of the theology (dogmatics and ethics) currently valid in the church. Naming the currently valid theology attends to the present historical moment. Thus Schleiermacher brings a deep sense of historical consciousness to his understanding of theology: it is always grounded in a particular context and changes as it moves through time and through different sociocultural contexts. The third and final moment evinces Schleiermacher's awareness of the contextual character of church and theology. Practical theology is the "crown and goal" of the theological disciplines for, taking up the results of historical work, it offers direction for the concrete practices of ministry.

Christian ethics, then, is an aspect of historical theology—the aspect that attends to doctrinal theology that is valid in the present. Ethics stands as a complement to dogmatics; only together do these two comprise the whole of doctrinal theology. Both theological disciplines are equally grounded in Christian piety, for piety includes both a sense of "interest" that finds expression in Christian discourse and is systematized by dogmatics and a sense of "impulse" that gives rise to action and is systematized by ethics.[19] Dogmatics answers the question "What must be on the basis of religious self-consciousness?" while ethics answers the question "What must come to be on the basis of religious self-consciousness?"[20] Schleiermacher acknowledges that it has often been the practice that the two disciplines have been treated together and that this can be appropriate in particular circumstances. He justifies his own separation on the basis of the benefit it has brought to ethics, the "advantage of undergoing a more elaborate treatment."[21] When ethics is treated as part of a dogmatic system, it is usually divided up and treated under a number of doctrinal loci, and it thus fails to be a "rightly ordered and well-shaped organism."[22] So in the interest of a holistic, comprehensive ethical vision, Schleiermacher develops his dogmatics and ethics as separate works. The *Christian Ethics*, then, stands with the *Christian Faith* near the very center of historical theology, proposing an ethical vision that can inform the present practice of the church.

THE SELECTIONS
FROM THE *CHRISTIAN ETHICS*

The selections from the *Christian Ethics* included in this volume represent materials from all the sections that comprise the work as a whole. As indicated in the "General Introduction" below, Schleiermacher identifies three distinct determinations of Christian self-consciousness and three corresponding forms of action. The forms of self-consciousness define piety and the forms of action define ethics:

1. Lack of pleasure gives rise to restoring action
2. Pleasure gives rise to broadening action
3. Blessedness gives rise to presentational action

Christian consciousness is a sense of communion with God in and through awareness of redemption in Christ. Redemption introduces the antithesis of sin and grace or flesh and spirit. Because the believer participates in Christ's perfect communion with God, the believer is aware of grace overcoming sin, of the dominion of spirit over flesh. This dominion of spirit over flesh is experienced as blessedness, a blessedness that is not absolute but in a process of becoming. When flesh or the lower self-consciousness gains the upper hand, there is a feeling of a lack of pleasure. This includes an impulse to restore the ascendency of spirit, and this impulse in turn gives rise to restoring action, reestablishing the prior state of the spirit's dominion. When the higher self-consciousness or spirit has dominion, there is a feeling of pleasure and a corresponding impulse to expand the dominion of spirit. This gives rise to expansive or broadening action. Since both of these forms of action seek a change of some sort—restoration or expansion—Schleiermacher calls these "efficacious actions." In addition to self-consciousness determined as pleasure or lack of pleasure, there is a moment of relative blessedness, a moment of satisfaction, that follows on the completion of an act of restoration or expansion. Schleiermacher understands this to be a sense of "rest" that does not include an impulse toward any kind of change. This determination of self-consciousness includes an impulse to present or express itself; thus it gives rise to "presentational action," an action that seeks no change but merely intends to express what is inward in an outward way.

These three determinations of self-consciousness, grounding three different kinds of action, provide the basic structure of the *Christian Ethics*. The first, restorative action, includes a form in which the community as a whole seeks to effect restoration of an individual. This is church discipline. There is also a form in which an individual seeks to restore the whole; this is reform or betterment of the church. Broadening action, the second kind of action, includes all forms of education and mission work. Education or formation seeks to expand the dominion of spirit in persons already included in the Christian community, while missionary activity introduces Christian piety to those not yet part of the community. Finally, Schleiermacher defines presentational action, the third form, as worship. In worship there is mutual sharing of Christian piety by means of liturgy and sacraments, but especially by means of preaching and congregational singing. Schleiermacher speaks of worship in both a narrower and a broader sense. The narrower sense includes both formal, public worship and household worship. The broader sense is the manifestation of the Christian spirit that is to accompany all that a believer does in daily life.

In addition to these actions that define the church's inner life, the *Christian Ethics* considers how Christians, as individuals and as a community, are to interact with the cultural world "in the outer sphere," that which is "not yet church." Schleiermacher recognizes that the social order predates Christianity, so the Christian task is not to create the social order out of nothing, but to discern how to relate to what already exists. Corresponding to the three forms of action identified in the inner sphere of the church, Schleiermacher analyzes restoring, broadening, and presentational actions in the outer sphere. Under restoring action, he considers criminal justice and social reform along with warfare and matters related to colonization—actions that seek to restore a previous state of peace. Broadening action includes all forms of economic and educational activity that seek to expand the sway of human reason over nature. Presentational action deals with the whole realm of artistic expression, play, and sport as well as informal social relationships. This analysis of cultural life in the outer sphere is comprehensive in scope, attending as it does to this wide array of social-cultural forms. Among its limitations is the surprising omission of explicit attention to the academy. There is also the matter of the artificiality of the structure in which functions of the state are considered under both restoring and broadening actions. This creates some odd combinations (e.g., criminal justice with social reform and warfare). Still, this analysis of the outer sphere constitutes the "first great Protestant theology of culture."[23]

The Structure of the Christian Ethics[24]

	Purifying action	Broadening action	Presentational action
Inner sphere The church	Church discipline Church reform	Christian education Missions Family: child rearing	Worship: Narrow—household and public worship Broad—virtue in daily life
Outer sphere Society ("not yet church")	Criminal justice International relations Warfare and colonization	Education Labor and industry Commerce	The arts Social relations

THE *CHRISTIAN ETHICS*
AND CURRENT THEOLOGICAL ETHICS

Schleiermacher himself would be the first to recognize that his *Christian Ethics* allows of no easy appropriation to a context almost two hundred years after he wrote it. He insisted on the historical rootedness of all theological and ethical thought; no transhistorical or final statement in ethics is possible. Persons in every generational, geographical, and ecclesial location must articulate their own understanding. Still, to stand in a tradition is to acknowledge the claim that those who have gone before have on us. In his *Christian Ethics*, as elsewhere, Schleiermacher models creative appropriation of inherited tradition.[25] Nothing less can be expected of us as we consider how the *Christian Ethics* might speak to theological ethics in the present. As a modest contribution to this ongoing conversation, I identify four aspects of Schleiermacher's theory of Christian ethics that may have particular salience.

1. *Moral agency.* Especially when viewed in the context of Schleiermacher's

overall ethical theory, the *Christian Ethics* exhibits a broad and robust understanding of ethics that includes an expansive concept of the moral agent who exists in a relation of mutual influence with her environment. In addition, Schleiermacher thematizes the role of human self-consciousness in reason's continuing manifestation in history. His ethical theory includes a rich and suggestive conception of humanity's moral task, at once the servant of and participant in a process much larger than any human being.

Schleiermacher's account of the moral agent informs his work in Christian ethics even if it is not worked out there. His position provides an alternative to Kant's, with its narrow focus on the will's motives—the will standing naked, as it were, before the Categorical Imperative, in the realm of noumenal freedom separated from what is phenomenal. For Schleiermacher, the moral agent is the embodied self that has been shaped by the natural and cultural world that bears down on it. He proposes a rich and suggestive understanding of the moral agent as an embodied self, existing in a relation of reciprocity with the "world" in which it exists and involved in an ongoing process of formation in which the agent's duty is to act in ways aimed at the highest good. Thandeka, whose important work on Schleiermacher's *Dialektik* develops this interpretation of Kant and Schleiermacher on the moral agent, appropriates Schleiermacher's view to found her "affect theology."[26] In doing so, one aspect of her agenda is to explore the nervous system and body as the site of religious experience and employ this as a basis for a theology of intersubjectivity, mutuality, and cooperation. Thandeka provides a significant example of Schleiermacher's appropriation for constructive purposes, drawing on his view of the embodied, other-connected, and formed self.

Another aspect of moral agency involves the fact that reason, always already present and active in nature, attains to a higher level of self-consciousness in human beings. Not only do humans act as organs of reason; we also are aware of the task that stands before us and our call to understand and name it. We are conscious of our role in reason's ongoing permeation of nature:

> Consciousness is irreducible because through it human power is released to shape its world and the self. We exist in a moral space defined by the power of conscious activity. Philosophically taken, the good of consciousness is the fashioning of nature into a reflexive whole, into a "world."[27]

Thus Schleiermacher's account of moral agency expands to include the way that the moral task comes to self-consciousness in human beings. Our task is not only to participate in reason's permeation of nature, but also to understand it. This is a complex and fulsome view of the place of humanity in the ongoing drive of reason toward the good. It remains suggestive for ethical reflection today, especially in its valorization of the human role in a larger process. This remains true even if our postmodern situation rebels against the optimism about the progress of reason that was prevalent in Schleiermacher's context and often in Schleiermacher himself.

2. *Philosophical ethics.* Another aspect of the *Christian Ethics* that has potential to contribute to current ethical thinking has to do with its relation to the parallel work in philosophical ethics. Since Hans-Joachim Birkner provided the baseline understanding of the *Christian Ethics'* place in Schleiermacher's larger ethical scheme, a number of scholars have built on his work, reflecting on the relationship between the *Christian Ethics* and the *Philosophical Ethics.* John Crossley argues that Schleiermacher may be unique among theologians in offering both philosophical and theological ethics, and that the way he allows each to have its own place and integrity avoids two opposite extremes. One is the move of Barth and Bonhoeffer to return to a precritical posture and subsume all ethics under theological ethics, while the other is the stance of Kant and Garrett Green to assert the reverse and claim that theological ethics has no contribution to make.[28] I have argued elsewhere that Schleiermacher's *Christian Ethics* amounts to an appropriation and transformation of the way religion and religious ethics are defined in the *Philosophical Ethics.*[29] Thus Schleiermacher allows both philosophy and theology to have a place in ethical theory, with the possibility of exchange between the two disciplines. He preserves the distinctiveness of Christian ethical theory even while acknowledging its need to enter the larger philosophical conversation in order to generate concepts for understanding human historical and moral life. William Schweiker sees the two works taken together as providing a model of "an ethical critique of reflexive modernization and also a constructive, public account of intrinsic worth that supports but also limits human action and aspirations in rationalized systems."[30] The *Philosophical Ethics* articulates the way that "reason does seem to drive to a total rationalization of nature as its own highest good."[31] This drive is on the one hand affirmed, since it is productive of good, yet it is dangerous because "it is not relentless activity that is the end of human life, but, rather, a life that manifests peace with and rest in the highest good."[32] The *Christian Ethics* provides the insight that "consciousness rests in community with God and with other persons even as the Spirit is the efficient cause of action in the world, action meant to realize the kingdom of God."[33] Attending to the rationalization of life in the modern world, Schweiker identifies how Schleiermacher is able at once to affirm and critique this drive by means of the dialectical relationship that obtains between his *Christian Ethics* and *Philosophical Ethics.* Here is a retrieval of Schleiermacher that sees great promise in the dual ethics he promulgated in relation to a specific challenge of the contemporary world.

3. *The church's role.* The third aspect of the *Christian Ethics* that can be suggestive for current ethical reflection has to do with this being a distinctively Christian and theological ethics that gives focused attention to the church as a community of formation. Schleiermacher recognizes that the faith community founds and funds the Christian life, and that the Christian life flows from the gift of redemption made known in and through the church's life. The living spirit of Christ animates the church as the church is constituted by distinctively

Christian practices. This valorizes the life and practice of the faith community as the locus of redemption and communion with God, and it outlines the task of Christian ethics: to describe how the church is to live out its calling.

In the *Christian Faith*, Schleiermacher articulates a revisionist theological vision focused on Christian self-consciousness or piety. This gives his theology a practical purchase, for theological claims have to do with what can be known in an experiential way. Schleiermacher's theology centers on communion with God through Christ, who is made known by means of the Spirit in the community. In its focus on the inner sphere, the *Christian Ethics* is an ecclesial ethics of piety for the church as community. The *Ethics* articulates how the church lives now and is to live. Stated in another way, the *Christian Ethics* is an ethics of *Bildung*, or formation, as it describes the actions by which individuals and communities are formed in the faith. All that the church does has one goal: strengthening the Christian disposition and building it up.

Here Schleiermacher valorizes the practices of communal life, for the Christian spirit is communicated as persons are enculturated in the community's life. He speaks of the "supernatural" having become natural. Schleiermacher's Christ is "relatively supernatural"; his perfect God-consciousness is supernatural, with a perfection that cannot be accounted for on the basis of the sinful world into which he was born. But he is only "relatively" supernatural since God-consciousness is an element of all human consciousness. Subsequent to Christ, the "supernatural" becomes natural since his perfect God-consciousness is now mediated by the natural means of people sharing in common life. By these natural means believers are able to participate in communion with God through Christ, thus being drawn into redemption or the "higher life." The task of Christian ethics is to contribute to leadership in the church by describing practices of the church that are valid in the present.

The *Christian Ethics* conceives of the church as a living process. This can be seen in the fact that the church lives in and through the actions that constitute it. Schleiermacher says that both broadening and presentational action presuppose and create community. "The outward expression of an inner determination of self-consciousness, presentational action, rests upon community and produces community," he writes.[34] Thus we might speak of the "event" of community.

What we have in Schleiermacher's "ecclesial ethics of piety" is sustained attention to the life of the Christian community and its call to formation of persons and communities in the faith by means of specific practices. This may well seem far removed from much of what counts as Christian ethics, but this ecclesiological reflection embodies the fact that Christian life is dependent on being nurtured in the faith by actual communities. In this way the *Christian Ethics* may be a conversation partner on the important matters of community and formation in general, and perhaps also in terms of specific practices that Schleiermacher names.

4. *A theology of culture.* The final aspect of the *Christian Ethics* that deserves

consideration is the comprehensive theology of culture that it sets forth. In this regard, the *Ethics'* basic orientation has significant affinity with H. Richard Niebuhr's stance on "Christ transforming culture." This approach affirms engagement with cultural life, acknowledges the natural and human good produced by culture, and offers critique and transformative alternatives where culture is deemed deficient or destructive of good.[35] Fitting this type, the *Christian Ethics* can be seen as a form of public theology: it enters into social discourse and contributes analysis and critique from a Christian perspective.

Among the noteworthy elements of the *Ethics'* theology of culture is critique of social-cultural practices that involve violence, corporeal punishment, coercion, or dehumanization. The critique is qualified in that Schleiermacher affirms a just-war view and argues that the state may legitimately implement violence in a situation of a defensive war to preserve order and protect weaker members of society. Nonetheless, he clearly rejects violence and punishment in the form of the death penalty, and he includes thoughtful suggestions for a process whereby society might move toward its abolition. Schleiermacher rejects dueling (a practice still current in his time), challenges the use of force in colonization, and decries slavery and forms of industrial production that reduce persons to "living machines." Moreover, he condemns as dehumanizing gambling and other forms of cultural expression that violate human subjectivity or intersubjective relations. Since issues of violence, coercive use of force, and dehumanization are with us still, Schleiermacher's critiques along these lines and the theological grounding for his claims remain highly relevant.

Among the values that undergird his critical reflection on cultural life are freedom from coercion, freedom for active participation in political and social life, equality and mutuality in social relationships, and brotherly love. These values are applied to society at large although they are grounded in theological claims in the *Christian Ethics*. Notions of freedom take root in Schleiermacher's understanding of human agency in the process of redemption. Redemption must be freely appropriated by persons to be genuine, and when a person enters the Christian community, there is a development from initial receptivity to activity. When someone has internalized the common feeling of the community, that person comes to be an active member of the community, giving expression to the common feeling in a unique way. This sense of freedom and respect for individuality is grounded theologically in Schleiermacher's understanding of salvation and ecclesial life. In the *Ethics*, the equality of all persons grows out of christological conviction as differences among persons shrink to nothing in comparison with the unsurpassable dignity of Christ. This is then universalized and becomes an affirmation of the equality of all persons, including those outside the community, for they are destined ultimately to be drawn into it.[36] This is an equality of "personhood," which for Schleiermacher does not mean that all differences in social station and function are to be leveled. Similarly, mutuality of persons is grounded in the character of Christian community, in which all persons must give and receive. This is the essence of "brotherly love," defined as the "continual joining together of self-consciousness which is separated by personal existence."[37] Members of this kind of community are both receptive and active.

In addition to the ethical purchase ascribed to christological and ecclesiological doctrine, it is the eschatological doctrine of the reign of God on earth that has the greatest ethical significance in the *Christian Ethics*. This is so because this is an ethics of the good, and the reign of God—conceived as the absolute community of all with all—is identified as the highest good. Thus for Schleiermacher, the reign of God is the goal to which all action aims. Christianity "intends the whole sphere of nature and talent formation for the broadening of the reign of God according to the Christian idea."[38] Schleiermacher invokes the absolute community of all with all to establish a norm that can govern international relations; although it does not exist concretely, it provides a standard beyond the nation-state to which nations are accountable. The absolute community also functions importantly as the goal, the measure of conscience, which commands the allegiance of Christians. While the citizen is accountable to the nation and contributes to the production of the good for the sake of the nation, the Christian may produce the same good for the sake of the reign of God. The reign of God can also function critically to judge the immorality of lesser goods that become ends in themselves. So Schleiermacher identifies the self-interest of the state as the most powerful force that can oppose Christianity. When a nation can be brought into the service of the reign of God, this represents the "most lordly triumph of the Christian spirit."[39]

Thus the *Christian Ethics* provides a comprehensive theology of culture that is transformative in its basic orientation. It provides critique of violence, corporeal punishment, coercion, and dehumanization on Christian grounds. It advocates for the equality and mutuality of all persons within a vision of civic life that affirms the participation of all persons and communities. The highest good, the reign of God, casts a universal net that comprehends within itself all cultural goods and provides them with a telos beyond themselves. Above all, this understanding of God's reign provides a vantage point from which to critique lesser goods that are elevated beyond their appropriate status—especially the self-interest of the nation.[40] In this way the *Christian Ethics* provides a model of engagement with the whole breadth of cultural life. It welcomes with appreciation its various goods and also retains critical leverage against ostensible goods gone awry (violence, coercion, and dehumanization) and those elevated beyond what is appropriate.

Chapter 1

General Introduction

Christian ethics[1] has been understood to be an organized compilation of the rules by which any member of the Christian church is to shape his[2] life. This general and indefinite notion of Christian ethics is not sufficient because we seek a scientific[3] presentation of the discipline. A scientific presentation is one in which all the particulars of the material taught derive from the general concept set forth as the form of the whole. Therefore we must define more precisely everything that is given in such a general notion and trace it back to a larger context.

Now, if we retain the name "Christian ethics" at the very outset, we must pursue the twofold opposition that is included here. As ethics, Christian ethics presupposes general Christian teaching[4] and also other Christian teaching, and so we naturally set it over against Christian dogmatics[5] as its coordinate and opposite, both belonging to Christian teaching. As Christian, Christian ethics on the other hand presupposes that there must be other forms of ethics as well. What, then, is the natural opposition here? This is not so easy to determine. "Unchristian" would be purely negative and provides no opposition. If we consider analogues that are the immediate neighbors to Christianity, we could consider Jewish, Islamic, and similar forms of ethics. However, we would be offering only a multiplicity, not a true opposition. These forms refer to distinct forms of faith and have in common that they are all religious ethics. In turn, the expression "religious ethics" impels us toward a simple opposition because ethics is generally set forth as a philosophical discipline, traced back to philosophical principles. What Christian ethics commands is binding only for Christians, while philosophical ethics makes a universal claim since it seeks to bind everyone who can raise himself to the insights of the philosophical principles from which it is derived.

[CHRISTIAN ETHICS IN RELATION TO PHILOSOPHICAL ETHICS AND DOGMATICS]

Since Christian ethics is therefore a division of Christian teaching, and dogmatics stands at its side as its complement, and since Christian ethics is the particular ethics of Christianity and philosophical ethics stands opposite as the totality of all ethics, this means only that our discipline on the one hand is to be Christian teaching, but not dogmatics, and that it on the other hand is ethics but not philosophical ethics. Is there anything here other than a sheer negation? Do Christian dogmatics and ethics together comprise the whole of Christian teaching and are there two forms of ethics, religious and philosophical?

We must see our discipline as an organic component of the totality of theological study. In the whole organism of theological science, is there a third that could coordinate dogmatics and ethics? Certainly not, for when we extract dogmatics and ethics from the whole scope of theological disciplines, what is left is either a τέχνη, an artistic teaching,[6] and moves outside the concept of Christian teaching, or pure history and as such is no longer subsumed under the concept of Christian teaching. This is also always generally understood, even if not in the same way by everyone. Customarily one names the two disciplines together: systematic, thematic,[7] didactic theology, which as such is distinguished from historical theology and practical theology. Whether or not there is for these three a fourth is for us at this point of no consequence, but if we ask whether within systematic theology one should reckon a third, the answer is a clear "no." Yet even this is not sufficient; we must prove that Christian doctrine can be nothing other than dogmatics on the one hand and ethics on the other. As we set ourselves to this task, we consider these as two, as distinguished from each other and as opposite of each other within this distinction. To begin, we inquire regarding the history of this matter and find that this distinction has not always existed; rather, the two disciplines have been treated as one whole within thematic theology. This division has arisen only of late and this fact necessitates that we consider the whole matter from another side at the same time: in relation to the matter of form.

Where has this division of Christian teaching into these two disciplines come from? If our answer were derived solely from the great scope of this whole, the answer would be purely mechanical and completely invalid for a scientific treatment. Thus there must be another basis for this division, or else it would be better to let it go. What sort of thing, then, is that which is identified as Christian teaching? Christian teaching, whether in its scientific or popular form, is wholly and exclusively grounded in and related to the Christian church. A doctrinal presentation is only useful when it contains what has validity[8] in the Christian church or what one is convinced should have validity in the Christian church, and what is also derived as such from the idea of the Christian church. Hence, from wherever it may come, every effort to demonstrate the truth of the Christian church itself, every effort to demonstrate by argumentation what no one may take away from a participant in the Christian church, would always be excluded from Christian doctrine itself. This has always been so; in the earliest time of the church it was designated "apologetics," and it was repeated also in later times in the same way: always excluded from Christian doctrine itself. Therefore, propositions that according to their content are analogous to propositions of Christian teaching, but are put forth without relation to the Christian church and are demonstrated on the basis of universal principles—these cannot be seen as propositions of the Christian church. All these [Christian] propositions rest not on the concept of humanity but on the concept of what is Christian, not on the concept of human society but on the Christian church; they must not be ἐπιστῆμαι, but rather δόγματα, that is, ἃ δέδοκται τῇ ἐκκλησίᾳ.[9]

Moreover, how do we distinguish propositions of Christian doctrine from other propositions? Whoever recognizes these propositions must necessarily be a Christian. But is this not an empty claim? Suppose that we return to the time of the origin of the Christian church, where for the first time people came to be Christian by means of oral communication, persuasion, conviction. What was conveyed to them by means of which they were converted? Nothing but the elements of Christian teaching. And so it appears that one cannot distinguish between propositions of Christian teaching and propositions that prompt the acceptance of Christian teaching. If we go further and ask, what is the relationship between the development of individual Christian doctrines from their presupposition—the recognition of the Christian church—and the development through which one offers what can bring others to this recognition? One cannot claim that these two are the same. This is so, for if different opinions about Christian teaching itself are to be harmonized, and if a person will not recognize that something belongs to Christian teaching, we must show him that we would have to give up interest in the Christian church and that the very presupposition of such interest stands or falls with it. When on the other hand interest in the Christian church is to be first aroused, one cannot proceed in the same way; rather, what is needed is to awaken something in the person that is not yet in him. That first kind of development—of the individual Christian doctrine from its presupposition—is an analytical process, but the effort to arouse interest in Christianity is not: the latter must be seen as a new creation. This distinction is in no way a mere conflict over words. Those in whom there is a development of Christian teaching are in perfect agreement about this presupposition and now seek only to remain in agreement in the more exact development of the same.

And here we have that through which Christian teaching is brought forth in a more scientific form, distinguished in a particular way from other disciplines by its content. In however strong a scientific way Christian doctrine is set forth, it always distinguishes itself in that it has its origin in that which makes a person to be a Christian, in faith. So that, standing fast with the characteristic content of our theological discipline, we must say that Christian ethics as Christian ethics conveys rules for life, but is Christian ethics only in that it indicates that one who would be a Christian must order one's life in this or that way and no other. Philosophical ethics also conveys rules for life, but not based on the aforementioned presupposition. Rather, making a claim for universal validity, they always go back only to the presupposition that one who wants to live one's humanity according to an already-established concept of humanity can only will to act as this concept prescribes. Again here one could indeed say that this distinction is empty and only a conflict over words, for here the Christian church sets no absolute boundary, but actually maintains that all persons should be Christian. In this way it is customary to develop from the universal concept of humanity that a person is truly human only if he is Christian in order to secure the universal validity of Christian ethics and to base it philosophically. However, this is nothing but an illusion, for even if the development of a universal necessity for Christianity were possible, it could never belong in the realm of Christian ethics; and a presentation that took this detour would totally lose the most inward unity of ethics: the inner connection of all individual propositions made known through an analysis of what is distinctively Christian.

This confusion about the boundaries between theological and philosophical disciplines did not arise directly, yet it is always protected against by the designation set forth above, especially by the designation "systematic theology." This is so, for we tend to ascribe universal and irrevocable validity to whatever we call a system, and it is natural that we also want to have knowledge that comes from only one system. So if one names Christian doctrine in its scientific form "systematic theology," its notion is promoted as an aspect of a system of all human knowledge. If we allow for Christianity to be conceived within the universal interconnection of all human knowledge in a purely scientific way, this would be right. However, the necessity of Christianity cannot be demonstrated; if one tries to do this, Christianity's essence is lost, because it never presents itself as a society of knowledge or as something that can be maintained or spread through demonstration. If it were otherwise, Christianity's dissemination would rest on using the technique of scientific method, in total contradiction to the clear declaration of Christ and his apostles, and in total contradiction to the whole history of Christianity. What can be demonstrated is purely human, but Christianity has always presented itself as arising not from a purely human process, but rather through a divine process—and indeed not a universal divine process, but a particular one. Indeed, a demonstration would negate Christianity, negate its distinctive character, and the desire to trace Christian doctrine back by showing the dependence of Christianity on the universal process of human knowledge will always have the same effect. This means that one can name Christian doctrine in its scientific form as "systematic theology" only with a particular restriction.

Now, in recent times some have chosen another designation and have said that the exposition of Christian doctrine is something purely historical. The truth of this is already indicated in what was said above, that Christian doctrine includes only propositions that have validity in the church. But this is also highly disputable. If the scientific presentation of Christian doctrine is an exposition of what has validity in the Christian church, and one deems it to be historical on this account, one must certainly decide what is valid in one time and what in another. One may then say that this is well and good, but there can be no universal Christian doctrine, and every presentation of Christian doctrine as something complete would always be dependent on a previous presentation. To be sure, this complaint contains something undeniable. But one must not forget that the power of movement of every historical whole has its own limit, and there is a presentation of Christian doctrine also for the present, though not one that is universally valid. This does not do the least damage to the matter. The presentation of Christian doctrine cannot be the same in different periods, because each has need of and the capacity to receive the other. Suppose there were something in the tenth century that was exactly the same in our day; this would hardly be recognized as Christian doctrine because at this time hardly anyone would be able to understand it.

In spite of all this, we can hold fast to the view that every presentation of Christian doctrine is historical, but it does not thereby cease to be systematic. The same is true of the other side, that any presentation that is systematic cannot be purely systematic but must always be historical-systematic. A presentation of Christian teaching that says, "This is the currently valid expression of the faith," would be purely historical. On the other hand, teaching that considers multiplicity not as an aggregate, but refers back to its unity and presents its interconnection; teaching that indicates that when a person considers one aspect, he must necessarily consider the other—such a presentation is no longer purely historical but is also systematic, and that means in this realm "scientific." The more its systematic character comes to the fore, the more what is historical will be pushed back, and vice versa, without thereby either one totally disappearing. The different forms of relation that the one has to the other will always have influence on the detail and exactness of the presentation. We have said that every presentation of Christian teaching can only be a presentation of what has validity as teaching in the Christian church. However, what has validity is not the same in all time periods; rather, if Christianity itself is to remain constant in the course of change, there must be something in it that remains predominantly the same in the form of Christian doctrine itself.

If one were to set forth only the elements of Christian teaching that have changed less than others, such a presentation would be less fully related to the distinctive way of comprehension in a particular time. If one were to abstract from the change to which the elements of Christian teaching are always subject, one could demonstrate that what remains is its most complete internal interconnection, but the substance of this interconnection must decline together in the same measure as the historical character is minimized and as the systematic character is maximally active. To accept the task of totally effacing its historical character is to take on a task that is not feasible. This is so, for to begin with, we have no other means of expression than language, which is subject to change in all its elements; each of its elements has its own history. This means that a presentation that remains the same for all time is totally impossible. Add to this understanding the fact that Christianity has spread itself over a great variety of peoples and over various language groups. This is so, for interest in doctrine and science never remains at the same point, but changes from one people and language group to another. We see Christianity dealt with scientifically first in the Greek, then in Latin, and now finally in the German language; it follows that the relatively most complete presentation of that which is unchanging in Christian doctrine cannot always remain the same because continually, from time to time, it must be translated into a different language.

And finally it must be considered that a separation of the changing from the unchanging in Christian doctrine cannot be done, certainly not in a mechanical way, but not even organically. This is so, for what is expressed in thought and word is already changeable. Indeed, behind thought and word lies what is innermost, and that is constant, identical [over time], but as such it can never be communicated in an outward way. Thus, even if, from other points of view, the basic principles of Christian doctrine can, with full justification, be distinguished from nonbasic principles, the unchanging element in Christian doctrine can never be named as "this" or "that." Whoever wants to set forth what is absolutely unchanging in Christian doctrine can do so only at the cost of exactness. Nevertheless, our main proposition is that Christ is the Redeemer of humankind. As long as one fastens on him in a general way and leaves "Christ" or "Redeemer" imprecise, one could certainly apprehend Christ in a heretical way, but as one begins to apprehend him—both subject and predicate—in a more definite way and thereby begins to present Christian doctrine, Christ also begins to be changeable.

Moreover, if we keep the historical aspect foremost in mind, its proportion must necessarily increase just as the preponderance of the systematic aspect must decrease. However, what pertains to extreme cases applies here essentially in the same way as there. For if everything is to be presented that was valid in the Christian church at any past time, everything in the measure in which it was valid, and if all private interpretations were to be set forth side by side, and also everything historical in Christian doctrine right up to its current arrangement—then on the one hand it would be an impossible and unfeasible striving, and on the other hand insofar as this could be accomplished, it would negate Christianity. The reason is that as the systematic element is maximized, Christianity is made so general that it contains nothing but what anyone, without exception, can immediately consent to because he is in a position to make of it what he will; in this way the historical element individualizes Christian teaching to the extreme point at which there could be no more thought of a Christian church. Then Christian doctrine is nothing but an aggregate of individual points of view, and there is no other unity but that of the subjective personal existences of individuals, so that the principle *Quot capita, tot sensus*[10] is posited, and thereby the dissolution of the church itself. This is nothing other than the negation of Christian teaching itself for it always rests only on the supposition of the Christian church.

If now in any statement of the whole of Christian doctrine, the systematic and historical characteristics must then be united, what is the status of the relationship between its branches: dogmatics and ethics? If there is no opposition between the two, how could they be separated? If they are opposed, how is it that for so long they were interwoven?

Clearly we must say that ethical doctrine is also faith doctrine (dogmatics).[11] This is so, for that which exists within the Christian church, to which Christian ethical doctrine always refers, is a matter of faith through and through. Moreover, without exception, the presentation of Christian rules of life is nothing but the further development of that which lies in the original faith of Christians. And is not Christian faith doctrine also ethical doctrine? Certainly, for how could the Christian faith be presented without the idea of the reign of God on earth being presented! But the reign of God on earth is nothing other than the way of being Christian that must always come to be recognized through actions. The presentation of the idea of the reign of God on earth is therefore nothing but the presentation of the way for Christians to live and act, and that is Christian ethics. In this way it appears that the two are not at all opposed: rather, the one is essentially included within the other. As a result nothing appears more natural than both being bound together, especially since the New Testament writings' didactic aspect approaches being a scientific presentation, and likewise the discourse of the most excellent teacher in that homiletical form by which the church always endeavors to preserve and heighten its Christian sensibility—all these know nothing of a separation of the two. If we look further in this historical consideration at how the combination has taken place, we cannot deny that the elements of Christian ethics are always underdeveloped. Why is this? Especially in the time of scholasticism, when the whole construction of dogmatic teaching attained a great expansiveness, matters were considered that seem to us to be peripheral—sometimes regarding practical contents, but totally inessential for Christian ethics, as for example the way to handle the sacramental elements, the adoration of the saints as a supplement to prayer, and the like. In this context the essence of ethics came but little to light, and the feeling thus emerged that this should be handled in its own discipline so that it could be set forth in full measure. If there had been produced nothing but an abuse of the union of dogmatics and ethics, there would have been an overcoming of the abuse, but not at all a giving up of the division into two disciplines. Thus this division must also be better grounded if we are to be able to justify it.

If we ask, "How can ethics and dogmatics then be made into one unified whole?" we must say, "In very diverse ways, because it is possible to conceive of each discipline on its own as configured in a variety of ways." Undeniably, the most ancient type of Christian ethics is all under the form of commands, which can be traced back to the Decalogue, which belongs to the dispensation of the Jewish law. The Decalogue has been divided into the two tables of the law, one containing duties to God, the other containing duties to the neighbor. How can this be placed in the whole corpus of Christian doctrine? Either one could return to the unity of Jewish and Christian revelation and present the whole of Christian ethics precisely in the locus where the theory of revelation is customarily addressed, that is, in the introduction; or one could divide the two tables and include the duties to God with the doctrine of God, and include the duties to the neighbor with the doctrine of the church or with the reign of God on earth. Finally, one could place the whole of ethics in this last locus. The first method—dividing ethics and blending the duties to God and to the neighbor with various segments of dogmatics—presents great difficulties. This is the case, for if the doctrine of God is handled in the usual way as the doctrine of divine attributes, none of the so-called duties to God can be connected to the so-called divine attributes, and the duties to God as a whole will be treated only as a corollary to the whole of the doctrine of the divine attributes.

The same thing, moreover, will happen with the duties to the neighbor if they are dealt with under the doctrine of the church: it is not possible to divide up evenly what can be divided and unified as Christian ethics under what can be divided and unified as Christian dogmatics; but ethics, divided and unified in its way, will always be presented under various loci of dogmatics, divided and unified in its own way. If this approach is not satisfactory, the other methods—where the whole doctrine of duty is either inserted into the introduction or appended to the doctrine of the church—are even less so. This is the way it is when ethics is treated as doctrine of duty. The results will not be different, however, if ethics is presented as doctrine of virtue together with dogmatics or as doctrine of the fruits of the Spirit—as Scripture names them—or as any other form. In each case ethics, as a whole or divided up, will be considered only under one locus of dogmatics or under several loci, and so it appears that no rightly ordered and well-shaped organism can result if one sets forth dogmatics and ethics in this unified way and if one nonetheless also wants the Christian rules for life to be highlighted in its own special form.

Now, these observations can certainly lead to separate treatments of the two disciplines, but we can only see this as a preliminary indication with a view to proceeding from here onward to orient ourselves in a more precise way and to ground the matter from the inside.

What then is the most basic presupposition upon which the whole development of Christian teaching is to be grounded? If we enlighten ourselves about this without binding ourselves to specific terms, this could easily lead to confusions and misunderstandings. However, it could also be taken as a very unscientific procedure, so that we must clarify this more exactly. The matter seems to be as follows.

When the terminology in an area of knowledge has been established in a fixed manner so that an expression has the same meaning for all people, then the subject itself is ready, and there can be no further change in any of the relevant disciplines. From this observation one can immediately conclude that the establishment of a terminology is the fulfillment, not the beginning, of a scientific treatment. The terminology itself cannot be fixed before the discipline's completion, nor can the terminology serve as a universal ground for it. Thus, there can be no blame at all if one makes one's start in a period before the completion has arrived. For a completely distinctive grounding of this matter is then possible for the theological disciplines. If it is true that the theological disciplines arise out of Christian faith and not the reverse (faith arising from theological disciplines), there certainly must have been a time when Christianity was not expressed in a scientific form, though of course it must have been expressed, otherwise Christianity could not have expanded. Here we see that the scientific form does not arise purely from a scientific motive. Rather, it is developed from an unscientific motive, the dominant motive being the spread of Christianity. What then is the relationship between unscientific and scientific use of language? This relationship can be traced back to two differences: on the one hand, every linguistic expression has a certain indeterminacy and a variety of meanings that must be overcome through scientific use of language; on the other hand, in unscientific use of language there exists a variety of modes of expression for each particular element, and no one is aware of the differences, so imperfect synonyms must be overcome through scientific use of language. It all comes back to these two points.

Now, it is certainly not possible to provide explanation for a subject unless it is one for which one seeks precision in language. However, there is one thing that precedes this effort, namely, setting forth the identity of the subject, which one must accomplish through many sorts of linguistic usage as long as no definite use of language has emerged within a given field. In general, before Christian teaching can be set forth in a general form, there must be a communion of persons bound together by that which constitutes a person as a Christian, and in which one has come to an understanding regarding the various ways of relating in life. Christian teaching arises out of a process. Yet couldn't it also be the other way around? Could we not say that it is presenting Christian teaching to persons that first constitutes them as Christian? This is also true, for how else do persons become Christian? They do so by means of a Christian's presentation of what is within, communicated in the form of discourse—through a presentation of Christian teaching. But where is the original source? In Christ, in whom resides originally what constitutes one as a Christian and from whom it issues, before any presentation or communication. Accordingly, this is the analogy for all expansion of Christianity whatsoever; being Christian is itself the presupposition for all Christian teaching, and the latter is only the developed presentation of that which constitutes one as a Christian. But what is this? Is it knowledge? Certainly. A way of acting? Also true. It is the same regardless of what comes first and what comes second; and we must say that if one puts a way of acting in the first place and then derives knowledge from it, or the other way around, both approaches are equally correct.

If one begins with knowledge and desires that the way of acting in all of life remain only something corresponding to knowledge, it will be natural to present Christian teaching as a whole, but in such a way that the character of dogmatics will be fundamental and ethics just a corollary. On the other hand, one who sets a definite way of being and acting as originally what constitutes one as a Christian will explain Christian teaching as a whole, but in the opposite way so that the character that ethics forms is fundamental within itself, and dogmatics is simply inserted as a corollary. When we consider the matter historically, before the division into two disciplines was made, then the first way just mentioned was followed. The second approach has never been the scientific way of handling Christian teaching, but this does not prove that the two viewpoints and modes of procedure are not parallel. Rather, this simply reflects a certain one-sidedness in earlier experience, the ground of which is easy to find in the overall condition of human culture at the time when Christian teaching began to take on a scientific form. This is so, for the theoretical and speculative approach dominated over all other approaches, and human circumstances had conformed so little to a regularized pattern that it was hardly possible to effect a presentation under the ethical form.

When we recognize that scientific presentations of Christian teaching always develop out of unscientific forms, we must say that this is where scientific form has its place since insofar as one seeks to incite a feeling for true holiness,[12] which is certainly a way of being and acting, one makes ethics the grounding. Accordingly, the way this is united with self-consciousness allows the development of rules for faith on this basis. Therefore, it would always be possible also to build a scientific approach on this basis. Yet for us, the approach does not work, and given that the division of the two disciplines has been instituted, this approach has no longer been feasible. If it is the case that the basic presupposition—what constitutes one as a Christian—can be conceived with equal right to be knowledge or a mode of action, which approach is taken remains a matter of indifference. We must search out which approach to take, and if we discover that there are different processes for the formation of modes of acting and for formation of knowledge, we will be able to comprehend the ground for the separation of these two disciplines.

What then is the difference between proclamation that produces Christian character and propositions of Christian teaching, which only represent such proclamation? It appears to be only that proclamation includes a moving element that scientific presentation lacks. Certainly one can say that the latter has a moving element: it is also grounded in conviction, and what makes something moving is that it convicts. But the matter stands this way. If we return to the experience of Christ and the apostles in their effort to ground the Christian frame of mind, we certainly go back to the effort to produce conviction, to bring forth this same movement, as in a scientific presentation. Of what did they seek to convict? That the criteria regarding the Messiah presented by the Old Testament are completely united in the person of Jesus. However, we cannot deny that one certain aspect of this process, that of bringing Jews into Christian community, was not actually original because people were connected with a situation already grounded in the Old Testament; above all else they had in view simply a corrective to the then-current understanding of it. Even more originative for them was the preaching of John. For since he was occupied with emphasizing in turn the forgotten idea of the Messiah and a disposition for bringing about the reign of God, this prior element was primary for him. Awakening a conviction concerning the person of the Messiah, as did occur in the apostolic preaching, was not his concern. We must indeed say that in every passing over from any individual form of religion to the Christian form, the original element is always mixed with the derived element.

Thus, if we imagine that a sheer opposition could be set forth between a pious person and an absolutely nonpious person, wherein then does the original difference between the two consist—a difference that must be overcome if a nonpious person is to become pious? This we immediately answer in the negative; it is not that one would have had a concept that the other would have lacked, or that one would have affirmed a proposition that the other would have denied. This is so, for if we suppose an absolutely nonpious person who also lacks the concept of God, would we not have to say he would become pious if this concept were communicated to him and by means of that communication? Surely this is not the case for it is certainly possible to think in the abstract here—and there are many analogies to this—that he would not yet have gained any interest in the idea of God even though he would have gained the concept. Of course, a person for whom such an interest was absolutely lacking, that is, an absolutely nonpious person, is a pure fiction. Now, however, even if we do not transgress the boundaries of actuality, we would still see that having the concept and having interest are very different from each other and that one cannot be the measure of the other. That is, there are persons for whom acquaintance with the concept is greater than their interest—those who deal with the concept in a purely dialectical way; also there are others in whom interest is vital but their ability to engage the concept is very slight. Here we see that it must be one kind of action to engender the concept and another kind to engender interest; therefore piety cannot be engendered by means of a communication whose only moving element is that which is able to engender the concept.

This being established, admittedly we still have not yet found anything regarding what we are seeking above all, for what we have said applies equally to doctrinal propositions and to moral propositions. Neither of these is original: both are secondary. Now, however, if the original ground that we presuppose is the condition of piety, and for us the specific condition of Christian piety, how then do these propositions, the so-called "dogmatic" propositions and those that form the ethical aspect of Christian teaching in a different way, relate to this condition? Answering this question is our real task. However, in that we have attached the condition itself to the term "interest" and have distinguished pure conviction from that condition, first of all we must indeed trace all this back to something more definite. What, then, is actually the essence of the condition of piety? As we have seen, it is not having certain notions; rather, the notions as such are always only secondary. Specifically, this distinction appears to posit only the contents and interconnections of the propositions of dogmatics as differentiated from piety itself. Therefore, we must seek another relation that in an equally specific way posits the propositions of ethics as differentiated from piety. These propositions contain notions, but only those whose object is actions and modes of action. Is it then possible that what is primordial in the condition of piety is action itself? If we imagine a person to be in a condition in which all action expressed outwardly is cut off, can he be considered pious anyway? Of course. Thus an external action is one thing, and piety is something else.

However, is there not also such a thing as an internal action? Certainly, for if we can resolve the whole being of persons into the condition called "action," then the person would be an agent and could be nothing else, so he must either be involved in some action by means of which something outside of him is changed, or in some action by means of which something within him is changed. Every meditation, for example, through which indefinite notions become definite is an internal action. Is then the condition of piety perhaps identical with such an internal action? Certainly not. A complete separation of the two can be only a fiction, but we can find the truth of the matter only in the difference as to circumstance between the two in each moment. That is, no moment in the life of a person disappears completely; rather, each moment has its influence on all the moments that follow; thus through each moment the internal being of a person is altered. Hence, to that degree each moment, including every moment of piety, is an action directed inwardly. However, are both of these moments always together to the same degree? Can we say, "Every moment is present within a person as piety to the same degree as a moment by means of which changes are produced in his inner being"? No, the two can stand in different relations to each other, both within each person at different times and in different persons at the same time. This is clear of itself and sets us over against all other domains. This is so, for whatever the change we may observe in a person or whatever the outwardly directed action that person may decide upon, motive and effect do not necessarily stand in the same relation to each other; rather, the one factor can be very weak while the other factor is strong, and vice versa. So, in a very definite way, we can then distinguish the action itself, that which is inwardly directed as well as that which is outwardly directed, from piety, just as we have seen a very definite distinction between concept and interest in the subject matter of piety.

Now, however, we also come automatically to the place where we clearly see that these two features are always essentially bound together in the condition of piety: on the one hand is interest in the object of the religious domain, which interest calls forth the concept of its subject matter in very different measures; on the other hand is impetus, ὁρμή,[13] or impulse that certainly must pass over into action, but in different persons and in different times in very different measures. These two features in their pure identity with each other are the actual originative ground that comprises the condition of piety. The distinction between a pious person and wholly nonpious one—if we want to imagine this possibility—refers to this originative ground. If a nonpious person gains the notions belonging to the pious person but not his interest, he also does not yet have piety; and conversely, if he is induced to perform the actions of the pious person but has not gained the corresponding impulse, he is likewise not yet participating in piety. What is the object to which the interest of piety is attached? God, the Supreme Being. And then, in terms of content, which propositions are "dogmatic" in the narrow sense? Obviously those that express the relationship of persons to God, but in terms of interest, as that relationship is expressed in accordance with its various modifications. Then which propositions, in terms of content, are the ethical propositions of piety? These are the ones that express exactly the same thing but as inner impetus that finds expression in a cycle of actions.

The formula for the dogmatic task is the question, "What must be the case given that the religious self-consciousness, the inner religious sensibility, exists?" The formula for our ethical task is the question, "What must come to be out of and by means of religious self-consciousness, given that religious self-conscious-ness exists?" Thus, the two disciplines present the same thing, but each considers it from a different side, and in this way we then see why it is appropriate to separate the two disciplines and how it was possible for the two to be united for so long. This is true, for as long as one does not separate the two questions— "What must be?" and "What must come to be?" on the basis of the religious self-consciousness—the two disciplines must be united. This status must continue as long as one of the questions is subsumed under the other, except that in such a case either moral teaching must be expounded under the form of dogmatics, or dogmatics must be expounded under the form of ethics. It is clear, however, that these two questions actually comprehend the two extremes of religious sensibil-ity. Thus a third form that would coordinate these two is not possible. Moreover, if one sees further that we cannot think of anything in a definite way—even including anything in terms of religious sensibility, except under the form of this contrast—then it is necessary to proceed from separation of the two extremes and present Christian teaching on the one hand as dogmatics, which presents

Christian self-consciousness in its relative state of rest, and on the other hand as ethics, which presents Christian self-consciousness in its relative movement.

The other question—that of the relationship between religious ethics and philosophical ethics—has its own not insignificant difficulties. If one thinks in a general way about two possibilities—the two disciplines are identical or not identical in relation to their content and to the totality of their particular elements—considerable predicaments arise in either case. That is, if the two are identical, it appears that one of the two is superfluous, and there is no place for the superfluous, least of all in a scientific domain. Everything superfluous arises, as does every deficiency, out of some imperfection; it appears, as it must, that if the two are identical in terms of their content, this is grounded either in an imperfect comprehension of what is religious or in an imperfect philosophical construction. Likewise it must be false to say that what is religious is derived from religious ethics or that what is philosophical is derived from philosophical ethics. On the other hand, if the two are not identical, the difficulties are equally great, for then either piety must contradict philosophy or philosophy must contradict piety. This could then mean either that a philosophical person cannot be pious or that a pious person cannot be philosophical, and that each needs its own particular ethics different from the other's ethics. Of course, this is often claimed. Still, from our theological standpoint, could we allow our neighboring discipline to be put aside? I think not. The reason is that if we wanted to hold fast to piety and say "farewell" to philosophy and could not do otherwise, we must at the same time say "farewell" to theology as well, because in its scientific presentation as concerns its form, it requires principles that can be taken over only from philosophy. Hence, we would be limited to the other case, namely, that it must be understood to be a false grasp of religious consciousness or of speculation for an ethics to be structured on the basis of both piety and philosophy and not only on the basis of the one or the other alone, since in any case there could only be one and the same ethics for the pious person and for the philosophical person. In this case, moreover, we would certainly be freer, for therewith the nature of theology is not yet endangered for us as it would be if an individual discipline as such were cancelled out.

Now, here we cannot determine in a scientific way whether a philosophical ethics simply rests upon a false way of conceiving speculation. That is, such a supposition must therefore appear to us as very doubtful, because the whole of history stands thoroughly opposed to this. This is so, for thus far there has been no philosophy that has not given expression to an ethics. Also, religious ethics, as we have seen, is very well grounded. So we must accept that both, the philosophical and the religious, can exist side by side. Generally, it is very difficult, however, to show clearly how these two stand next to each other. This is so in that if we begin with the supposition that every distinctive form of religion can come to a scientific presentation, there will be a great variety of religious ethics. These could not all be identical, for as its ground each has a different way of being, a different formation of religious self-consciousness, so that the moments in which impulses become actions must be very different from each other. The same is also true about the actions themselves and no less true of the theories about all this—that is, ethics. All religious ethics, however, would be in the same relation to philosophical ethics. Among themselves they are not the same, and it is not possible for them to become the same. Now, certainly one could say, it is not the case that all forms of religion postulate a scientific presentation; polytheism does not attain to a scientific presentation, and among monotheistic religions neither the Muhammadan religion nor the Jewish religion but only the Christian does so. Even if we could work through all this diversity, however, we would still not be helped thereby because in Christianity itself we also find differences not only among different periods but also within the same period, and these differences are so radical that doctrine and church communities have separated and split.

Accordingly, both philosophical and religious ethics must nevertheless be the same as regards their content if we as theologians do not want to be caught in an irresolvable contradiction, to feel bound both to perform and not to perform a given action. In this light, then, how does it stand with philosophical ethics? Are different expressions everywhere and always self-identical? Certainly to the degree that one construes an ethics together with a philosophical system, one will hold that ethics alone to be true and will want to adhere to it. Yet even with this claim we see at all times a great many of the most diverse construals come to the fore, and unanimity is never to be found. Thus, we can say that the differences among religious ethics cannot be denied, and if there were just one philosophical ethics, the identity of content between religious and philosophical ethics could not be affirmed at all. However, differences among philosophical ethics are also undeniable, and so between religious and philosophical ethics there is nothing absolutely intractable; rather, the differences among the one in itself are parallel to the differences among the other, and both kinds of differences also have some things that disappear in parallel ways. Thus it is not necessary for us to give up our theological point of view; as the highest result, we have Christianity as the actual completion of religious consciousness.

Moreover, if on the one hand Christianity could come to completion within itself so that it were able to overcome all the mutually negating oppositions within its realm, and if on the other hand speculation were also able to come to an absolute and universally recognized completion, then in the resulting Christian and philosophical ethics every contradiction would be impossible. But then would not one of these two be superfluous? This we must deny because each has different sources and a different form. So neither is superfluous: rather, Christian ethics is an essential element of philosophical construction when philosophical ethics completes its full course; if we desire to take Christian ethics away, we rob philosophical construction of an organic component. And philosophical ethics is necessary to the completion of the form of Christian consciousness, so that it is an organic component of it; or if that does not suit someone, in any case if Christian ethics is laid aside, Christian consciousness fails to achieve its highest level.

As in terms of content, no element of one can contradict an element of the other; in terms of form, no element of the one is identical to the other; so the two remain two, in one aspect completely identical and in another aspect completely nonidentical. Religious ethics always presupposes religious self-consciousness in the form of impulse. We now may set aside the question of whether philosophizing can exist apart from consciousness of God, but we must note that there is a philosophical system[14] that grounds the necessity and inner truth of the postulation of the Supreme Being in the moral domain; hence, even this approach comes to a consciousness of God, the reverse of what we experience in the religious realm. As long then as this reverse approach is possible in the area of philosophy, the coming together of philosophical ethics with the form of religious ethics remains purely incidental. This is all the more the case as long as there exists a variety of approaches in the area of Christian ethics alongside a variety of approaches in the area of philosophical ethics. Because the differences among the one in itself parallel the differences among the other in itself, and because the differences in the one area are of a different sort from the differences in the other, they ground wholly different ways of acting and make more difficult any coming together in terms of form.

Add to this the fact that philosophical ethics coheres exactly with the philosophy of history, since it is clear that system-of-life rules for the individual cannot be constructed out of the pure idea of reason without claiming that a noncontradictory common life would also be developed out of it. At that point, however, it is natural that all that is imperfect will only be seen as a transition to what is perfect and that every appearance will be compared to its distance from the archetype. Therefore the development of the religious element in the human race must have an essential place in philosophical ethics, and the latter cannot take up within itself all the differences among religious ethics together with the differences in formation of religious self-consciousness.

For an individual religious ethics, however, this is not at all the case. It is not appropriate to its idea to extend beyond itself. Rather, it closes itself up in the particularity from which it originally came forth, as does its great hope: always to spread itself more widely. If religious ethics cannot have this universal or universal-historical tendency, it is therefore strictly distinguished from philosophical ethics in its form. Indeed, up to this time Christian ethics has not had a similar experience, but very much to its disadvantage this already displays a historical consideration of the matter. Under the domination of the Leibniz-Wolffian philosophy, not to go any further, Christian ethics has taken on the scheme of this philosophy in a complete way and has used it to displace the popular philosophy, resulting in a mishmash of rational and empirical elements, and the principle of happiness has come to prevail over the principle of perfection. In the same way it has taken from Kantian philosophy the Categorical Imperative. Since then it has come to a more definite decision, treating philosophical ethics as a system of commands—that is, a doctrine of duty, as a presentation of an organism of moral power—and thus as a doctrine of virtue and as a doctrine of the highest good. It has not hesitated to appropriate for itself these three ways of methods of treatment. One could say that handling the matter in this way could not lead to any harm and that the content remains the same whether the dominion of the Christian sensibility is expressed as happiness or as perfection, whether self-consciousness that has taken on Christian form in its highest impulse is presented as a system of duties, and/or whether it is expressed as an organic union of all moral powers or results.

Let us ask now, however, whether the bridge from the one development to the other was grounded in Christian ethics itself. This we must deny. All can stand well next to each other; that one follows the lead of the other is precisely what commonly happens in philosophy and in the theological domain. What follows from Christian ethics not having its own form but always following whatever changes there are in philosophy? This fact—that it has no choice but to deteriorate into the difficulty of the various philosophical orientations crowding each other out and of always considering the main issue that is being contested, however much it may be a secondary matter for Christian ethics. It cannot fail, however, that whatever its main issue is will retreat, that the actual character of Christianity becomes ever less visible, and that at the most there will be nothing but philosophy clothed in Christian speech.

Yet is it possible for Christian ethics to have a form that is independent of philosophical form? Scientific form first makes Christian ethics into a theological discipline, the minimum being an easily perceived complete organization, the maximum a more fully perfected organism in which the content and the interconnection among the elements is identical. History indicates that the nearer one comes to the minimum of scientific form, the more Christian ethics remains free from being subordinated to philosophical form, and vice versa, the more the concept of scientific form is strengthened, the more the analogy to the contemporaneous philosophical ethics comes to the fore. History thus seems only to provide the conclusion that the level of independence of theological disciplines from philosophical stands in an inverse relation to the level of the purity and completion of their scientific presentation. This fact need not disturb us, however, for it is one thing for a scientific presentation of religious ethics to have the same form as the philosophical discipline, and it is quite another thing for it to be dependent on philosophy insofar as philosophy contains the principles of scientific presentation and controls the language used, and for it even to be dependent on a particular philosophical construction of a particular philosophical science. So we ask, if we want to let theological ethics loose from the form of the philosophical, how can we attain this and let theological ethics gain its own particular form without losing the rigor of scientific presentation? We cannot resolve this problem as long as we consider religious ethics in general in its difference from philosophical; we must now move to consider the particularity of Christian ethics more closely and ask, "What is the essential and distinctive character of Christianity that can be the constitutive principle of ethics?" In answering this question, we must hold together the identity between ethics and dogmatics as well as the ground for the difference between the two.

Where self-consciousness is bound together with the consciousness of the Supreme Being, there religious sensibility exists, there piety exists. Since this union of being with religious sensibility can be expressed, it can be grasped in the following formula: it is the communion of persons with God, for we exist in communion with all that goes into our self-consciousness immediately and determines an aspect of the self, just as we say that we posit our sensations, our communion with the world, as something outside us that is codeterminative of the self. If this formula is correct, we must also say that there is always as much religious consciousness in persons as there is communion with God in self-consciousness. What is specifically Christian, however, is that all communion with God is seen as established through the act of redemption through Christ. Even this basic proposition will certainly not be universally recognized, but even those who deny it cannot but admit that the distinctiveness of Christianity rises and falls with this claim and that without it only what is generally religious remains and can emerge only as such. This must be sufficient for now, for a demonstration of what is distinctively Christian, which must always be presupposed by dogmatics and ethics, does not belong here but to apologetics.

[THE CHARACTER OF CHRISTIAN ETHICS]

Here we must leave undecided which formation of Christian dogmatics can be accepted based on this point. We can only ask, "How must Christian ethics be organized?" It must be a presentation of communion with God as determined by communion with Christ the Redeemer, inasmuch as this is the motivation for all Christian action. It can be nothing other than a description of those ways of acting that arise from the dominion of Christianly determined religious self-consciousness. In our naming this process as "description," there appears to lie a narrower determination of the form—one that is quite remote from the usual determination. It is by far most customary to deal with Christian ethics in the form of a doctrine of duty, thus a system of commands. It might appear that we, too, presupposed this when we said earlier that it contains rules for living, and so we seem to be in contradiction with ourselves when we now claim that it is to be description. However, the word "rule" indicates not only how something should happen, but also how something does happen, and we have used the word only in this latter sense, as an exact synonym for "description." But then it appears that we contradict the notion that ethics is to contain commands. This claim also disappears by means of closer consideration, and the remaining difference appears to be only incidental.

Let us compare two expressions. If we say, "Christian ethics presents the way action should be," the question comes, "Who should act in this way?" Evidently those in the Christian community, because Christian ethics can extend no further than its presupposition, can only be for those in whom the Christianly determined religious consciousness is living. However, if the Christian church is the place where action should be like this, where is action actually done in this way? Only two answers seem possible. First, in the Christian church; and second, nowhere in human society on earth. Both seem very justifiable. If we think of Christian consciousness as the dominant impulse, then it will actually be enacted in the way Christian ethics prescribes. The Christian church is precisely the place where Christian consciousness is the dominant impulse. Against this position one can only say, "It belongs essentially to Christians also to be conscious in such a way [as to understand] that Christian consciousness is not yet the ruling impulse in them in an absolute way." If we say, "Communion with God in Christianity is conditioned by communion with redemption through Christ," each person must be first established in this connection; this takes place in time and thus has a beginning. This means that the life of the Christian is posited as a becoming that develops throughout the whole of one's temporal life, by means of the whole temporal development up till then, and from this perspective is always only a matter of becoming pervaded by the particular Christian formation of the religious consciousness.

Further, one can thus also say, "The Christian church is always the first place where Christian religious consciousness is the dominating impulse; insofar as it is not yet dominating, it is the place where there remains something imperfect or totally lacking in communion with God through Christ." However, when actions in the Christian church are not yet done according to the prescriptions of Christian ethics, the latter as description is always also a command, and it must remain indefinite whether one means the one or the other. Moreover, is there no point where both command and fulfillment are so completely equalized that they are absolutely identical? Certainly in Christ the Redeemer, in whom communion with God is absolute, not a becoming, there is absolute agreement between action and the commands of Christian ethics. So we must say, "Christian ethics is a description of Christian ways of acting insofar as these are traced back to the Redeemer, and precisely as description it is also command for all who are in the Christian church, for whom nothing is command but what may be developed out of absolute communion with God as it existed in Christ the Redeemer."

Now, if Christian ethics is thus a description of Christian self-consciousness insofar as it is impulse, the question becomes, "How is it then impulse, and how does it pass over into action?" All this we must now explicate. Since our discipline strives to be a complete whole, which is composed out of a series of individual propositions, what is presented must itself be a multiplicity that has a unity for its ground and a unity that becomes a multiplicity. Following on this process, however, next we must investigate whether Christian consciousness is but a simple impulse that first becomes multiple through joining with something outside it, or whether it is already a multiplicity in itself. Religious consciousness is originally self-consciousness. We proceed from this fact. Yet we have specified it more narrowly as communion with God under the form of self-consciousness proceeding from what is distinctively Christian, viewed as communion with God as determined by redemption through Christ. This concept includes within itself a host of other claims. First, such a condition is also possible for human nature because without this it would not be possible for this condition to be brought forth through Christ. Second, this condition cannot be developed out of human nature left to itself, for without this a person could develop it without the intervention of Christ. Now, whether the inability to come to communion with God outside of connection with Christ is something originally posited, or whether it is something learned that has simply been lost—this does not concern us here for we are not considering the whole history of human consciousness but only that which is in the church, and this latter does not go beyond what is manifest in Christ.

[THE THREE FORMS OF ACTION]

In consequence, regarding action in the church, we are completely indifferent to this question. However, if we posit communion with God as determined by Christ, we also posit that outside of Christ it does not exist; for us, a person who is separated from redemption is thus in a condition of separation from God, with no possibility that the separation can be overcome. We can think of this condition as only being in opposition to the Christian condition; for since in this condition God is determinative, we can think of it only as opposition to God—that is, only as sin. Hence the whole presentation of the distinctiveness of religious consciousness in Christianity is essentially determined by sin's being posited as the unavoidable universal human condition outside of communion with Christ. Yet if we think about the condition of communion with God as mediated through Christ and being perfected, thus as completely separated from the condition of humanity outside of communion with God in Christ, this is the condition of blessedness, the condition in which we lack nothing in our own consciousness, and in which we are actually absolutely perfected, thus having consciousness of our own being as totally fulfilled. When we say that this is the condition of Christians in which the religious consciousness is perfectly developed, we say at the same time that it is not the being of persons in and for themselves, but the being of persons in communion with God mediated through Christ, that it is such only insofar as consciousness of the Supreme Being is completely coposited in self-consciousness through communion with Christ.

Now, how can such an existence—which we can represent to ourselves only as in itself completely at rest—thus become an impulse? It is as difficult to think of these two ideas together as it is for us to teach two opposing considerations. First of all, if we think of God without the world but with absolute blessedness, it appears that there could be no transition at all that would allow God to move out of Godself in order to produce the world. The creation of the world appears to our thinking as something totally ungrounded, as something arbitrary, and this is the deepest ground of all objections against the idea of creation in time. Then, if we look at humanity and consider its activity, we are always inclined to ascribe activity to a consciousness of deficiency. Certainly, the oft-spoken proposition that need is the source of all human activity offends our feeling in several ways, and we would gladly let go of it. On the other hand, however, we would still have to say that in order really to let go of it, we would have to be in a place to conceive of persons already in a state of absolute blessedness and in a state of activity, and we will never succeed if we want to prove this for the individual. Rather, we must always return to the proposition that every activity presupposes a deficiency. This is so for when we say, for example, "There are activities through which a person seeks to achieve no goal"—and all presentation, all play is certainly of this kind—yet on closer consideration we see that an inner urge is always presupposed, and it follows that the condition before a given presentation is less perfect than the condition after that presentation. And so it appears that religious consciousness that is viewed as blessedness can never become an impulse.

Nevertheless, the matter can be viewed from another perspective. How do we come to think of the condition of humanity as blessed? If we consider any given condition, we must abstract much from it in order to be able to think of it as blessed: on the one hand, everything in it which still has some share in being outside of communion with God, and on the other hand, everything which is not yet perfected activity, which we believe must be coposited in communion with God. Based on this latter observation, however, it follows that we can posit blessedness being perfected only, as it were, after an assemblage of perfected actions. Also, to this extent we cannot posit that blessedness is being and impulse simultaneously. Based on this consideration, we conclude that the two concepts, blessedness and impulse, can only be united when we conceive of the blessedness of Christians not as being but as becoming.

There is an objection to our proposal, the removal of which will be fruitful for the whole further development of our presentation. We have said that in Christianity communion with God is mediated through Christ, determined by connection with Christ. However, in this way if Christian faith is actually to proceed from this connection, we must conceive of it in such a way that the communion of Christ with God is original and perfect, and on the other hand that in us communion with God is derived from Christ's communion with God and is continually becoming an approximation of his. This is so, for if Christ's communion with God is not a state of being, ours cannot be derived from his. Yet if his communion with God is absolute, his condition is simply and utterly that of blessedness itself. It would follow from this that we could not even know how this could become an impulse in him in the way that we could think of ourselves as, like him, simultaneously blessed and acting. Thus, between our condition and his there would have to be such a distinction that the two could not be grounded in the same concept. The effort to resolve this difficulty could easily move us to posit the relationship between Christ and our communion with God in a fixed way; this is a dogmatic issue that we need not take up here. Instead, we must seek to depict the matter directly at this point, and we must say, "If we think of Christ as a child coming into the world, we cannot think of perfect blessedness as included in this form of life, for the condition of a child is deficient, because his nature is not yet fully developed in him." Yet this deficiency does not lie on the side of communion with God but is something purely organic and is located in the child as the impulse to all action.

If, then, we now think of Christ with all the spiritual and organic powers of human nature fully developed, we can still think of all activity in him in analogy with the early development, for the adult person can and must always be learning more. However, in terms of being able to think of his blessedness as impulse and as communicated to us, we must let go of the viewpoint we have held to this point and no longer think of Christ as isolated, but think of him taking up the existence of all other human beings as the communal feeling of his self-consciousness, and think of him carrying our deficiency of blessedness in a sympathetic way, so to speak, so that our formulation also finds application to him, and a deficiency of blessedness must be posited in him so that it can become an impulse. This deficiency originates in him in his expanded self-consciousness, in his feeling with us our lack of blessedness, and this is in him the impulse for the whole of his redeeming activity. In this way we can retain the position that blessedness and impulse can coexist only insofar as blessedness is simply a matter of becoming.

Now, in order to fix our subject aright, we must make quite clear the distinction between the becoming of blessedness and absolute blessedness. If we return to our own self-consciousness, we do not find pure blessedness to be present at all. How, then, is the becoming of blessedness manifest in us? It is manifest in the alteration between what is pleasurable and what is lacking in pleasure in relation to that which is the measure of blessedness. This can only become clear when it is also clear that in absolute blessedness this alteration cannot be posited. In relation to this, one element in and of itself is evident, for the lack of pleasure cannot be thought to be present in divine blessedness. However, neither can pleasure be conceived for it lies in the realm of decrease and increase, of change, of oscillation. In this realm, however, which contains less and more and is wavering between the two, there is never perfection in itself; if we think of absolute blessedness as a negation of all lack of pleasure, we must also think of it as the negation of all pleasure. Although they are unequal, pleasure is itself as essential as the lack of pleasure; it is something that must be essentially lacking in absolute blessedness.

It does not yet follow from this, however, that blessedness in the process of becoming must necessarily have these two characteristics that absolute blessedness cannot have. That it can be nothing other than this does follow when we consider that communion with God can only be grounded through Christ because there is no other way to establish it. This is the case, for if it could be established by other means, Christianity would be only something incidental. Implicit within this position is the notion that the life of a Christian in communion with God would proceed from the negation of this communion. However, if we consider communion with God to be negated in human self-consciousness in such a way that no claim can be made on this basis, the lack of pleasure is also negated.

The possibility of the lack of pleasure rests in the first place on a claim to communion with God. In absolute blessedness, however, the lack of pleasure can no longer be imagined since just as earlier, before communion with God was established, it could not yet be imagined. Thus it lies necessarily between two points, one in which communion with God can first be responded to, and another in which it is perfected as absolute blessedness. Also, the same thing is true of pleasure, for in each moment between the two points, both pleasure and lack of pleasure must always exist: pleasure, insofar as communion with God has begun and is compared to its negation; and lack of pleasure, insofar as it is compared with absolute blessedness.

We posited pleasure and lack of pleasure as equally essential factors in the domain of blessedness in the process of becoming, in such a way that each moment must comprise both elements; hence, we must admit something common between the two that always passes over into the two opposed forms, and this is the claim to communion with God thought of together with its realization but without this being determined as given in any one moment. If the condition of communion with God were seen as a stage in human life, it would continually be compared with a lower stage toward which communion with God would act negatively, but this influence is also not claimed. Moreover, in this constant comparison with a lower stage of life, which is the same in moments in which becoming blessedness appears as pleasure and the moments in which lack of pleasure appears, we have the constant consciousness of a higher life potency overall. This is precisely the consciousness that Scripture calls "joy in God" or "joy in the Lord," that constant consciousness of the same higher stage of life that is the basis for our communion with God and from which our consciousness of pleasure and of the lack of pleasure proceeds in each moment. Thus, if we want to describe the life of the Christian as pious—purely from the side of self-consciousness and abstracting from actions proper—the constant greatness therein will be this joy in the Lord, which in some moments will be experienced as pleasure insofar as the content of these moments is felt as a drawing near to absolute blessedness, and as lack of pleasure insofar as negation of communion with God is predominantly called to mind.

Through this consideration the matter will become clear up to a point: a pure negation appears nonetheless as something positive when the contents of individual moments are determined. Here we will simply return to the way in which

Scripture presents this comparison between the higher and lower life potencies. In the opposition set forth between flesh and spirit, flesh is the lower and spirit the higher, and the former in comparison with the latter is its negation; but as a stage of life it is positive, and precisely this positive feature is that which in the comparison is experienced as lack of pleasure. That is, it is not that the locus of the lower life potency in persons will be abolished or destroyed, but only that the difference between the two will be overcome. Each moment is to be determined by the higher life potency in that everything that belongs to the lower life potency will become its instrument, and all self-determination will be renounced. If the lower life potency comes independently into a moment, it must nonetheless be felt as lack of pleasure as the two are related to each other, because the higher life potency is negated as a determined power and because not only is the higher life potency negated, but the lower also comes forward independently, so that the negation is at the same time something positive.

[Restoring Action and Broadening Action]

Now, how does this consciousness pass over from being self-consciousness that is simply at rest to being an impulse? If we posit the claim to communion with God and the reality of the same compared in every moment to the idea of communion with God in itself, yet always as something that is not yet complete, it is not possible to think of this moment in real life without an impulse being thought of at the same time, which the moment does not yet fulfill, yet the impulse seeks to realize the communion with God that has been claimed. We can divide this proposition into two others of which it is composed, which are expressed in a negative way. The first proposition is, "There is no impulse in absolute blessedness, because it cannot be conceived without thinking of all action as completed. Here there is no longer any difference whatsoever between the way in which the claim and its satisfaction are in consciousness." Then what corresponds to the first proposition is the second: "As long as the claim to communion with God is not yet established in self-consciousness, no impulse to activity is possible that could be included in a presentation of Christian ethics, for the nonexisting condition would then be negated in an absolutely identical way, just as, for example, the notion of a human being flying is negated."

Moreover, if we take these two propositions together, it follows that all activities that aim to produce absolute blessedness must lie between these two points. Also, between these two points there is no conceivable moment in which it is not the case that religious self-consciousness must necessarily become impulse. Now, is there a different impulse for blessedness as becoming on the basis of whether pleasure or lack of pleasure is present? We must compare these two more closely with each other from the viewpoint of how self-consciousness passes over into impulse. Lack of pleasure is posited when the indication is that the claim to communion with God has been negated in a given moment. If we consider more closely how this can be, we must say, "Beginning at the moment when communion with God is claimed, an impulse is also coposited." An impulse conceived as being without any actual activity, and an activity conceived as being without any result—either one is impossible. Thus, it seems as if the condition of persons in the beginning of such a moment must then be a constantly growing pleasure. That would be the case if we could explain everything within it in terms of this impulse. However, the moment in which communion with God begins to be claimed is very remote from the beginning point of human life. This is our basic presupposition, even if this is not the place to justify this claim. As a result it is clear that before the beginning of the higher life potency, the lower life potency is already in possession of all impulses. If that is the case, however, it is also inconceivable that the higher life potency, in the sheer emergence of claiming communion with God, can also directly overcome all the possessions of the lower life potency. If that is to be the case, it must be able to effect, within an endless process and through endless moments, what is not sustainable in the form that human life takes.

Thus, there is always still an opposition in the consciousness of Christians, always a vestige of the independent existence of the lower life potency, a desire of flesh that opposes spirit, and the restraint that proceeds from this is what is experienced as something lacking in pleasure. However, if that sense of something lacking in pleasure is in place, the effort to overcome the independent activity of the lower life potency is also in place, for as the sense of something lacking in pleasure is only the feeling of an impediment to the higher life; so also the effort that proceeds from the midpoint of this life does not allow itself to be impeded nor to rest until the lower life potency is not destroyed—because if it were destroyed the higher life potency would also be destroyed, for it can only exist as it is bound together with the lower life potency in the form that human life takes; rather, in this way it becomes the organism for the higher life potency, and also this higher life potency is its sole agent.

Along with the sense of a lack of pleasure, there thus exists an impulse to action through which the very idea of the relationship between the higher and lower life potencies that has been infringed upon, the normal situation that has been negated, is to be produced, and since it should not stretch out beyond the subject's actual self-consciousness, the size and scope of which is not at all to be determined here, we can appropriately call it restoring action. What is to be restored is not simply the particularity of what was at one time present. Rather, what is to be restored is what is always established with the beginning of Christian moral life: that spirit has dominion over flesh as its organism even though the obstinacy of flesh in an individual is as yet never completely overcome. However, the pleasure that stands in contrast to the lack of pleasure is posited not when we are conscious of the subordination of the lower potency under the higher potency being perfected in one moment or domain, for if that moment were also pleasure, it would not be the kind that could be an actual impulse, since this would proceed much more out of a perfected action, including within itself the kind of rest that is analogous to absolute blessedness. Rather, pleasure is posited when a lower power of life comes under the claim of a higher power and when that same pleasure is posited without resistance (for if there were resistance, a sense of something lacking in pleasure would arise), as willing and insistently inclined in such a way that its subordination under the higher power is immediately possible. Moreover, the impulse toward a widening, broadening action is identical with this pleasure.

[Presentational Action]

Do these two forms of action—the restoring and the broadening—embrace the whole domain of action? Just consider the possibility that if a task of broadening action were completed in terms of self-consciousness, it would be seen in this respect as absolute blessedness, and only rest could proceed from it. Self-consciousness would then consist in the following, that everything in this realm had already been done. So if we have said that self-consciousness would be analogous to absolute blessedness, now we can also say that in this particular connection it would be absolute blessedness itself. Moreover, both of these positions are correct: quantitatively, it would be analogous to absolute blessedness; qualitatively, it would be the thing itself. Now is it possible, then, that a partial self-consciousness of this kind can be quantitatively distinguished from the absolute, which is qualitatively identical to it? If so, we would have the right to say that it is absolute rest and could not become impulse. If not, however, then it would only be relative blessedness and must become an impulse. So how does this matter stand? If we think of any relation of consciousness in which the lower power of life is perfectly subordinate to the higher power, it is certain that at that point no action can proceed from this consciousness that would want to change something in this relation; to this degree it would certainly be analogous to absolute rest, which must be thought of as included in absolute blessedness. This is the case, for if an action in this connection wanted to change something, there must still be an imperfection in the subordination, an obstinacy of the lower power of life must be present, and from this state no peace could emerge. Alternatively, there would have to be no unity in self-consciousness; rather, it must be a composition from two elements, from the consciousness of perfection and from that of possible unity, and this too would not be able to produce peace, for a possible unity always remains nothing more than a task.

Now, however, in that this self-consciousness in life would always be only partial, we would nonetheless always actually have to present the matter in this way: "We are conscious in ourselves of a certain portion of that which constitutes the lower life, in its complete subordination to the higher life." Yet this portion does not admit of being completely isolated; thus we can be conscious of this portion in ourselves only as it belongs together with the whole, and in virtue of this fact it would still have to unite the two opposing characters in itself. That is, this portion on the one hand includes in itself the capacity and the willingness to subordinate itself to the whole, and to this degree there would be coposited at the same time an element of aroused pleasure that can become impulse. Yet this portion on the other hand is in place in connection with the whole and to this degree with obstinacy of the lower against the higher; to this degree the specific task would be coposited at the same time to overcome this obstinacy in all the remaining portions.

Likewise we must say, considering the matter from a different standpoint: "Such a partial self-consciousness that represents absolute blessedness can always only be momentary, for how could we ever rest permanently on a portion of the whole?" Now, just as self-consciousness is incited and determined from another point, however, in turn it cannot be such that what is analogous to absolute blessedness would be the determination of self-consciousness; rather, it would be one or another of the types mentioned earlier. Thus it is posited that if such a self-consciousness were absolute blessedness, absolute without any opposition between what is pleasurable and unpleasurable, then we must think the impossible—that from absolute rest there is a transition to activity—or give up entirely [the effort to] construe an action that is interconnected with the relation of the lower power of life to the higher power of life. Accordingly, either there is no condition whatsoever that represents absolute blessedness, or there must be some condition of this sort that has the capacity to be an impulse.

Perhaps we want to say, "There is none, there is no moment in which we are actually conscious in ourselves of the subordination of the lower power to the higher power." Fine; then all moments are either pleasure or lack of pleasure of the kind noted above. Now, if self-consciousness were determined as pleasurable, how then is the broadening action that emerges therefrom to cease if not in a moment of satisfaction? It would have to continue indefinitely. On the other hand, if we consider self-consciousness in us determined as lacking in pleasure, how could it have been so determined? How could it begin a restoring action if there were no moment of unification of the lower power with the higher power, in which there would have been relative satisfaction? All that remains to be said now is that between the moments of pleasure and those lacking in pleasure, a moment of satisfaction must necessarily enter; that cannot be posited as absolute blessedness, but only as relative blessedness; it must be impulse and must pass over into action. What kind of action then? Evidently only a kind such that it is not essentially and immediately related to any aspect of life and is not destined to produce any sort of change.

Even apart from religious self-consciousness, in other domains we find actions that are not distinctively destined to produce change, actions that express what is inner without being actually efficacious. We call everything "play" when it appears in a lower and formless gestalt, and "art" when it appears in higher and developed form. Both are actual actions, but neither has a specific tendency to change something in the relation of humans to the world; they are not directed toward the accomplishment of a purpose but are purposeless; they are not of such a kind as must have as its ground a specific pleasure or lack of it, a momentary determination of life. Rather, they proceed from the general consciousness of life that is the innermost source of all momentary determinations of existence.

Certainly, if we could completely isolate an aspect of life and within it also the moment of such relative satisfaction, then we would hardly be able to conceive even how the expression of a purposeless action could proceed from that state. However, a person is never given to us in isolation; only the totality of humanity, given as a living unity, can be isolated. Moreover, such an individual moment is isolated just as little. This is so, for if it were isolated, it would be nothing but the absolute origin and disappearance at one and the same time. Thus, it only exists as it is interwoven in the whole in a living way as originating from the earlier moments and passing over into the later ones—that is, if it is, in a certain sense, something enduring. How then can it still be a moment? It must be able to be repeated; thereby it becomes something enduring, and it nonetheless also remains a moment. So now we see that for a moment that proceeds from a state of rest, that moment's connection can be produced in no other way than by an activity being produced from it, yet an activity in which the predominant tendency is to fix on "the moment" from which it actually arises so that the moment can be repeated. How is it then in this respect with what we have found to be the general type of such an action? If we simply consider play, it interrupts the succession of efficacious actions directed toward a purpose and essentially has only the tendency to express freedom in motion through certain fixed forms in order to ensure the repeatability of those moments and to hold its own identity fast. The moment does not disappear, because through a fixed form of expression it becomes a self-repeating and constant aspect of the whole of life.

It is no contradiction that the moment holds within itself both rest and activity, because both are only relative, not absolute. The activity is only relative for in itself it is nothing other than expression of the desire to continue in the given condition without any tendency to change anything therein. Rest is only relative: if it were absolute, it would be a complete negation of all temporal life; rest expresses itself in precisely such a way that in its activity only rest itself is fixed and real, not that the condition itself is to be altered in any way. Moreover, if we set aside the individual in himself, which we can as little isolate as we can the individual moment in life, and we consider the individual in community, in common life with others, we find this individual only insofar as his existence is taken up in the community's consciousness, and this consciousness in turn can be true only if the succession of the different moments—which is the only way that the inner unity of life can be manifest—is taken up with it. Where the inner determination of humanity passes over into efficacious action, the manifestation in others is already coposited. However, even the moments—about which we are speaking and without which the existence of humanity would not be complete—must be taken up into the consciousness of others; this could not come to pass if it had a tendency toward absolute rest, for in this state there is nothing to be recognized.

Thus we see also from this side that there could only be a relative satisfaction. There must be an impulse to activity but only in such a way that it will be taken up into the consciousness of others, and consequently there can be nothing other than a pure passing over of the internal into the external in order to be taken up again in the internal. So from these two observations we find two formulas for our activity: (1) One that is pure expression and negates all efficacy, because in this the only effort is to fix the moment. (2) One that is purely a presentational action: it has no purpose other than to make its own existence such that it can likewise be appropriated by others, wherewith all actual efficaciousness is excluded that can only proceed from what is pleasurable or what is lacking in pleasure.

Bringing together everything that has been said to this point, we have thus found two main ways in which the inner determination of Christian self-consciousness becomes an impulse: these are impulse to an efficacious action through which a person desires to move from one condition to another, and impulse to a presentational action through which a person does not move out of his condition but only wants to fix the inner determination of self-consciousness in an outward way. The first impulse is also twofold in turn, as to whether self-consciousness is determined as pleasure or lack of pleasure. The second impulse cannot also be twofold because it is the transition from one determination of self-consciousness to the other and is essentially indifferent toward both. Instead, what we have found are only formulas; we still lack the pictures wherein they are realized. So we must ask whether we can actually find the general classes of actions that correspond to the formulas we have presented.

If we look first at nonefficacious action, presentational action that is nothing but the expression of our communal Christian condition, we will have to say, "The general type of this action is everything that we bring together under the name of Christian worship." Two objections can be raised against us. In the first place, one can say that Christian worship is not at all to be such a nonefficacious action; rather, it belongs to the broadening side of efficacious action since it establishes and increases Christian piety. Furthermore, neither do the given actions of Christian worship proceed at all from a condition that we have taken to be the origin of presentational action, that is, not from consciousness of relative fulfillment, but from consciousness of deficiency. This is so, for if we look at how Christian worship is constituted, we find everywhere in it a certain spontaneity and also a certain receptivity. Thus, keeping the receptive side in view, one could say that insofar, for example, as a congregation were listening in worship, it would also be receptive; and insofar as it were receptive, we must also presuppose a desire to receive, thus a feeling of deficiency, a feeling of a lack of pleasure. On the other hand, if we look at the other side of worship, the active side, without which worship could just as little exist for it cannot be thought of without speakers and writers, it appears that what must be presupposed is not a consciousness of deficiency, but rather its opposite, the feeling of pleasure that ends in broadening action. Thus one could say here that, combining these two aspects, the whole of worship is put together from the receptive activity of those who feel themselves deficient and from the communicative activity of those who feel themselves strong enough to provide fulfillment to those who yearn to receive in themselves a greater measure of what is religious.

However, suppose we doubt that the contrast between these two functions, that of communication and that of reception, is nothing of a personal nature in worship; but that, if one looks at each participant in himself, the communicative function is necessarily also receptive and the receptive function is just as surely also productive and not purely passive. Thus if we suppose that both factors are always present on both sides, then the conditions for worship's fulfillment would also be posited as being present everywhere. The indifference toward pleasure and lack of pleasure that we seek, and the expression, the presentation of fulfillment—these would be posited as the very nature of worship. It is clear that people have also constantly viewed it only in this way. This is the case, for if worship had been held to be merely a means of establishing and increasing Christian piety, one would never need to exclude those from worship who are most in need of enlivening, and yet this has been done from the beginning, thus presupposing that participants in worship need not proceed from a feeling of deficiency. Thus for the time being we can state as a well-founded fact that the only requirement is the expression and communication of the condition of relative fulfillment that we have found to be the impulse from which worship proceeds.

Let us look more closely at efficacious action that proceeds from pleasure. As we have seen, this action presupposes that in self-consciousness we can find cognizance of the presence of an inclination that has come from somewhere to raise the lower life to the higher and a feeling that the inclination has the strength to begin the corresponding broadening action. Therefore, however, we find it obvious that the main type of action in what is education in any sense of the word is, accordingly, not just action of the mature on the immature, but is above all action of the mentally[15] stronger intelligence on the mentally weaker. This is so, for one could never come to the point of educating persons instead of merely drilling them if they were not already in a time when, though the higher life potency still appeared to be sleeping in them, an inclination was perceived or at least presupposed for uniting the lower life potency with the higher, and if the perceived inclination were on the other hand not to feel itself to have the power to awaken the higher life potency in itself; thus if both of these conditions were not present, the basic presupposition for action that proceeds from pleasure would be lacking. However, whether the whole of efficacious action that proceeds from this determination of self-consciousness is always only an action of one person toward another, or whether there are also some efficacious actions that have the character of a person being an object to himself—this is not a question to be decided here. We can only observe that self-formation, an action of a person on himself, is conceivable only to the extent that a twofolded-ness in the person within himself may be presumed, be it a twofoldedness that exists in a moment of time or in some place—since this twofoldedness must be presupposed in educational activity; thus an action of a person on himself is conceivable if there is no opposition in him to his desiring something on the one hand viewed as a higher process of life and on the other hand viewed as taking this higher process of life into himself.

Finally let us examine the efficacious action that proceeds from the impulse belonging to a lack of pleasure of a religious sort, which would either restore the proper relationship between the congregation and individuals if it has been interrupted or dissolved at some place or other, or would return anything what-soever that is part of the power of the lower life to obedience toward the higher life. Accordingly, it is self-evident that everything that is in any sense punish-ment, discipline, or penitence belongs to this category. This is so, for all of this, dealt with in the general way that we have given here, is nothing but an action that proceeds from the strength of higher life, with the presupposition that that relationship between the lower potency and the higher is disturbed.

Now, however, if these are the general types of modes of action that we have found, do we have the probability that the whole of moral action would be covered by this typology? Or do other areas of moral action still remain that do not come from this typology, for which we would thus still be lacking the principle for judging and for their presentation? Let us assume that humanity's external vocation is to be lord of the earth and its internal vocation is to present the image of God, which is originally only in Christ. It is evident concerning our broadening and restoring actions that each concerns itself completely with both of these vocations. Suppose we look further at the fact that all actions that are interposed between these two actions, and that have as their task human being's self-revelation, correspond completely to our presentational action. Then it would appear that the whole of moral action is in fact encompassed by our three forms [of action: restoring, broadening, and presentational].

Now, however, is the moral life truly comprehended by means of this typol-ogy? We have proceeded on the basis of the fact that a determination of self-consciousness belongs to each action; therewith pleasure or lack of pleasure or indifference toward both must be presupposed. Now, however, there is no moment in life in which there could not be a basis for each of these determina-tions and for each of the corresponding modes of action. Thus it follows that the entirety of moral life may be completely attended to in each of the three forms and may be constituted from each one. It may seem to be a matter of indiffer-ence from which action we constitute it and whether we do so only out of one form or out of all three. However, as a result the construction would be subject to arbitrariness, and thus a scientific presentation would not be possible.

Nonetheless, this difficulty resolves itself when we recall our finding that the contrast on which our division is based is not absolute, but only relative. This is so, for we found precisely this when we were required to concede that that determination of self-consciousness abstracted from the content of the moment—excluding absolute pleasure and lack of pleasure, yet not absolutely but only relatively—would be blessedness that included pleasure and lack of pleasure within it as a minimum since it is actually coposited with the understanding that pleasure and lack of pleasure do not totally exclude each other. "The difficulty resolves itself," I say, "for if the contrasts are only relative, this means that the whole of life can be attended to by each of the three forms of self-consciousness, and none of them is superfluous. On the contrary it is clear that if one wanted to convey only one of these forms of self-consciousness completely, one would have to convey the others in order to account for that which is contained even as a minimum in those others." Thus all three forms must necessarily be conveyed in order to be able to indicate the predominant and less important elements in each moment of life.

PART ONE
EFFICACIOUS ACTION

DIVISION I
RESTORING OR PURIFYING ACTION

Chapter 2

Purifying or Restoring Action in the Christian Congregation

INTRODUCTION

The presupposition for this kind of action is, above all, the partial negation of the dominion of the Holy Spirit over the flesh, that is, sin. However, from which side does sin appear in this? That is, how is a partial negation of that relationship between spirit and flesh possible once it has been established? It cannot proceed from spirit, the living principle, for what proceeds from the spirit is necessarily sin's opposite; it must have its ground in a condition of sensorial nature—one, indeed, that does not rest on the already-existing general dominion of spirit but one that is independent of the latter. This is our second presupposition.

In Christ we posit the dependence of sensorial nature on spirit as original; thus we posit sin as impossible for him. However, concerning all remaining persons, the matter is actually as follows. The relationship of flesh to spirit is two-fold, a relationship to spirit in oneself and a relation to spirit in others. In the beginning of our life, the Holy Spirit—in cases where we also want to take the Spirit into ourselves—is obviously as yet able to exercise no sway over sensorial nature. However, the Spirit is at once active and holds sway through the repetition of the Spirit's activity, through indwelling presence. However, because the individual exists only in community with others, his sensorial nature is always dependent on the spirit that dwells within the community. Now in Christian community this dependence is never lacking anywhere; thus it is clear that, based on our presupposition, every action of the church against sin in it can be seen as a restoring action.

Further, as was said earlier, in Christ we imagine the self-sufficiency of spirit over flesh to be absolutely original, the originating action[1] of spirit needing no help and absolutely preserved from all the influence of the sinfulness of the whole human race. Now, if we suppose the Christian community to be perfect in this way in any moments of this life, the individual would indeed be formed—certainly not through his own personal power like Christ, but through the power of the whole—in a way completely devoid of sin, and all restoring action in the church would be superfluous. Therefore the task to perform restoring action can arise only on the presupposition that the existence of sin in the individual has its basis in the sinfulness of the whole. However, it is also certain that we have a point here that we can regard in this respect as the null point of our task, and we must at least grant that to the degree that the Christian community approaches perfection, the need for purifying actions in it must be correspondingly removed.

Now, however, if we consider the other characteristics of these actions, on the basis of our suppositions it seems that if purification were necessary, presentational action would not be able to begin at all; and also on the basis of our supposition it seems that if the broadening or presentational actions were in progress, purifying actions would be completely superfluous. That is, since the only efficacious action conceivable would be broadening action if the Christian community were absolutely sinless (we are still abstracting here from presentational action), it appears that as long as the absolute sinlessness of the church cannot be admitted—even when the church is making progress toward its perfection—the more perfect the broadening action in the church is, the less room would remain for purifying action. Thus purifying action would rest only on the imperfection of broadening action. This is how the matter appears in the whole. For the individual, however, it appears as follows. If we imagine the life of an individual as an ongoing series of actions that belong to widening or broadening actions, we have no actions but those that proceed from the impulse of spirit and for which the object is the raw material of nature not yet united with spirit. Between the two, between spirit and nature as raw material, there lies then the organism of spirit, everything in humans that is already united with spirit, that is, the whole sensorial nature of an individual person when spirit is effective in him without exception.

Thus with continuing efficacious action that has contributed in every moment to the expansion of the reign of God, the individual's sensorial nature would also be animated and governed by spirit, out of which [perfecting] practice would result of itself. For with each such action it must be easier for spirit to regulate sensorial nature and easier for sensorial nature to allow itself to be governed by spirit, for without this there could be no moral experience at all. Consequently, given this presupposed continuity of broadening actions, the organic union between sensorial nature and spirit would have to become more complete in every moment, so that along with it even what would exist as abnormality in sensorial nature, as sin, would have to disappear of itself. Thus, at least in the Christian community, no purifying action would exist if it were in the position of being able to engage its members in uninterrupted broadening action that is efficacious.

Yet does it not appear therewith that the whole form of this action would be brought to nothing where the Christian disposition is purely constitutive? Would we not have to say, "Since the continuity of broadening action would still actually be lost, would the possibility of restoring action not rest on sin, and would every actual practice of the same not rest on some continuing remnant of sin?" Would we not have to say, "Belief in the necessity of purifying action itself would be nothing other than an outgrowth of sin"? Therefore, against this inference it is reasonable that we would have to be greatly suspicious if we were to consider that, in actuality, there can be no action that would be exclusively broadening. The right place to develop this further and to ground it more precisely will become evident shortly.

However, first let us likewise still consider purifying action as compared with presentational action. This comparison appears to yield a twofold result. On the one hand, a person could say, "Recognition of the necessity of restoring action includes within it at the same time some incapacity for presentational action." This is so, for what is to be presented is the pure relationship of spirit to sensorial nature, the power of spirit over sensorial nature. Where this is not the case, there is nothing to present, and presentational action could only begin if purification were no longer necessary. On the other hand, one could say that presentational action would make purification unnecessary. For since we have also said that presentational action could be distinguished from the positive side of efficacious action in that it would not produce anything and rather would be a pure expression of what is within, it is clear that spirit could never carry out presentational action entirely on its own; but spirit could carry out presentational action only by means of sensorial nature as its organ. However, if this is the case, presentational action always includes a practice within itself that directly conveys the dominion of spirit over flesh, and to this degree it appears to be able to replace purifying action altogether.

Now, these two observations seem to contradict each other. One cannot contest the first, that no one in whom the right relationship between spirit and sensorial nature is negated is capable of pure presentation. Nor can the other observation be contested, that presentational action includes within itself a practice of increasing the dominion of spirit over sensorial nature. Thus if presentational action were completely a matter that only involved individuals, nothing would be left to do but to choose between these two points of view. Yet we would still always have to say, "The view that individuals must be excluded from presentational action because of impurity is certainly stricter; however, it must still be moderated a great deal if another presentational action is ever to take place since in actuality we are never absolutely free of all impurities." The other view—ignoring impurities in the hope that they would disappear with time through the formative practice connected to presentation—is certainly the laxer view, but still it proceeds correctly from the fact that presentation could never take place at all [if complete purity were required] and that presentation must be begun with what is imperfect.

However, the matter looks differently when we consider that presentation in the Christian community is actually not a matter for individuals alone, but proceeds from the church. For then the task is for each individual to participate in the presentational action of the whole in a way that his imperfection does not endanger it. If this is possible, there is no conflict between purifying and presentational action as exists between purifying and broadening action. It is easy to see that the task cannot be fulfilled with complete rigor, but only in an approximate way, thus only in an oscillation between more strict and more lax viewpoints.

If we consider all this together, we find therein the germ of the different theories of purifying action in the church, theories that have actually been put into practice. In the first place, it has been claimed that there would be no need for action that is especially directed toward purification either from the side of the whole community or from the side of individuals because purification would turn up along with vocational faithfulness in broadening action completely by itself. Another theory that is compatible with the former says, "Whether a purifying action would take place or not, this much is certain, that the Christian community would have to exclude from participation in presentational action all those in whom an impurity occurs on a particular day." The former theory is the negation of all penance in the church except the positive side of discipline; the latter theory is the recognition of excommunication as the negative side of discipline, not directed toward producing purification of individuals, but only directed toward protecting the self-presentation of the Christian community from contamination.

Over against this is a third theory saying that this strictness would make it impossible for presentational action in the church to be initiated; however, presentational action would have to happen, and one could depend just as much on the purifying effects of this action as one could depend on the effects of positive efficacious action. And so all purifying action proper remains completely empty. Against these there is a fourth theory, which recognizes both the positive side of discipline, penitence, and the negative side, the ban, to be necessary. This view excludes individuals from equality of participation not only in presentational action but also in the efficacious action of the church, as long as there is impurity in them. This is the theory of the Roman [Catholic] Church in its opposition to the Evangelical Church and in close connection with the contrast between clergy and laity in the Roman Church. For in the spiritual leaders as such they decree there to be no impurity because for it the totality of the clergy represents the pure spirit of the church. At least, this is the Roman Church's idea even if it is not so strictly expressed in a didactic way. They ascribe to the laity only a passive role in relation to the clergy in all broadening and presentational actions; they suppose that all spontaneity in the church is only in the clergy. For the clergymen set forth its doctrine, order the rules for living, watch to see whether life itself is in accord with the rules, provide laity with the impulse to all actions, prescribe penance to them, and have the right to exclude them from presentational action. Thus the Roman Church must affirm the infallibility of the clergy.

On the other hand, in the Evangelical Church all the non-Catholic theories find a place side by side. For even if the Evangelical symbols [confessions] never say that there can be no activity that is restoring in an explicit way, that is affirmed so frequently by individuals that it would be hard to find a moral system that lacks this theory as its ground. On the other hand, there are unions in the Evangelical Church that allow the church ban as something temporary because the imperfection of individuals can hinder the presentation of the whole, and also there are unions that even contest the community having the right to apply temporary exclusion from worship, precisely because for us presentational action must replace purifying action.

This is how it stands in general. Now, however, as concerns our position on this matter, we of course admit that if an individual is thought of as being in a continuity of broadening action in and for the reign of God, in each moment something happens in him through which the dominion of spirit over sensorial nature is increased in a general way. However, this in no way makes all purifying action superfluous. If we look at nothing but the totality and consider all actions as common, the church only as a unity and individuals only as a part, the principle is completely correct, for here we will say, "The perfection of the Christian church, the final goal of which is absolute perfection, is an approximation, and thus something that is gradually growing, and it increases infallibly in every moment, when the church is conceived of as a unity in a continuity of broadening action." What happens in each moment does not matter since the approximation can still come about only in a gradual way. The task itself is a true totality, and everything is included within it, everything that will be seen as purification from another point of view. Thus along with the completion of the task, all purification will also be effected, and there will no longer be any individual imperfections in the church, so that we can claim with full justification, "The church as a unity requires no special purification."

However, the matter is very different when we consider the individual in himself and see the perfection of the individual as the goal. That is, the vocation of an individual is not a perfectly uniform efficacy in all directions. In civil life, in the common task of the human race, which has as its object dominion over the earth, we are in agreement that each individual's task must be partial because only through a distribution of work can an organism be found such as is necessary for the completion of the task. Now the matter is certainly not as clear in relation to the spiritual[2] task of the inner perfection of persons in the church. For even if we bring the whole human race together here, we can still only see the task as completed when each individual is utterly perfected in himself so that, accordingly, agreement must be sought for the completion of the task in the whole and in each individual. However, something analogous must still take place here, in turn. There is already a one-sidedness in the individual nature of each person, and yet we can never regard it as a task to change nature itself, but only for it to be subject to spirit as it is. And in this there already lies the truth that something can be accomplished for the reign of God by means of one individual that cannot be accomplished by means of another. So here too the usual division of labor must take place, and the vocation for each individual cannot consist of identical activity in all directions.

Now, however, if an individual is to be utterly perfected, here accordingly arises the current possibility that the two tasks will not coincide: someone may remain in the process of the continuity of his broadening action without overcoming the disturbance between spirit and flesh that has taken place. Accordingly, however, if this is so, it follows necessarily that in individual cases there would have to be a special purifying action that balances the unevenness between the two tasks—the one for the whole and the other for the individual: we would certainly contaminate our conscience, and it would not be sufficient for Christian consciousness in the form of impulse if we would want to set forth a theory that does not allow such a method of balancing to be a form of purifying action. If one could say that every action is morally insignificant or empty that is not interwoven in the true vocation of a person, then certainly there could be no special purifying action. However, this would be totally against the spirit of Christian piety, which must unify both—the necessary one-sidedness of a person in that which is entrusted to him insofar as he is at the same time an organ of the whole, and his effort to bring himself closer to absolute perfection; a restoring action as a supplement must necessarily be introduced if the broadening efficacious action of individuals is not sufficient to overcome a disturbance of the right relation between spirit and flesh.

Thus we could have established this point to this extent. Now, however, precisely here is also the right place to ask, "Suppose then that the place for purifying action is ascertained; from whom, then, is the impulse to proceed for that purpose, and through whom is it to be determined? From the whole and its representatives?" That would be the theory of the Catholic Church. From individuals themselves? Then we would have to set forth another theory, one different from that of the Roman Church. So we must address this question next.

We have seen above that the self-consciousness from which all impulses proceed includes two sets of oppositions: on the one hand is self-consciousness as common feeling versus personal feeling; then on the other hand is self-consciousness determined in general versus individual ways. Now, in relation to our questions it appears that opposing decisions must be made, whether one proceeds from the one opposition or from the other.

To begin with the second distinction, we have determinations of self-consciousness and actions that are relatively opposed and can be classified under the following formulas: (1) Under the same circumstances these determinations and actions would be incumbent upon each and every individual. (2) Only a given individual and no other could be determined and act in precisely this way. In the latter case the individual predominates, and in the former case the general predominates. Now, insofar as a purifying action is to be of the individual kind, it appears that it could proceed only from the person himself; however, insofar as it is of the general kind, it appears that it could proceed from both individuals and the whole. Do we find a bifurcation here, or must this matter be considered from both points of view at the same time?

As concerns the other opposition, we had set forth an opposing relation between the individual and the common life. We said that in individuals it often is simply the spirit of the whole that predominantly expresses itself, and at that point the personal feeling would be subordinate to the potency of this common feeling and would then be moved by that common feeling. However, if in the common life progress is to arise from within [and move] outward, this action would have to begin with individuals, and something must be present in these individuals that is not yet present in the whole; at this point the individual would step forward predominantly as an individual person. His determination would predominantly express only his personal condition. Now, in this respect our subject seems to stand as follows: If the whole is in a condition of imperfection, then a purifying action directed toward it could proceed only from an individual who is not in this condition. If, however, we imagine the whole to be relatively perfect and individuals not to be up to the standard of the whole, it appears that a purifying action could proceed only from the whole. From this side, then, the question becomes whether these two cases can actually occur or whether only one of the two is possible.

We direct ourselves first to the opposition between what is of a general nature and what is of an individual nature and consider first the case in which the right moral relation between spirit and flesh is partially negated in an individual. Now, in this case, can a restoring action proceed from an individual life determined in an individual way? At base, this question is not answerable. From where would that partial negation of the right relationship then manifest itself? It can be made public only to the extent that it bears the character of a general action, for if an action belongs under the formula that only this individual and no other could act in this way in this case, then the criterion by which to judge this action would be lacking in all others. It is not as if another person could have no feeling of approval or disagreement regarding the individually determined action of another. However, another person could not by himself supply the criterion by which to bring about rectification. That criterion could be found only in the gradual drawing together of what is general and what is individual, and therefore between these two no absolute opposition can be formed.

In this way it would appear, however, that in the same degree that what is of an individual nature is affected in the person who is in need of purification, this purification can proceed from no other place than from the individual himself. Yet how is this supposed to be possible? It would be possible only provided that the individual can be seen as a twofold person—that there is something in him from which purification can proceed, separated from the place where the purification is to be carried out in him and not contaminated by that source. Thus we will have to say: "If in a person who is in need of restoration that which is of an individual nature is affected, the purifying action can proceed only from that person insofar as, and only to the degree that, an agent within him can be thought of that is itself free of the impurity that is to be removed. If this cannot be conceived of, then there can be no special purifying action in relation to what is of an individual nature in him; instead, purification must result, in a supplementary fashion, from other modes of action."

How is it then with such a duality in persons and with a separation of what is pure and what is impure in them, if an individually determined purifying action of an individual worked upon himself were required? This question leads us into psychology, a scientific domain that is both distinct from and presupposed by our field, and it is simply a bad thing that there is no solid, generally recognized ground in this field that we can build on with any surety. Thus we have no alternative but to set forth a fragment from psychology with which we are in agreement. To be sure, since here we must stay with the purely Christian standpoint, it may appear that we have gone beyond the realm of customary or so-to-say "natural" psychology. There is no particular fragment in a natural psychology regarding the capacity that a human being would possess in all situations, from which a purifying action could proceed, for Christianity presupposes that a new agent, the Holy Spirit, is necessary for that to happen. Christianity also presupposes that everything that belongs to the natural person, reason not excepted, is infected with sinfulness and, as polluted by sin, stands in opposition to the Holy Spirit. If we did not want to accept this position and reason were without sinfulness, then reason would be able to bring about the most complete purification purely on its own, and the original presupposition of Christianity would be overturned.

Now, does Christianity have a specific and generally valid view of this matter as to whether and how, given the presupposed impurity of individuals, the Holy Spirit can influence the individual himself from the individual himself? No. Rather, here we are bereft of any general definiteness, and we enter into a realm of contesting notions of the kind that can in no instance find any general placement within dogmatics. It is evident that, originally, the Christian idea was that the divine Spirit had its place in the community and in the individuals only insofar as they were members of the community. If we trace this view back to the original state of affairs, the emergence of the Christian church in the community of the Redeemer with his disciples, and if we restrict ourselves to the biblical and theological expression that the divine in Christ is the divine Spirit communicated to him without measure, then we must say, "This Spirit is communicated from Christ outward to each individual according to the measure of the individual's sheer receptivity." Moreover, if we consider the time when Christ was no longer among us as the original communicator and then consider how the divine

Spirit is seen as the common possession of Christianity, then the Spirit can be in no other form in the church than the Spirit's being in individuals except that the Spirit cannot be viewed as a special and heterogeneous Spirit in each one.

How then does the individual's participation in the divine Spirit relate to the Spirit's total power and efficacious action in the whole? It does so unequally, and indeed not only in such a way that the power of the Spirit shows up more strongly in one and more weakly in another, but also in such a way that in each individual, in turn, the Spirit does not work to an equal degree in all respects. Patently, this different measure of the Spirit lies in the differing makeup of persons in whom the Spirit is present and on whom the Spirit works. Thus, the more one's sensorial nature's resistance and obstinacy to the Spirit is present, the weaker is the efficacious action of the Spirit, and vice versa. And how is it, then, with someone who is in need of some restoration? In and of itself, we certainly have no reason to believe that the efficacious action of the Spirit in that person would suffice to effect a purifying action because it would be limited by the partial negation of the right relation to which we have referred, and so it would appear that in every instance the individual must be referred to the whole. This might well be true, except that, as we have said, the activity of the Spirit in the individual is unequal, and this allows still another view, for which we are pointed back to the domain of psychology.

Here, however, we want to stick with nonscientific terminology since for the most part greater scientific precision is not required in this case. In ordinary life we name what is highest in a natural person and that which is the distinctive stage of human intelligence as "reason." For a long time, even in science, people have made a distinction between theoretical reason and practical reason, and we will adopt this usage since we can reduce this distinction to common parlance, to the relative opposition between understanding and will, which is what it essentially comes down to. This is so, for people assign understanding to theoretical reason and assign what moves persons to practical reason. Now we are accustomed to saying that simply the reason of a person can be the immediate organ of the divine Spirit; accordingly, we say that this Spirit is manifested first and foremost by influencing understanding and will. However, in that we distinguish between these two functions too, we view them to be unequal in their possibility, and they are actually unequal at each point that is not yet absolutely perfect. Accordingly we can say, "It is conceivable that wherever some purification is necessary, the reason for it lies not in an absolute impotence of the Spirit, but in a relative impotence of one of these two aspects or the other."

This is generally the case, for example, where a partial negation of the right relation between spirit and flesh exists, and the person does something against his better feeling, against his convictions. So here there is clearly no absolute weakness of the spirit, but rather an unevenness in its influence on one's understanding and on one's will. In this way it thus appears that a purifying action can proceed from an individual himself, for when the individual's spirit manifests itself more strongly in the individual's understanding, it can be the agent for overcoming the cause of the will's being not yet so strong. Yet this is true only under the presupposition that a carryover from understanding to will would be possible, thus [enabling] a working within the individual himself from one function to another function. This carryover remains one of the mysteries of psychology in that it can on the one hand be viewed as an everyday experience, and it can on the other hand be viewed as nonsense; for if one can say that understanding is able to bring about a different direction in a person without the will's being at that same place, this is nothing but an empty show. Given this uncertainty, we must also say, "This matter will be decided only by the speculative conscience of the individual."

One who is convinced that will can be moved by understanding must try to perform a purifying action on oneself by oneself and then observe to what extent this purifying action can be achieved. One who does not have this conviction but instead has the conviction that there is a gap between theoretical and practical reason must plunge himself into the collective life and say, "Influence on my will cannot proceed from my understanding but from the collective will. I will sink myself into it in order to emerge again as an individual will, with the collective will having become mine, and I would stand there purified."

We cannot remain where this matter stands, after considering it only from the viewpoint of the individual, for the individual and the whole could indeed each have a differing viewpoint concerning it. The whole could turn one individual away and say to him, "You will have to perform restoring action on yourself," and the whole can reprove another individual and say to him, "Trying to effect restoring action on yourself will be of no avail; rather, it must come from me." So we must see how the whole relates to the needs of individuals and to what extent a rule can be set forth that corresponds to these needs.

Each totality is, in comparison with other totalities, something of an individual nature. As we cannot think of any people without its own distinctive character, so it is for any religious community. As within this kind of community each individual in turn has also his own distinctiveness, so the whole to which he belongs is not something of an individual nature in relation to him but carries the character of a general nature in itself, and it is that out of which the individual forms his own distinctiveness. Yet if that is the case, we must also say, "As the individual personal distinctiveness arises out of the common life, so it is also sustained as such through the whole and, where it is necessary, can be restored." So there must be a process for passing over from what is of a general nature into what is of an individual nature, which we can only construe in such a way that we say, "An influence of the totality upon the person as individual must also always be willed by this person." This is the rule that we must never allow to be out of sight, because here it can never be a matter of force of any kind.

However, this will of the individual is nothing other than his living receptivity to the influence of the whole, and we cannot think of this in him as divided between the character of the totality and his own personal distinctiveness. Rather, this receptivity is rooted in the innermost unity of his own life. Further, if the totality is to exercise influence upon the restoration of a person in his individuality, then this influence can only proceed from a determination of his own self-consciousness within the totality; thus a consciousness of the negation of the right relation of spirit and flesh occurring in the individual must have been communicated to the totality. Because the personal distinctiveness of the individual is not present as such in the whole, this negation is only possible to the degree that the character of the whole has been wounded in the individual and therefore insofar as the individually determined and generally determined aspects have not been allowed to be totally separated from each other.

Now the matter stands this way: the totality is affected through what is of a general nature that is wounded in what is of an individual nature in the individual. Moreover, to the degree that the totality is affected, it cooperates with its own character of an individual nature, which is in turn what is of a general nature for individuals. In contrast, in the individual person there exists a vital receptivity; he allows the whole to work upon him in a purifying way, and thereby what is of a general nature passes over to him from the totality and is for him something of an individual nature in that it also has an effect on what is individual in him. The general formula for the relationship of the individual and the whole—in that he on the one hand is a member of the totality and in turn on the other hand is nevertheless also of a distinctive character in and of himself—is that in every person the character of the totality is individualized. Moreover, every influence of the whole upon the individuality of a person must be able to be resolved in terms of this formula. As a result we can say, "If the whole desires to effect purification upon an individual under some other formula, that is, without the character of the totality being individualized in the person, it wills something that cannot be justified." And then this rule will lead us in the whole presentation of purifying action, particularly in the assessment of the Catholic Church's practice as compared with the Evangelical Church's practice. . . .

CHURCH DISCIPLINE

As indicated above, we are convinced that a purifying action upon individuals in the proper sense can take place only under the presupposition that the vocation of an individual is not equally directed toward all of its various aspects: in and of itself, an individual's vocation is not a complete moral totality. We have also seen that presentational action can replace restoring in a certain way insofar as it includes practice within itself. On the other hand, as long as the right relation between spirit and flesh is negated, it would seem that it would be impossible to give up purifying action. A general task remains, however, that cannot wait until purifying action is no longer necessary—that is, until the end of all things human—so we must seek to unify the two. Now, based on these two considerations, though based particularly on the first one, the individual is yielded up to us as our focus. What we obtain from the first consideration is a negative rule: we cannot view any restoring action as rightly done that does not bear the tendency to produce what the broadening action that is the object of purifying would have produced if his vocation had been a moral totality. Or, as we can say following another more general proposition that has already come up, we can view no restoring action as moral that does not include broadening action at least as a minimum within itself, an action accordingly through which no result whatsoever arises that was previously not yet supposed. That these two expressions are identical surely requires no discussion.

Now, if we ask, "What does this rule exclude?" this question directs us to the historical domain, for a negative rule cannot be heuristic but can only be critical: it can only serve to evaluate what has been given.

Precisely at the time of its emergence, the Evangelical Church opposed numerous penitential practices that the Catholic Church held to be features of purifying action, above all forms of physical self-torture that were freely undertaken, among which forms of flagellation stand out as prime examples. What must we say about this practice on the basis of our rule? Flagellation can be considered from two points of view: on the one hand, as suffering that one inflicts upon oneself, and on the other hand, as a reduction of physical strength that results from its use. Now, we can never say that it lies within a person's vocation to inflict pain on himself or on another. Certainly it does belong to our vocation to bear physical pain, and so one could believe that through such practices one could gain readiness to bear pain. For this reason, however, it should not be carried out arbitrarily. Rather, the ability to bear it must be gained through the endurance of pain that is necessarily tied to the fulfillment of one's vocation.

Moreover, as to the reduction of physical strength, this reduction is something that broadening action runs against because it disturbs the very organism that such action has need of. Just as our rule opposes this reduction, it is also contrary to Scripture. This is so, for when Scripture demands that we care for our bodies so that they do not become soft, it does this so that we will be capable of bearing physical evil. That is, we are to guard against pampering ourselves, but at the same time it is specifically forbidden that we willingly inflict pain of any sort upon ourselves. The reason is that the concept of care means nothing other than that physical powers in their totality should be preserved. Thus, reducing physical powers, even in the smallest measure, would be to oppose the maxim of Scripture. To be sure, not to become soft requires ongoing effort, but vocation of itself provides sufficient opportunity for effort, so that all artificial arrangements are useless. Suppose, however, that some vocation is always limited to something one-sided. Once in a while, something is then lacking in terms of physical efforts, and in this regard some supplement is thus required. Then the rule that we have set forth must be followed in every instance: no restoring action is right that is not at the same time broadening action—that is, nothing can be produced by it that of itself inveighs against someone's vocation. It is no more clear for this exception than for any other that something in the form of general precepts could be arranged for by the whole, but that the whole should still only step forward with counsel in such situations and must leave to the conscience of the individual whether and how far he wants to comply with it. . . .

[INFLUENCING THE FLESH,
INFLUENCING THE SPIRIT]

This brings us, however, to the transition to what is still lacking in our account. That is, our rule was only negative, and we have applied it to the main differences that are apparent in our area between the Roman Church and the Evangelical Church. At this point it is appropriate to define the rule more precisely and to give it real content, so that it does not remain purely critical but can also be used heuristically. If we look back on what has been considered up to this point, we must confess that in everything we have rejected thus far, there also remains some inner truth. This is so, for if we ask, "What can a purifying action possibly consist of?" we come back to these two main forms: on the one hand, prayer; on the other hand, exertion and privations. That is to say, either there is a great permeation of the whole person by the religious principle, and in general this will always be prayer, or there is an intentionally employed activity that is to fill out what is lacking in each person's vocation, and then it is—depending in each case on whether one expresses the matter positively or negatively—an exertion or a privation.

From here onward, if we want to arrive at a still more definite account, we must return again to our presupposition. We have said that if moral vocation were not one-sided, there could also be no particular purifying action because every relapse would negate itself. At the same time, we have admitted that the one-sidedness of vocation, if individuals are yet to form a whole, would be a relative necessity. Consequently, we must also assume that there are cases in which the complete fulfillment of one's vocation is not sufficient to restore every disturbance in the right relationship, but rather a special action must be postulated for this purpose. In what can this then consist, and how many kinds can there be? We presuppose that the relation between spirit and flesh has been altered and that the task is to restore it. Thus we can begin from two different points. That is, we can say, "An effect on the flesh must be produced that in turn subordinates it to the spirit in willing obedience," and we can say, "An effect on the spirit must be produced that increases its ability to affect the flesh."

In addition to these two themes, no third [theme] is thinkable. Our two forms of the task are in relation to each other in such a way that if either form is completely executed, the other is made superfluous. Yet precisely on this account it also follows that if either form is incompletely applied, the other form completes it. Both forms of the task are practicable, and it is an imprecise task—which can only be resolved according to what is appropriate in individual circumstances—to try to define which of the two forms of the task or which combination of the two would be able to reach the desired goal. If here too we ask, in turn, "From whom must an action of this kind proceed, from the individual or from the whole?" we will come to the following result, from whatever aspect we try to consider the matter: both the self-initiated activity of the person and the effective action of the whole must concur. This is the case, for it is already clear in general terms that if the individual in and of himself had the power to restore the disturbed relation between spirit and flesh, he would not have come into the position of needing such restoration. Thus, if he had need of restoration, he could only have participated in it with the help of the whole or of a representative of the whole.

This will be even clearer, moreover, if we look at both aspects of the matter in particular, as follows. If the individual were on his own to subordinate one or another of his physical functions to the spirit by means of influences on it, this could happen only through free actions. If he then had enough love of the truth so as not to blind himself to his situation and had perseverance enough to follow through on such action, it would be unintelligible how he would be able to come to special purifying action working against the flesh on the basis of this already-existing relation between spirit and flesh. In this respect the presupposition of a need for a special purifying action thus presupposes the incapacity of the individual to be able to effect it on his own and the need for the community to come to his aid. This is even more the case, on the other hand, when it comes to the point of influencing the spirit so as to strengthen spirit in the individual. This is so, for what can the individual want in himself but a strengthening of his highest agent, inner spirit? Only spirit in the whole can accomplish this task in an individual. Thus the individual must sink and submerge himself in the whole in order to emerge strengthened.

As we have seen, however, the whole in its relation to individuals can either be in the condition that the efficacious action has a definite form—that is, that the whole effects this action through a specific organ—or in a condition in which it is lacking in this organization. When the latter is the case, every action of an individual must still make an effort to bring about the former situation. In this way, then, we will always take a formless condition back to an organized state, and we can set forth a normal observation of a given object only under the presupposition that such organization exists. When we have proceeded further with this matter so that, by means of the individual['s initiative], the whole comes to a position of working in a purifying manner upon that individual, then the individual must complain to the whole of his need and lay claim to its influence because the whole's activity is based on the incompletion and one-sidedness of the moral relation of the individual. Just so on the other side it must not be overlooked that we can also imagine ourselves in the opposite case—that the completely organized whole perceives the imperfection of the individual before the individual himself does. Nevertheless, then we will not be able to say that a purifying action of the whole upon the individual is to take place immediately. Rather, this action must always be completely of such a kind that the individual has a share in it because, moreover, the individual could also oppose the whole. In this way restoring action can only emerge in life when the individual requests it, supposing also that the whole must first arouse the feeling of deficiency in the individual.

Now suppose that in our initial consideration of the method of influencing the flesh, we begin with the observation that in the church it must be possible that an individual, in his connection with the whole and out of his specific vocation, is not able to generate or to allow to be generated an action on his sensorial nature by means of which the right relationship of flesh to spirit is established. Then the distinctive life of the church must bear within itself a relationship through which the one-sidedness of vocation can be complemented and any detrimental effects of it can be overcome, so that discipline is simply a matter of each person, according to that person's need, occupying a place in the life of the church through which such a complement can be produced for him. Thus for those whose vocation would not permit sufficient exertion, for example, the church's life must have available certain opportunities for toilsome service in poor-relief or nursing the sick. The principle involved here is also expressed in organized forms of charity in the church—which in earlier times, widespread especially in the Middle Ages and in the establishment of institutions that the Roman Church still has—in which persons of both genders and even from the highest stations are occupied in caring for the ill. To be sure, it was not justifiable that these spiritual and secular brotherhoods were allowed to occupy the whole of their lives with purposes that should be only supplemental, and the superstitions connected to them in various ways were even less justifiable. Yet it was not justifiable either that the Reformation uprooted all institutions of this sort without laying any ground for reorganization of them corresponding to the Christian spirit, or that the Reformation thus allowed what was good in them to go to ruin instead of directing itself only against the abuses therein. That is, if a purifying action of this sort is not organized in the church, then such action does not proceed from the church at all; and if it does not proceed from the church, it also becomes a purely private matter, and the arbitrariness of the individual becomes so much the greater.

Hence, the task of developing in our church community a way to restore some organization for purifying actions remains before us. This matter also has another aspect: the necessity for such a purifying action rests on there being situations in which it is not readily expected that persons are prepared to exert themselves very much. This is so, for the one-sidedness of vocation fails by far to offer all the necessary practices. This is a bad situation, one that must grow to the extent that the inequality among individual members of society grows. It is also true that medieval institutions were grounded in this inequality, at the time when serfdom, this analogue of slavery, existed in full force and was much greater than it is today. Now, if the most elevated members of society were to participate in the strongest personal way in the church's organized care for those who suffer, this would express the fact that all inequality is to be leveled out in Christian community, whether or not inequality continues in the governmental and social domains. Yet inequality must also be removed from the civil arena, certainly in a gradual and not in a revolutionary way. The more this occurs, the more members of all classes are obliged through their vocations to exertions and privations, the more the need for such institutions would be removed and the actual purifying action provided in those institutions would be established by means of broadening action. Thus there are, in turn, two different movements that must finally come together at one point.

Yet we must still say that a great deal would always come off badly if the ecclesial community were to allow all the means for restoring the proper measure of exertion and privation to be lacking. This reflection, moreover, brings us to a third line, which also goes to that same point. That is, we can view such moral deficiency as a negation of the right relationship between spirit and flesh, thus as in need of purifying action, insofar as we presuppose that in the educational process there is already a gymnastic for exertions and privations, and that the readiness to bear these is simply lost through a later emphasis on leisure and the life of luxury. If we then say that the church should bear witness wherever this readiness is lost, then the church must also be concerned that, after the early educational process, there should still be the same kind of ongoing and resumed gymnastic.

Moreover, if we consider Christian history from this viewpoint, we find that a great number of voluntary privations and purposeless exertions have already had the character of this ongoing gymnastic. Like this is the hermit life, for example, which some who would like to work as teachers in the church submit to after their education and before taking some position. In our locale we cannot approve of this sort of gymnastic, for no purifying action is moral that is not productive, that does not, while it is completing the one-sidedness of a vocation, at the same time produce something of what would be produced through another person's vocation. So the hermit life is of negative value, because it produces nothing of this sort and still cannot be acquitted from the reproach of having decreased a person's powers. Already the ancients disapproved of gymnastic effort insofar as it gave itself over [solely] to athletic effort, because people would lose broad-mindedness to the extent that they pursued gymnastics exclusively and for their whole lives; in its own area the hermit life has precisely this characteristic of athletics.

Even if the old institutions of the church were also wrong, the quest for a better organization of the community regarding the resumption of our gymnastic may not be given up, and the main features of what is to be achieved are given in all our considerations when taken together. If the practices are not to be pointless, the church will be able to properly organize these practices in no other way than as its activity for the poor and the sick and its concern for everything that goes with being poor or sick and similar activities. Yet in doing so the church may never allow that some give only their money while others give of their own person and time; this temptation comes from a worldly viewpoint that lies close at hand and is very powerful. This is so, for inequality would be spread by means of this, and thus the whole would lose its original character, both its churchly Christian character and its character that provides completion. In the recent

German struggle for liberation,[3] this matter came to the fore in a pure and lovely way, however in a way that was only temporary; in this instance those who cared for others completed what was lacking because of the one-sidedness of their vocations. The task of the church is to organize itself so that this activity can be practiced in an ongoing way.

However, concerning the other method, influencing the spirit, since the former method rested upon the consideration that the power of the spirit is not lacking in and of itself, but only in connection with particular functions of human life, influencing the spirit proceeds directly from the opposing consideration. The opposing consideration says, "Although in each individual life the power of spirit always turns out to be stronger in some areas and functions of life and weaker in others, yet it can prove itself to be stronger in the weak areas when the power of the spirit is raised overall." How is this to happen? As we have seen, it happens by means of the individual sinking himself into the common life and experiencing life-giving influence from it. Now, this appears especially in the worship life of a religious community, for here the individual appears as an individual and the community also appears as a community; here the whole manifests itself in an organic way and by means of this totality influences each individual in a living way. However, did we not earlier say that worship is to form the true bulk of presentational action? Now, how is worship to produce restoring action? The answer to the first question is clear. This is so, for where the power of spirit over nature is present and expresses itself, this expression is purely presentational action as such; and where this presentation, where religious life appears in an organized way, there is worship.

Yet the other idea is not contradicted by this at all, for restoring action is also based on the power of spirit over nature and thus can certainly attach itself to this emergence in worship without worship ceasing to be essentially presentational action. However, since with this method we will make reference to presentational action in just this way, as with the former method we made reference to broadening action, we now will begin by returning to the former two opposing viewpoints, the first of which claims that one who needs purification may not participate in presentational action, while the other viewpoint declares that all purifying action proper is superfluous precisely because it would be covered by presentation action. This is so, for to the same degree that the individual were to participate in worship, the true condition of the whole would be reflected in him, would remain in him, and would gain a purifying influence on his artistic actions. However, when the first viewpoint is pursued in a strong way, presentational action as such is totally negated. This is so, for since there is no member of the Christian community who is still not in need of purifying action, all persons without exception would be excluded from presentational action, and this can never be allowed to happen. Thus insofar as this viewpoint calls for what it wants to guard against, calls for its own restriction, it can only be recognized as true if we say, "Presentational action carried out by those who remain in need of purification themselves will indeed always be imperfect, nevertheless it must be organized and will always also be right insofar as at the same time it contains within itself the remedy and produces improvement and purification in individuals, that is, as purifying and broadening actions are established within it as a minimum."

Then, however, the other viewpoint is perfectly right, and thus those who are in need of purifying action must be immediately asked by the whole to participate in its presentational action in order to partake of purifying action that is contained within it. Presentational action cannot suffer thereby since the purifying that is given in and with presentational action always also includes within itself improvement of the latter. That is one way to settle the dispute. However, the difficulty can also be resolved as follows. By its very nature presentational action calls forth a contrast that is modified in a distinctive way only in relation to the conflicting viewpoints we have been discussing. That is, two factors are always present in these two viewpoints, one from whom an action proceeds, and the other for whom it is intended. This is so, for an action is always only presented for another. Those from whom the presentation proceeds are predominantly active; those for whom it is intended are predominantly receptive. If we imagine the presentation as something done utterly in common, as is the case in the actions of worship, this contrast is no contrast of persons but only of functions. Each individual contributes to presentational action as a common work, and each also takes it up into himself. Yet these two functions are never equally established among all individuals. However, the difference that arises as a result is truly always only a contrast that is passing away. This fact is certainly not to hinder the contrast becoming settled and fixed as long as organized activity is included within the contrast.

Now, as we have seen, a perfected condition of the community includes organizing the influence of the whole upon the individual. Thus it is also completely appropriate to the moral development of the church that out of this fleeting contrast a more permanent contrast has been created, a contrast between those who represent the efficacious action of the church and those toward whom this efficacious action is directed, a contrast between clergy and laity. This contrast can never be absolute; rather, members of the clergy, as persons, must also always remain receptive, and members of the laity always also remain self-active; yet it lies in the nature of the thing that there will be different elements of presentational action in worship, some pertaining to the clergy that are predominantly self-active, and others in which the predominant role for the clergy appears to be to join in—this pertains to the laity in just the same way. Surely this consideration is actually not appropriate here, but in the elaboration of presentational action itself.[4]

However, this leads us to what certainly is appropriate here: the organization of this contrast insofar as purifying action must be bound together with presentational action. Indeed, in this connection we must say, "The task of developing a purifying action that comes out of presentational action belongs on the side of those in whom receptivity dominates; on the other hand, the task of not allowing presentational action to be contaminated by the participation of those who are in need of purification belongs to the side of those who are predominantly self-active and represent the organization of the whole through which the community influences individuals."

And with this formula we now also have a solution to the difficulty that has been occupying us currently. This is so, for according to the formula all those who are in need of purifying activity may participate in the activity of worship as long as they belong to the group of those in whom receptivity dominates, not as they belong to those in whom the activity of the whole is to be expressed. . . .

CHURCH BETTERMENT

Let us now consider purifying action of an individual on the whole, which in an entirely general way we have called "church betterment." It may appear that it has occurred much too infrequently for it to be taken up in a theoretical reflection such as Christian ethics. However, we have this action in view not only insofar as it produces some advance in the church at large, but also insofar as a tendency toward advancement exists, quite apart from any results produced, and put in this way the action is not at all rare. If we look to history, the efforts of those who in the earliest period of the Christian church wanted to make Judaism again dominant belong entirely to this category. They proceeded from the idea that Christianity arose from Judaism and should therefore be seen merely as a modification of the latter. However, this was different from Christianity's original tendency, in which a portion of those who confessed the faith denied an obligation to the Mosaic law. Consequently, there was [thought to be a] need of restoration, a return to the notion that the Mosaic law is to be binding on all Christians without exception. Precisely in this way every effort to hold fast to something that another party regards as antiquated would belong to church betterment.

On the other hand, soon there were also those who stood in the area on the other side of efficacious action and sought to bring about something new, whether in teaching or in modes of life, and we must admit that we find this tendency as much as the other one almost always side by side in the precincts of the Christian church. Suppose, however, some wanted to say that actions directed at betterment of the church should nonetheless not be taken to be a general tendency inasmuch as it can always begin only with those who lead the church; this would likewise be incorrect, as experience teaches. This is so, for we certainly have no basis for seeing such Judaizing movements as proceeding from the organism of the whole church. Rather, we can be sure that those movements were not recognized by that organism. Thus, those who led them acted as individuals on their own authority. Moreover, we find similar movements in every time period, inclinations of the so-called laity to change existing conditions, even to separate from the larger church community because it did not want to remedy some deficiency that had crept in, and in many ways to want to intrude into what is essentially the business of the representative body of the church and indeed even precisely into what the representative body had made into a firmly established organism.

Thus it appears that our domain here is an entirely general one, as can then be shown from yet another side. That is, we are already of one mind regarding the fact that the capacity of the Christian church to move in the steps it takes toward completion arises from elements set over against each other; thus [we are also of one mind] regarding the fact that progress never spreads over the whole in an uninterrupted fashion, but that reactions will always have been registered. As soon as this happens, opposing viewpoints about the state of things also arise. Moreover, this always does happen, except in times when an impulse toward progress continues on in the first power of its enthusiasm; such a power is never able to endure over a long stretch, or in times when stagnation is so dominant in the church that, accordingly, there can be no talk at all of movement forward. Hence, repeatedly the course of the Christian church between these two points will always be set forth in accordance with the very formula mentioned above. Thus some will view a given movement as progress, others as a destructive innovation.

Now should anyone need to stay out of participating in these contrasting tendencies? Certainly not, for if the answer were "yes," one would be for one's own part supporting a condition of stagnation in the church. Thus every member of the church must participate in purifying action arising from a condition of stagnation on this basis. Light needs to be shed only on the fact that not only those who want to prevent what is new in the whole—for this goes without saying—but also those who want to bring the whole into a new path—both groups almost always find themselves in the situation of viewing their actions as falling within our domain. Yet this fact will not be immediately clear in itself. It will become evident, however, if we become aware of how the two—action of the whole upon the individual, and action of the individual on the whole—actually limit each other. How does the opposition that has been indicated come about? We will seek to make the process clear by means of an example, yet without binding ourselves exactly to what is historical.[5]

As long as Christianity existed only within Judaism, the question could not at all arise as to whether commitment to the Mosaic law must continue or not. Yet as soon as Christianity set roots down in the Gentile world, a decision became necessary as to whether Christianity could be communicated only along with Judaism or also without it. If we then assume that Paul had been the first who had taken in the Gentiles without them also becoming Jews, the whole Christian church, insofar as it had a representative body, would have remained with the old ways; Paul would have appeared to be a rank innovator, and people would have had a right to say that this tendency had originated in his not being suffused with the true religiosity that binds together Christianity and Judaism as one; thus the whole would have had to direct a purifying action to him. As a result, to that extent there could not have been any talk here of a purifying action of an individual directed to the whole. Yet how would Paul's action have to be understood? Apparently not according to the formula "My opponents are not yet Christians at all; so first I want to act toward them for this purpose." Rather, as a purifying action directed to the whole, as an action according to the formula "I would receive Gentiles into the Christian community without at the same time making them into Jews, and since I desire that they be universally recognized as Christians, I would influence the whole so that along with me it would properly distinguish between what is proper to Christianity and what is proper to Judaism. As a whole, the community does have an idea of Christianity. However, it is one that is obscured by attachment to Judaism, and I want to free it from this retrogression." Accordingly, one who aims at producing something new in the church, but in such a way as to declare that what persists in the church obscures an earlier moment or is a contamination of an earlier moment—this person is practicing a purifying action upon the whole.

Now, let us look at our current situation, which is different from that of the earliest church in that we have Scripture as a source on the basis of which to recognize what the original Christian message is. We must say, "If an individual seeks to bring something new into the church that he himself says he knows is not to be found in Scripture, however also that for him Scripture is in no way the absolute norm for everything that is deemed to be Christian, then his action directed at the whole would not have a purifying nature, but a broadening nature." On the other hand, if an individual seeks to propose and arrange something in the church, the opposite of which may have always had currency up to this time; yet if he is convinced that he could call upon Scripture in doing so, he works in a purifying way upon the whole for he presents what is new as already included in Christianity's normal state of affairs, and [he presents] the current state of affairs as a deviation from Scripture. And now still more. Suppose also that it is asked of no one at all that the church move into the new thing that he has proposed; instead, he is satisfied with communicating what is new to individuals, and he even strictly avoids demanding that the church embrace the new and takes on the new only in and for himself—then his action would still be a purifying action directed to the progress of the whole. This is so, for on the one hand the intention is not altered if someone says, "I see clearly that I will not succeed in changing the whole so I will content myself with educating some people about my view." Rather, as a result the influence on the whole is only delayed until sometime in the future.

On the other hand, however, the whole always remains the object of such an action. This is so, for the individuals are still always only members of the whole and are in the organization itself. However, in an organic whole an absolute interconnection is always to be supposed, so that any influence on a point is an influence on the organization itself. Thus if an individual were only to refrain from absolutely isolating himself by leaving the church altogether—however, in this case the individual would not even be an object of our inquiry any longer—he acts in a purifying way on the whole in that he does not influence only himself nor escape from what he takes to be a corruption of the whole. Thus the occurrence of the kind of action about which we are speaking is not as unusual as it appears on first view, but is as common as any other action.

Still, under what circumstances and in what form is this action moral? Naturally, at this point we must return to the relationship between individuals and the whole. We have said that we as Evangelical Christians could only declare the church in its appearance to be something living, to be a whole that is understood to be advancing, but not without also making retrogressive movements. However, the progress of the whole must proceed from individual points; thus an individual's action must influence the whole; hence, the same thing must also be valid regarding the way a retrogressive movement is overcome. Thus our basic proposition is, "Just as certainly as there are retrogressive moments in the course of the whole's progress, so purifying actions of individuals on the whole must happen in the Christian church." Still, we will not be able to perceive the whole in a better way than we will if we seek for an endpoint immediately as we establish a point of departure and say, "Thus supposing there is a purifying action on the whole that proceeds from an individual, when does it end?" Since in this instance we must aim exclusively at specific retrogressive movements in the church, thus only at some such specific moments after which another moment follows in turn, we must say, "Apparently a restoring action ends when a retrogressive movement in the whole is overcome and a condition of pure progress is restored." This is the first answer that we can give.

Taken alone, this formula does not have one simple meaning but a double meaning, depending on whether we consider the whole as an organic unity or as an aggregate, as a totality of individuals. In connection with the latter meaning, however, the formula would be false. Thus an individual's action directed to the whole is not to last until the retrogressive movement in the totality of all individuals is overcome, but only until it is overcome in the whole seen as an organic unity, that is, accordingly, until a purifying action that proceeds from an individual is taken up into the organization of the church. Hence there follows at once for us a conclusion by means of which we are able to determine more exactly whether an action of this kind is moral. This is so, for if a person who has begun such an action still wants to bring to an end, in the most perfect way and by the most perfect means, what appears to him to be a retrogressive movement of the whole, he must also want the purifying action that proceeds from him to be followed by another that proceeds from the whole; and it is clear that his action is only moral insofar as it concludes in an action of the whole, and thus clear that he wants to call forth such an action of the whole. Without this intention the action is immoral and has a motive completely different from one directed toward effecting a true purification of the whole.

This is in perfect agreement with what we have already set forth above in a general way: every action of this sort presupposes an unorganized condition and must set out to establish an organization. This is so, for if we presuppose a retrogressive movement in the whole, this means the organization that existed during an earlier and better state of affairs has ceased to exist, and the whole as it is must appear to us in this connection as not being organized at all, or it must appear that its organization is unhealthy. Thus the task of establishing an organization belongs precisely to individuals. However, that the activity of individuals as such must cease as soon as the organization's establishment is accomplished is based on the fact that an organic state of affairs is more complete than an inorganic state of affairs; accordingly in addition an activity that proceeds from the organization of the whole is to be preferred to every other kind of activity. . . .

Thus we have now come from a different point to the same result that we had already reached earlier: a restoring action may never perpetuate dissolution of the whole or negation of interconnection with the whole. This is so, for every self-isolation of the kind referred to above, which we have shown to be immoral, is a negation of the whole. However, if the following claim remains firm—that each individual who feels in himself an impulse to a purifying action on the whole must also necessarily advance to the point of acting efficaciously on the whole—then on this basis we will be able to set forth the following general rule that summarizes what has been said up until now: from each point onward an individual must give the greatest possible public character to his conviction about the whole and to his agency upon that condition.[6] Every way of acting that departs from the aforementioned amounts to a return to self-isolation and thus is immoral, since deficiency of public character and a separatist nature are always necessarily found together. However, this rule surely refers to something much greater, for the individual would certainly not be in a position to follow this rule if public character were not already a matter of concern in the state of affairs of the whole and if a way of making matters public were not already in place.

In this regard, let us consider the history of the Christian church. We admire how quickly the church produced a method for bringing about this public character. For when Christianity first arose, it appeared as if it aimed solely at communication by means of speech that still can always be limited to only a small circle of persons. Nonetheless, Christianity's literary character emerged very early, so an impulse for organization of this most comprehensive method for public expression must have been deep in its nature. Let us go somewhat further: we surely find, among those who treat the history of Christianity in an impartial way, not a few who speak with only a bit of displeasure about the intention that manifested itself so early of producing that which we call the Catholic Church. But what was this intention in actuality? None other than precisely an intention for the greatest public character. Certainly the intention was also for the assimilation of people, but not originally. Instead, the original intention was for public character—public character that can and must have come first, before there were efforts to harmonize the great range of differences in teaching and efforts for regulation of the common life, and efforts to overcome retrogressive movements. Thus assimilation is rooted exclusively in public character. Hence, this [public dimension] constitutes the essential character of the Christian church, and the proper resolution of our task is only possible if the church retains this character.

This is so, for without that happening, it is certain that every purifying action of an individual on the whole must be repressed.

Misunderstanding the whole of this intention, the Roman Church has reversed the subordination of assimilation to the public character and said, "As long as assimilation comes about, public character is no longer required, and then an individual may no longer need any means to influence the whole." Thus we have now come again to a point where we must say that our presentation is essentially Protestant; this is so, for since we presuppose that the whole in its oscillation can only continue its progress insofar as there is influence of some individuals on the whole, our task can be fulfilled only with the presupposition of an unlimited public character; we could only affirm that it is right for any individual to escape from a church in which the principle of public character is completely obstructed, for in such a church there would no longer be any means of overcoming a retrogressive movement, and all errors would be permanent.

And let us consider the procedure that our Evangelical Church has employed from the very beginning: it also indicates that the church made use of the greatest means of public expression—namely, the printing press—with the greatest energy. Would the Reformation have occurred before the invention of the means of printing books, or if from the beginning the right to restrict this medium of communication had been in the hands of the clerical estate? Surely not. Instead, it would have been lost in a fruitless effort. Therefore, even in the whole of a society that always has the means needed for progress, the principle of openness must never be encroached upon. Yet openness does not remain unencroached upon if the outward expressions of individuals whose goal is a purification of the whole—regardless as to whether they are right or in error—result in something other than the matter being discussed freely in the whole of that society, and if its goal is achieved or is set aside solely on the basis of whether it is fair to living conviction.

Thus it is impossible to fulfill this task in a moral way without calling for opposition to the whole if, on the one hand, there is not an aim that nothing foreign is mixed into the concern to be worked through between the individual and the whole, and on the other hand, there is not an aim that the reaction against the whole—when it is believed by individuals that a deviation must be presupposed—remains within the limits that we have indicated above. Now, however, this rule is, on the one side, only a presupposition that in the whole a public character is to dominate and make possible the most perfect mutual communication. On the other hand, in relation to individuals it is a genuine rule. The individual has the duty to act with the greatest possible public character. . . .

Chapter 3

Purifying Action
in Which the Civil Element
Is Co-constitutive

INTRODUCTION

Now on the one hand we will discuss discipline in the home, and on the other hand discipline in the state. When the Christian church came into being, it found the state already in place; thus we cannot view the state in advance as a product of the Christian life. The relation is not precisely the same regarding the family. Certainly the family also existed when the church came into being, and originally it was always the case that family members became members of the church only as individuals. Christian upbringing that was an interconnected whole was not yet possible, nor could there immediately be any Christian household discipline or any purifying action as an aspect of discipline. However, this was the case only in the earliest beginnings of the Christian church, and already quite early the family could be seen as arising out of Christianity. This means that, keeping the above-cited reality in mind, we cannot at all avoid presenting the home as a product of the Christian life and household discipline as an aspect of Christian restorative action. Certainly one could say today that we have the same case with the state: it should be within the church as the family is. However, in practice an important distinction stands out in this regard. This is so, for while we must say plainly that in the Christian church domestic life[1] never

79

came into being except by means of specific action of the church, this we must quite certainly deny in relation to the state; the state was not formed through any ecclesial action.

Thus if household discipline must always necessarily be seen as something that also proceeds conjointly from the church, for the time being this idea certainly remains thoroughly problematic for us in relationship to state discipline. Of course, it could appear as if this uncertainty were only a result of the way we have chosen to arrange our presentation. This is the case, for if we had begun with broadening action, we would have known already whether establishing the state would have been included in the nature of the church, whether or not the church would have discovered the state already existing or not, and this is so, for thereby all uncertainty in this connection would be negated. However, our presentation would then also be in danger of losing a certain general validity: it would be valid only for the time in which the state could already be seen as adopted by the church, and exactly at this point general validity would have to have for us the greatest importance because Christianity remained outside of the state and alien to the state for a long time because it conceived of all other viewpoints as derived from the Old Testament period.

In any case, it is already clear from what has been said that discipline in domestic life stands nearer to discipline of the church than it does to the discipline of the state. Thus it will also be completely natural that we begin with household discipline.

HOUSEHOLD DISCIPLINE

If in the present the family is also formed by means of the Christian church, nevertheless nothing in its essential constitution is changed because of this. Both before and after Christian influence, the family is formed by the twofold distinction between parents and children and between lords and servants. Yet here we do not have to take all of these elements into consideration. For the relationship between lords and servants is variable, and in connection with the spiritual realm they relate to each other as individuals in community. And even spouses relate to each other only as members of the community relate to one another in terms of the restoring action we are here considering. Thus what remains for us is only the actions of parents toward children, that aspect of upbringing that has the character of purification: discipline regarding children.

Certainly, insofar as the Christian church produces domestic association, the parents are only the organs through which the whole has an effect upon the children, and so it appears that here too we have been returned to the ecclesial domain. However, what is different is that children are members of the community only in an incomplete sense, and actions upon them thus stand in the middle, between actions of the whole upon its members and actions upon the whole mass of those who do not yet belong at all to the community. If we were able to count children among the latter group, then education would be wholly comprehended under broadening action.

Still, the boundaries must be designated from another side. That is, there is an established theory in the science of education—pedagogy—which has as its task configuring all restoring actions by the parent upon the child. It is clear that we cannot now take up the entire discipline into this discussion. Thus a determination should be made as to what we appropriate from pedagogy and what we let go. Here we need to consider a twofold relationship. On the one hand, educational theory is an applied, subordinate discipline, the principles of which derive from philosophical ethics. Thus at this point we can only set forth the principles for the area of education that concerns us; the realization of these principles we leave for pedagogy, as a truly technical discipline. Accordingly, here pedagogy is not considered exclusively from the religious viewpoint; rather, it is an applied and subordinate theory that stands in an immediate relationship to philosophical ethics. Pedagogy's principles are completely and properly found in the latter discipline. Thus, here our task is to see the particular way in which these principles are organized from the Christian viewpoint.

So that we may connect as closely as possible to what has been stated before, we must return to it throughout our discussion. The principal distinction that we have found was that between actions of the whole upon the individual and actions of the individual upon the whole. It is clear that there can be no discussion of the latter here; it does not befit children to act upon the whole. Thus we will concern ourselves exclusively with the first member of that opposition. Still, regarding this matter there are two methods, as we have seen. The two methods, resting on the opposition between spirit and flesh, complement each other. On the one hand, the spirit of the whole works on the flesh of individuals, and on the other hand, it works on the spirit of individuals. So, precisely this perspective can now also lead us regarding domestic discipline. It can, for insofar as our general discussion here concerns purifying actions, truly the dominion of spirit in the children must also be presupposed already, since otherwise there could be no restoration but only an awakening and enlivening.

However, when does Christian education of children then actually begin? The communication of the Christian spirit in its essential unity with the idea and actuality of redemption rests, on the one hand, on the fact that Christianity has been given in history, and on the other hand, upon the feeling of sinfulness and the need for redemption. Religious maturity does not exist where these two things are not developed in their completeness. In children, both first exist only in a process of becoming; thus the spirit also first exists in a state of becoming within them. Yet if we posit the presence of spirit in them and certainly with a definite dominion of the spirit over flesh, this can only mean that we suppose that spirit in the general human sense is present in them that allows for the communication of Christian spirit. By what means, then, is the dominion of the spirit over the flesh manifest in them? Through conscience. Accordingly, before its development in children, there can be no restoring action upon them, only one that seeks to establish the conscience.

Now, from one perspective it would seem unnecessary to say anything about this, for no one will dispute that there can be no dominion of spirit over flesh where there is no conscience. From the other perspective, however, one could say that it is entirely conceivable that conscience could already be present but no dominion of spirit over flesh is yet present. The first claim is clear, for if one wanted also to assume that there also exists a dominion of spirit over the sensorial nature given without conscience because, of course, conscience is based on a subsuming of the individual and the particular to the general, which as an act of understanding still could be lacking even while the being and action of spirit on flesh under the form of will has existed for a long time; yet it is unmistakable that this power of spirit over flesh would only seem to be present. The opposition between spirit and flesh would not yet have appeared at all; nothing would be present but what we call, in the language of everyday life, the good heart, natural good-heartedness, whereby the intention would indeed always be to ascribe to spirit the fact that sensorial nature manifests itself in a particular way, but [ascribe this] to spirit without consciousness of this opposition.

However, when consciousness arises, then conscience also comes into being, and from this point it will also be easy to make clear what value there is in the notion that conscience could exist where there is not yet the dominion of spirit over flesh. The content of this notion can now be determined more exactly if we consider something being forbidden a child by his own inner consent; conscience then makes itself felt as soon as it acts against this prohibition. Yet it does not at all follow that the child will be in the place where he is able to comply with the prohibition. Thus it appears to be certain that without considering whether conscience is already awakened, there can be no talk yet of a purifying action but only of a broadening action that generates the dominion of spirit over flesh. Of course, if the act of recognition of the law were purely an act of understanding, then there would not yet be an establishment of the power of spirit over flesh. That is never the case, however, for the ability of the will to follow the law is always included.

If we consider an act that transgresses a given law, this certainly can happen in very different ways. There is a sophistical form in which the act is accompanied by a refutation of the law that had been previously recognized, and there is a purely "pathematical"[2] form in which the law always continues to be recognized, but the admission that the power to follow it is lacking. Yet in either case there is always nonetheless an earlier condition to which the case can be traced back, though the earlier condition has been revoked. In the first case, the conviction has been disavowed—though this can always only be something momentary; in the second case, the resolve is to act in accord with the law, without the lack of willpower having been recognized beforehand. Hence we can certainly say that as soon as conscience has been aroused and in every case in which there is an action that goes against a recognized law, then a restoring action is indicated. However, just as domestic discipline begins with the awakening of conscience, so everything in domestic discipline is contingent only upon it, and this is true not only in general, but also in every individual case; and all pedagogical measures that need to be justified here, but proceed from a different principle, have nothing in common with Christian discipline of children. . . .

PURIFYING ACTION IN THE STATE

Introduction

At all times Christianity has found the state already in place, and when new states have arisen since the origin of Christianity, these new states have still not come into being by means of Christianity but only in connection with previously existing states and by means of their agency. It is also clear that Christianity has not appropriated the state in a way that created a new organization of the state, unlike the way it has appropriated the family such that the latter is now always inaugurated and sanctioned by the church. Thus we must also consider purifying action in the state as something already given, so that it is not at all a matter of us asking whether purifying action should exist or not. Rather, the question is to what extent a given purifying action is to be approved or condemned by Christianity, or modified or allowed to exist as it is. However, if this is the way things stand, the question is always only the following: "How is an individual Christian to relate to this form of action in the state?" Now, every individual in a state is either a magistrate[3] or a subject; thus at all times this distinction must be taken into consideration and must be specified in order to determine what is fitting to a person insofar as he is a subject and insofar as a person is a magistrate in relation to the purifying action in the state. This much is in advance about method in general.

Now, however, as to the idea of purifying action in the state as a whole, there is an inner aspect and an outer aspect, just as there are inner and outer relations for the state itself. This is so, for in its very nature the state is in a law-oriented condition, a union of people under law, and this always includes a specific way of establishing and changing laws in the state. All this concerns its inner relationship, which is, accordingly, included in the distinction between magistrates and subjects. However, the state also has a relationship with those outside, a relationship to other states, and a relationship to those who do not yet live in any kind of state.

The inner purifying action in the state presents itself as having two aspects. In the first place, analogous to discipline in the church, it exists as criminal justice, as a reaction of the whole to those of its members who—in that they have not obeyed the law—have fallen back into a condition of immorality, therefore a condition requiring reestablishment of the obedience that has been abrogated. Then [the second aspect is] analogous to church betterment, viewed as the action of an individual upon the whole when the whole is moving backward and thus is in a state of corruption that must be overcome, and when a healthy, living movement of the whole is concentrated in individuals from whom health can in turn be spread over all the elements. Accordingly, our questions in this connection are these: "What is fitting for the Christian in relation to criminal justice if he is a subject, and what is fitting if he is a magistrate? What is fitting for the Christian as subject and as magistrate in relation to the need for betterment of the state?"

It is also clear that the outer purifying action is twofold. In the first place, there is the purifying action of one state upon another. Certainly there is no law-oriented condition for a people in the same sense that there is a law-oriented condition in the state, but wherever relationships of states to each other are to be judged as moral, the idea of a relationship of universal law among the states must also be presupposed and must be established as a ground. Now, if a state moves against the free efficacious action of another state, it negates the relationship of law that is presupposed and makes a restoring action directed toward itself necessary, thus [calling for] either negotiation, analogous to the awakening of the conscience in the realm of household discipline, or war, analogous to criminal justice. A special handling of the matter is required here regarding war; consequently the opposition between magistrates and subjects also comes into consideration again. This is so, since it is always the magistrates who decide for war, and it is always the subjects by whom war is waged; so it is to be determined whether subjects do all they do in this regard exclusively out of their relation to magistrates, or if something else comes to bear in this regard. The second direction of the outward purifying action is one that will have to be done in connection with the whole portion of the human race that does not yet live within a civil society, especially those states that are at the point where the civilized world and the uncivilized come into contact with each other. This is the case, for here too a law-oriented relation is presupposed, and if this is violated, it must be restored through the state and its citizens; accordingly, the question is, "What is the right behavior in this regard for the state and for its citizens?"

The whole treatment of this area is enclosed in these questions. However, it is appropriate to begin with the one that is directly next to household discipline.

1. Civil Criminal Justice

If obedience due the law is abrogated, a purifying action is indicated as well. This is true since a state is only an actual state when obedience to its laws exists. If the obedience due the state is abrogated and the original relationship is not restored, the state is in a condition of disintegration that it must face with more certainty as more disobedience recurs. At this point we agree that the questions we will put forward are twofold: insofar as a Christian is a magistrate, and insofar as he is a subject. However, it appears that there is no proper place for the subject in this arena. This is so, for we presuppose that subjects are to give way out of obedience; the authority seeks to lead them back to obedience, and to the degree to which this happens, there seems to be no room for participation [in purifying action] by subjects. However, the matter stands this way. If a subject breaks the law, then another subject might have an interest in this, and the question becomes what the latter then is to do now. What must be determined regarding conflicts arising among Christians over this—all the more so since there have always been some who have held that it is unchristian to have recourse to the authorities if an individual were offended in the realm of his free personal existence. Regarding the first aspect of this question, what is required of a Christian insofar as he is in a magisterial position, this is well established: it is self-evident. This is so, for wherever there is disobedience, it is natural that magisterial authority has to be restored in regard to it, and thus the question to be posed is whether, when this kind of action is carried out by one who is Christian, a modification is to be permitted or not.

Thus when disobedience against the law is ongoing, the state must respond in order to prevent its own dissolution. Yet how is obedience to be restored? Either obedience was violated unknowingly, in which case the only thing that can be indicated is for the one who has violated obedience to be brought to awareness. This is so, since the reparation that must somehow be accomplished belongs under another rubric: that of the civil court. So here we have an analogue to the admonition and instruction in the realm of ecclesial discipline. Or the violation was done knowingly, and then it is to be presupposed in the one who has violated obedience that he had not been led by the idea of the state regarding some particular state of affairs, and not that he had no idea of the state at all. What is to happen now? In analogy with influence on the spirit considered above, is the political idea to be revived? Or in analogy with the previously developed notion of influence on the flesh, is there to be a counterweight to the sensorial motives that have gained the victory over the power of the political idea?

Certainly the first thing mentioned must occur, but this cannot be the goal of the restoring action in the state: rather, the Christian finds the place for this in the Christian community, on the one hand, and in the institutions of political education that belong to broadening action, on the other hand. Thus only the second alternative remains; accordingly, since a person can only be moved to violate obedience by means of selfish motives, only this remains: that there will be self-seeking motives of an opposite kind available for him that can return him to obedience; thus a system of punishment and reward will be put to use. The question then concerns the degree to which it is fitting for a Christian who is a magistrate to make use of such a system, and the degree to which it is fitting for a subject to submit himself to such a system and to make claims upon it.

Thus in the first place we ask, "Is it appropriate for a Christian as a magistrate to implement a system of civil criminal justice?" One could say that a Christian is to overcome evil with good[4] and thus may neither assign nor inflict punishment, and that if the state were organized in a Christian way, there could be no question of any penal legislation. Actually the question is often raised from this point of view as to whether it is fitting for a Christian to accept a magisterial office, and many answer this question "No." Now, however, there are in turn also sayings in Scripture that take an opposing position and certainly sayings that are much more distinctive, and in order to be in accord with proper rules of interpretation, the more particular must have more weight than the general. This is the case because the question always remains with a general proposition as to whether the author had actually considered all the individual possibilities since in every general proposition the general model was the relationship between a Christian and his opponent; however, the situation of a Christian being a magistrate was certainly not considered.

Hence, when Paul says in Romans 13:4 that magistrates wield the sword in order to punish the evildoers and has indeed already said in verse 1 that the magistrates are established by God, he presents criminal justice as grounded in divinely instituted authority. Thus the Christian can have no doubt as to whether a person in a magisterial office, in acting to effect punishment, seeks to fulfill the will of God. Moreover, this is not at all on the topic of overcoming evil with good, which surely cannot be accomplished through punishment, and it is also the case that punishment is not something evil in and of itself. And yet punishment always inflicts evil, and this in itself also appears to contradict the law of Christian love. Still, we must consider this matter more fully in terms of its origin. Punishment is to work as a threat, and the actual application of punishment is only necessary so that the threat is real. Criminal penal law that is only for show—with no intention that the punishment will be carried out—has no meaning. However, one could not ever give out that penal law could have retroactive power. Thus if it is always to be presupposed that penal law is to be recognized, then merely by means of remaining within a state, one consents to penal law; and if any person later breaks the law and incurs punishment, he is the one who inflicts it on himself, not the magistrate who obtained the impulse to action from the person himself. Thereby, however, the Christian magistrate can be completely at rest provided no other evil is imposed as punishment except what every person is ready to impose on himself.

Now, no one is permitted to kill himself, so it follows that the death penalty should never be found in a Christian state. From time immemorial this point has been contested, but when it is carefully considered, there is nothing that can contradict our conclusion or endanger our result. The true purpose of all penal legislation is to maintain obedience to the law. This is true; yet in relation to evildoers who are put to death, this no longer has any meaning. Thus one could only say, "The death penalty is carried out on one individual and thereby has a more powerful influence on all others than is possible by any other means." Suppose that it works this way: can the state then have a right to purchase the most powerful form of threat at the price of a human life? Surely not. For as often as the state employs the death penalty, we have no feeling except that the state is preserving a barbaric time or that the state is indicating that it has become politically bankrupt because it lacks the power to maintain the dominance of the political idea. The former feeling occurs when the state imposes the death penalty on common criminals, the latter when it imposes it on those criminals against the state that we call "traitors."

However, suppose someone were to say, "There are crimes that will not allow persons who have committed them to ever have a happy feeling about life again, so that to impose the death penalty on them is an act of human love and the greatest blessing for them." We must reject this out of hand as unchristian because the grace of God is greater than any individual human action. Yet, apart from the Christian perspective, a person can only say one of two things: Either, "The feeling that one is not able to live with the consciousness of certain crimes is an individual feeling, thus no other person is able to make a judgment concerning it." Yet then the only thing that could follow is that the freedom must be granted to the criminal to kill himself. Or, "The feeling is a communal one, about which the state is thus in a position to judge." However, if the state then punishes a criminal with death, this would only be morally justifiable given the presupposition that a partial self-murder by the state is allowable.

Now, how is a Christian to behave in relation to this matter? If it cannot be denied that the death penalty as an aspect of civil law comes out of a condition of barbarism, from this war that individuals have with each other, and in relation to public law from a condition of rashness, from this war between the whole and individuals—hence, along with the formation of the state, the effort to abolish the death penalty must grow, and along with the Christianization of the state, the consciousness must grow that the death penalty is not only superfluous and unnecessary, but also immoral. And if this does not actually occur, it is always a sign of dullness.

Next comes the difficulty for the princes. They should thus begin by approving no more death sentences and always substitute another penalty for the death penalty, in order to abolish it legally, as soon as experience provides evidence that neither individuals in the state, nor the state as a state, is judged to be more evil when there is no longer a death penalty. Yet princes of course do not act as individuals but feel themselves bound to the whole and consequently believe that the authority of law may not be transgressed when a law's abolition is demanded by only a few at first, and when the law provides a kind of security for the majority. Yet what follows from this is that the guilt resulting from the death penalty is collective and not individual, but that does not mean that it can be seen as justified. The Christian must strive resolutely for the death penalty to be abolished. . . .

2. In the State, Restoring Action of Individuals upon the Whole

If civil society has regressed, it is in need of reform, which yet can only proceed from individuals in the measure that the whole is in need of it. We set the whole in contrast to the totality of all individuals, and regarding the latter we distinguish individuals who are members of the leading principle in the whole or of the magisterial organization, and individuals who are not. Now we ask whether or not the two groups stand in the same relationship to restoring action. Two opposing theories immediately come to the fore: one theory puts the two on a par; the theory holds that only magisterial persons have a right to do this [restoring action]. However, here the difference between magistrates and subjects shrinks to a minimum, for neither group can do anything essentially different from what the other does. As a result it becomes all the more clear that each individual may act only in accordance with the form of his political placement.

Suppose we think first of all of a state in which legislation depends in part on a council that, for its part, was instituted by the subjects. In this case each individual in whom there is a reforming tendency can convey this tendency immediately to the organization by only choosing representatives he knows to desire the same changes that he desires. However, he must then also content himself with this influence, no matter how slow its effects appear to be. For if he were to do more, he would be acting violently and thus immorally, as would soon be pointed out. Yet he would also completely fail to accomplish what he had intended. Or would it indeed be possible for a movement to last that was based on something other than the living conviction of the whole? Impossible. And for that reason it is also the case that those who are constitutionally denied all political influence in the state can contribute to the restoration of a better condition only by means of seeking to influence the convictions of those who have the authority to make changes. Indeed, these latter themselves, who after all take steps in the organization of the whole, have no other way before them than that indicated above. For what happens in this state always happens only under the form of the general will, and each individual act of will is either the effect of a passionate impulse or of enthusiasm or of thoughtful consideration.

Yet enthusiasm most often comes solely from the unity of one personal life; thus where a greater number of persons are working together, acts of will proceed from a passionate impulse or from thoughtful consideration. Now passionate impulses are plainly immoral, so it follows that all betterment of the state must come predominantly from thoughtful consideration. And everything depends upon each individual contributing his highest consideration in those moments in which a reforming tendency is present. Hence one can say that even those individuals who are not part of the organized political structure can effect it in the same way as those who are members of the structure, except that they begin from more distant points. And even members of that structure, when that structure itself is on the whole entangled in a regressive movement, can effect it only in the way that any other individual also does, the only difference being that they are in a position to spread their reforming impulse more quickly and in a wider variety of ways.

Now, however, it is easy to make clear that proceeding in a different fashion contradicts the Christian spirit. Of course some say that if the state is moving in a retrograde direction, those who have occasioned it and have opposed reform are its enemies, and it is entirely right to act against them, just as it is right to act against the external enemies of the state: thus the use of physical force is right. However, they themselves must nevertheless admit that the state would cease to exist if a portion of its members were to consider themselves justified in regarding and treating others as enemies of the state. It also follows acting in this way would be to regress back to the state of nature. Although Christianity too does not prohibit one from protecting oneself against force in the state of nature, it does decidedly prohibit initiating an element of action bearing on other persons with use of force. This is so, for accordingly Christianity has already prohibited making right a previous injustice by means of force. So Christianity must be much, much more opposed to trying to change the moral condition of another by means of external force.

Thus, given that it would be right to treat those who had occasioned a retrogressive movement in the state in the same way that external enemies were treated, it would always be against the spirit of Christianity to restore a better condition by means of force. Or disregarding the genesis of a state's worsening, yet simply granting that a retrogressive movement is at hand, still those who want to restore a previous better condition, for which the state makes no provision, must first put an end to the current organization of the state. But this would be in direct opposition to all Christian principles. This is so because, as we have seen, Christianity pronounces the government, including every valid authority in the state, to be a divine institution. Thus it can as little allow destruction of the state in a very small way as it can on a grand scale, just as it has then also never approved what admittedly the classic ancients counted as a great glory: neither the greatest of this kind, murder of tyrant, nor any other violent movement in the state. When, in spite of all this, such actions also occur in a Christian state, above all else it must not be overlooked that much is reckoned to belong in the Christian state that in its grounding nevertheless really belongs under another rubric. In this regard we cannot allow ourselves to draw specific limits, for that would lead us too far into details, but we want to set forth a general viewpoint.

Where the existing conditions of a state rest on a real contract, not only in terms of individual points, but also in terms of the whole—certainly this can never be the rule, but only happens as an exception since every state comes to be without a contract since a contract becomes possible only within a state, and what is valid for the emergence of a state is also valid for essential changes of the state, for these have the same character—if subjects break the contract, magistrates have the right to punish them. However, if magistrates break the contract, they cannot be punished by the subjects: in that case the whole contractual status would be overthrown and a situation of chaos established; this means that the task can only be to produce an entirely new order. Hence it is a purely Christian propensity for taking care that the highest power cannot violate the contract, and in most states thus far the tension between the inviolability of the monarch and the responsibility held by the highest public authorities rests upon this propensity.

Essentially interconnected with this is the idea that an action of the highest power in the state is valid only if the two parties in tension with each other come to agreement concerning it. When a real violation of a contract arises, blame then falls to the responsible persons, and they are to be punished; however, the result cannot be that the state itself would be dissolved. Where this protective regulation is not found and yet a contract does exist, the whole form of the state is negated if the authorities have violated the contract; the only principle that can then be set forth is that everyone has a duty to assess the morality involved and according to one's conscience to restore the social condition in the most peaceable manner possible. Yet it is also clear that in cases of this kind the civil society was not destroyed by the subjects, but that the constituted authority had undone itself. There are cases that rest on quite special circumstances and that do not fall at all under our Christian rule, that no individual may dissolve the governmental authority, an institution of divine origin, but such cases fall under rules from a presumed state of nature that seeks to protect against outbreaks of raw power; in that case a Christian would never be justified in doing harm in the face of an injustice visited upon himself.

Where authorities violate a contract, there is no longer a state, but an eruption of raw power; but Christian action responding to such a situation would still be very limited by the fact that no person may engage in this action unless he is certain that the contract with the state has been broken and that no one can be certain of this unless he sees himself obstructed in the fulfillment of his duties by this violation. On this basis it is already clear that even in this case the action of a Christian can be only a peaceful one; this is so, for no process can be violent that has its basis solely in an effort to avoid being thwarted in the fulfillment of one's duty.

Now, however, revolution is appropriately considered here and unfortunately proceeds too often even from individuals in Christian states, who have no scruples about first undoing the state in order to be able to improve it afterward. This is to be explained in a twofold manner. That is, first it lay in the nature of the case that because the Christian spirit originally only took hold of the lower classes of society and penetrated the actual circumstances of the state only late and only very gradually, accordingly it is no wonder that even political theory itself is still contaminated today with pagan vestiges and holds fast to pagan models. However, this situation is never to be approved, for if the intention of Christianity is to put an end to every situation in which nothing rules but external force, then no Christian can approve a rule that, even if it is only provisional and is no more than a means to a particular end, has no capacity in turn to produce anything other than a condition of sheer external force.

Second, however, the consciousness of what is right in political matters can scarcely be made clear and correct and brought into an adequate theory before the political condition itself is brought clearly to a certain level. Everyone knows how little this was the case in the Middle Ages; thus, although this is also not a matter for praise, yet it is very easy to declare that a true Christian political consciousness was not to be found in that time. A right judgment about this matter was first established with the Reformation, and if we consider what the Reformation has to teach on the one hand about the Peasants' War and such matters, and on the other hand about the duties of Christian princes, it articulates the genuine Christian sensibility that rejects all illegal power and provides us with generally sufficient grounds for the principles we have set forth. . . .

3. Purifying Action of One State upon Another

Up to this point we have only defined the actions of one state that is self-governing[5] upon another state that is also self-governing, so the question that remains is this: how subjects themselves are to relate to this situation. Here, however, we meet with a variety of opinions deriving from equally confused sources, all of which still are intended to be viewed as based on a Christian standpoint. We will not be able to take the right position regarding a single case unless we first come to an understanding in general terms as to how war is to be evaluated in relation to the lives of individuals. The usual approach is to think about this matter as if in war only the life of the enemy were in view, but this is actually not the case at all. Rather, it is always only an arbitrary matter when a certain number of the enemy come to die by war. It can never be moral for a state that is waging war simply to order its subjects to kill the subjects of an opposing state wherever they meet them; thus the state would never have killing enemy subjects as its purpose; rather, what it would actually want is only indemnification and security for the future. Surely, both of these goals are to be achieved by means of physical force, so there is no other means for this purpose than to weaken the opponent to the point that no other rational way remains except for the opponent to grant what has been demanded. However, the enemy is not to be weakened by killing its subjects; rather, it is by taking possession of what provides its power: land and people.

The less that war is waged in this manner, the more it is barbaric and immoral; this is so, for if the state may not punish its own subjects with death, even less may it do so to foreigners. Thus, that the enemy is killed is not the result of a determined desire to kill them, nor the result of it being known that they had established themselves in a particular position, but only that they offer resistance of their own free will. Indeed, in previous times the situation was vastly different, but for us there can be no doubt at all which way of waging war is the more moral one, the old way or the current way. Of course, greater personal bravery was developed when one fought only with sword and lance. However, because a fight to the death resulted more easily from those means than from the currently dominant use of guns that seeks only to cause the opponent to retreat in the face of a certain amount of force having been built up, so the current way of waging war is by far nobler.

Our waging of outpost warfare[6] and use of sharpshooters are the only unchristian elements of contemporary warfare; by these means individuals are disregarded, and also precisely the least effect is also achieved. Now as to what concerns the subjects themselves, the issue cannot be that they are simply being led to death or go to their death in war; rather, the issue is that a portion of the subjects are exposed or expose themselves to a greater danger of death in order to reach a particular goal. However, this cannot be unjust. Rather, just as a false teaching about divine providence can bring about a view that lightning rods and vaccinations are sinful, just so a false teaching about the preservation of human life and about responsibility for self-preservation can lead to the view that every enlistment for military service and every participation in war can be declared to be unacceptable. With the same justification as is applied to military service, every dangerous activity such as seafaring, construction, and other similar activities would have to be forbidden and avoided.

So if someone has put forth the theory that a magistrate cannot command the shedding of human blood since Holy Scripture forbids it, according to this theory magistrates could not require anyone to participate in war if his conscience also forbade it. This whole presupposition is wrong; since Christian communities like the Quakers and Mennonites have set forth this theory, in this way they have actually placed themselves outside of the state, and it seems to us a great indulgence on the part of our government when they are tolerated in the state in spite of this. If there is no personal duty to do military service, such as in England and Holland, the matter stands in an entirely different way. This is so, for then participation in war is a freely chosen occupation.

However, if the matter stands the way it does with us [in Prussia], where participation in war is a universal duty of all citizens—and this is clearly the nobler state of affairs—then no exceptions are allowed. Where this higher state of affairs is not yet in place, where there exists a special class of soldiers with no universal duty for military service, the transition to this more perfect situation will be made more difficult the larger the number of those who would not permit Christians to bear arms. Thus it certainly is very important to declare one's conscience on this point. And this is not at all difficult, but certainly one may not trace everything back to the unconditional obedience that is owed to the magistrate, as is the usual practice. Rather, the sole sufficient viewpoint is the truth that nothing at all may be required of an individual in war that involves knowingly and willingly shedding human blood.

Yet if it has now been established that a Christian subject may not refuse to participate in military service because this would be completely unchristian, we have also nevertheless come to agreement that Christian ethics can only allow for a defensive war, not a war of aggression. Yet it is still possible that a magistrate can call for a war of aggression, and in this case one might then say a Christian is not allowed to participate in such a war without taking a portion of the guilt on himself. However, the matter actually stands this way. Above all else, a Christian as subject has no means at all by which to decide with certainty whether a war that the magistrate calls for is justified or not justified. This is so, for a war is always enclosed within a series of negotiations between states over a violation.

Now let us also suppose that all the deliberations in the state had the greatest possible public character, though in matters of war and peace this is to be least expected. Yet in this case, as one learned in the law and as a politician, an individual who would want to make a judgment as to whether the government is in the right overall and did not omit any intermediate steps even in the negotiations would have to have, in addition to perfect information about what actually occurred, all the insights that the various branches of government unite within itself, and no one will be able to boast of this easily about himself. At that point, however, also suppose an individual, not himself having magisterial authority, who unites all this information in himself—this individual may still never presume to refuse a magistrate's order to go to war on the grounds that the war does not seem justified to him. This is so, for his doing this would mean nothing but dissolving the state on his part.

Moreover, if a number of people were to act in this way, the state itself would actually be dissolved since all assurance that the magistrate would always find the obedience he needs would disappear. And finally it is clear that a subject incurs no guilt if he takes up arms at the command of a magistrate. This is so, for generally responsibility can rest only on those who are members of the governmental structure, and precisely only in the areas to which they have been appointed and about which they are responsible to act strictly according to their own judgment. In any other area they can only have influence in the way that any other person would, by advocating publicly for their views, but never by means of disobedience or resistance. Moreover, before all else they are able to presuppose that by their advocacy they can have a weightier effect by virtue of their social position; and only as they take up this advocacy are they able to make it contingent on the extension of their magisterial function. If in spite of this, something is carried out that one is not in a position to approve, one is free of all responsibility if one, now being nothing more than a subject, complies with the command of the magistrate as all subjects do.

If one desires to give currency to a different rule, one looks at how conscientiousness fails to attain its true mark and must fail in a most dangerous fashion. To exclude oneself from war because one does not find it to be justified is plainly mutinous. It is also completely pointless to say regarding this matter, "I do not want to participate in an unjustified war so as not to share in the guilt." This is so, for warfare includes more than merely bearing arms, and those who do not bear arms are no less participants in it. "But still is it not the case that they take part in a purely indirect and unconscious way?" There is nothing to this idea. The reason is that on the one hand the state in a time of war immediately lays claim to all activities, and on the other hand even those who themselves bear arms participate only in an indirect way. And if it is true that some participate in war in a conscious way and others unconsciously, this changes the matter only insofar as the latter still bear the particular guilt that they are generally lacking in any vital participation in civic life.

There are only two possibilities: either one must participate in a war ordered by a magistrate, or one must refuse ever to be in a state that does not declare once and for all that it will never wage war. On the other hand, to declare one's conviction that a war is unjustified and to seek to influence the magistrate with all one's power based on this conviction, while still remaining in complete obedience to the magistrate, is everyone's duty, and if one conforms to this in a conscientious way, one can be entirely at peace in one's conscience.

We cannot expect scriptural evidence for our propositions to be found in the New Testament since Christianity only came later to be present in the Roman army. Still, John the Baptist must not have held it as a matter of conscience never to be a soldier; this is so, for otherwise he would not have been able to give instructions to soldiers over the particular conduct they were to follow. But to be sure, he is only on the border of Christianity. Nevertheless, Paul too cannot have had the thought that participation in military service is absolutely disloyal to Christianity. This is so, for he was the first to bring Christianity into those areas from which many surely went into the Roman army. Thus he would have had true cause to speak his mind about this matter if he had held this view. Christian ethics permits the bearing of arms if commanded by a magistrate in such a general way that individual exceptions to this permission cannot be valid.

4. Purifying Action of the State upon Individuals Completely outside of the Bounds of Any State

It is easy to see that a regressive movement is also possible in a relationship between a state and those who do not yet live within a civil union, and likewise that where this is the case, a purifying action is indicated. Now, if subjects of the state are the ones who disturb the existing conditions of social relations through treachery and deceit, the magistrate must also exercise justice against his own subjects on behalf of those who belong to no state and thus also have no one to advocate for them. This is so, for it would only be a heathen notion and not a Christian one to grant rights to its own citizens in relation to each other, but not to its citizens in relation to others, and for a Christian magistrate it cannot matter at all against whom injustice has been perpetrated by his subjects, but only whether or not they have committed an injustice of any kind. Now, however, what if those who do not yet live in a civil union are the ones who violate the good-faith relationship in social relations? We can only comprehend the significance of this question if we consider history, particularly the time since previously unknown but inhabited regions have been discovered.

The dominant point of view that we find is that Christian states would have the right to take possession of people who do not yet live in a civil union and to bring about a civilized condition among them by means of force. Yet hardly anyone would claim this right in an unconditional way, so on what pretext would it be exercised? When one meets unknown people with whom it is not possible to speak, the first relationship that arises is a real one so that the effort to come to understanding by means of symbols is naturally set aside. In this case, one gives and receives gifts, practices exchange by bartering, and so forth. Now, based on this original circumstance, how could one come to the point of moving into the use of force? Obviously this would be done only on the presupposition that an injustice has occurred and that a civil condition is not actually present as yet, so that there is also no government to which one could turn. And from where could this presupposition arise? Obviously only out of social relations and the perception that these relations have been violated.

Based on this perspective, however, is the use of force that one employs to be justified? Every form of social relation proceeds from the supposition of an agreement to a social contract. Yet where there is no civil society, there is also no agreement to a social contract in the strict sense; this is so, for only in a state does there exist sanction that belongs to the concept of a contract. It follows from this that an agreement to a social contract is presupposed between individuals just as the rights of peoples are presupposed between states. And indeed this is so even in the case of a contractual agreement that is gradually realized by means of having been accepted as a sheer presupposition. If, for example, a bartering exchange is initiated, there is always an interval between the promise and its fulfillment, and this interval is occupied by trust that the word that has been given will be kept. The more and the longer people act on this presupposition, the more inner validity the presupposition has even if an outer sanction is lacking. However, a true contract is not yet present.

So if those who are not yet living within a civil union do not live by their word, the first natural result of this process is that barter exchange within social relations is invalidated. However, those who have had the advantage of this practice, as long as a good relationship exists, will take pains to restore it and to make the broken trust good again, and from this a kind of guarantee must have arisen that is an approximation to civil society. This is so, for if a case of this sort were to occur, a process of arbitration would arise; the majority who desire social relations will make use of physical force against those individuals who created the disturbance through their faithlessness, and clearly this is a foundation for use of civil power. Now of course, civil society is beneficial for all persons because it is here that an acceleration of the dominion of humans over nature is first possible; certainly it is in conformity with the duty of Christians to assist those who are not in a state toward living within a state. However, can the use of force be justified in doing this work? This is all the less so since a civil condition brought about by the use of force is no civil condition.

For this reason, when social relations are violated, there exists no right to introduce civil society by means of force; for where this occurs, it naturally makes the force that has been introduced into a dominating force. In that case, however, the usual custom is precisely to suspend all relations. Yet this customary procedure is always difficult to effect because the individuals who already live within a state by virtue of their superior position in relation to those who have no civil status—these people do not believe that in this respect they are strictly subject to the law as they are in all other cases. This, however, is absolutely false;

here as elsewhere magistrates must be followed, and magistrates have the right to determine the limits to social relations. Now it is quite clear that if one holds oneself to these proper limits, the truly free and natural formation of civil society is to be expected.

If we compare the results that come from two different ways of establishing civilization with each other, it appears that the use of force reaches its goal more quickly. If one subjugates uncivilized people, a civil condition is present very quickly; however, if a civil condition is first to be grounded on an inner need, it will only come into being very slowly, and thus one would be able to say, "If it is a responsibility to spread civilization, it is also the case that the quickest way is the best." However, this quickness is only apparent. This is so, for those who are brought into a civil condition by means of force lack the consciousness from the very beginning that civil society exists among them; rather, they feel that they have been merely suppressed. The consciousness of being within a state can first come to them when the power that influences them builds to the point that it succeeds in bringing forth the opposition between magistrates and subjects among them. Until this occurs, they will always have an inclination to repel force by means of force, subjugation by means of rebellion.

However, this scenario disregards the fact that Christianity knows nothing of the right to bring civilization to uncivilized peoples by means of force. Christianity demands that everything be avoided by means of which the Christian name can be defamed among peoples, and there is nothing that can defame it more than suppression. We are reasonably surprised when Christians have social relations with non-Christian peoples for centuries without any inclination toward Christianity being developed in them. But the reason for this is not so much that these Christian peoples had no interest in Christianity as it is that they have created hatred in a scornful way by using force. If this had not happened, the good-natured races with whom people had contact in the fifteenth century would have long since been Christianized; that they are in part not yet Christianized is and remains a scandal among Christian peoples. Perhaps this comes somewhat late in Christian ethics; however, theory always comes somewhat late, and unfortunately it is not coming too late, for violent actions have never yet ceased to occur.

DIVISION II
BROADENING ACTION

Chapter 4

Introduction
[to Broadening Action]

The positive side of efficacious action has the character of education, formation, further development. We have seen above that the opposition between rest and movement is grounded in immediate feeling itself and that presentational action rests upon the former and efficacious action on the latter, also that efficacious action has the character either of pleasure or of a lack of pleasure. Now, the action previously described proceeds from a lack of moral pleasure, upon which the whole nature of Christianity rests insofar as it must be viewed as redemption, as restoration. The action to which we now turn arises from a feeling of pleasure, from the consciousness of unchecked power, or if conceived in relation to its object, from receptivity, which, insofar as it is conscious of itself, is a desire. Now, if we are to hold fast to the standpoint of Christian ethics, then all actions of the Christian are as such actually continuations of the action of Christ himself. These actions have established the reign of God, at which all Christian action aims, and have indicated its characteristics, so that all action of the Christian church is nothing but the realization of these characteristics.

Thus, if we return to the idea that the different forms of action always accompany each other in actuality, it follows that each form can always be seen as presenting all forms of action. This also means that the whole saving action of Christ can be comprehended under the form of broadening action. Christ himself described the distinctive life of those belonging to him as being one with him, so that they together with him constitute a whole. When he said to them, "You did not choose me, but I chose you,"[1] he established this unity and the total activity of those who have become one with him as proceeding solely from him. It follows that his action must be able to be recognized as broadening action and as the universal prototype of our action, which manifests itself everywhere in individuals. Let us return to the opposition between spirit and flesh: insofar as it is to be overcome, it is the foundation of purifying action. If [this opposition] were overcome, if the ἐπιθυμεῖν[2] (acts [desires] of the obstinacy of flesh against spirit) were overcome, this does not mean either that flesh as a whole or every relationship of flesh to spirit is brought to nothing. Rather, it means that a new relationship has arisen.

We can express this new relationship in two ways. On the one hand, in this new relationship we can see spirit as the agent, and then we see flesh as the organ by means of which spirit acts. Or if we suppose spirit being at rest, then flesh is something outer while spirit is manifested as something inner. Conceived in the latter way, we have the basic type of presentational action; in the former way, it is the basic type of broadening action. This is so, for if we suppose that spirit is the agent, then the general formula for this action is to unite another with oneself. Now if we apply this to Christ, we must say that in him there was no opposition of flesh against spirit to be overcome; thus, neither is there a new relationship between flesh and spirit to be established. That is, the divine nature in him was able to hold his sensorial nature in the most perfect relationship as organ to agent and as external manifestation of what was internal. Thus his action in this connection proceeded completely from himself, and the ground for this action was perfect in itself. This is the case, for the beginning point for the universal unification of all flesh with spirit could proceed from him and come to others through his influence only insofar as this unification would have already been perfected in him.

So this is the first feature of the general type for all broadening action: it is always a transitive action, always going forward out of itself, yet one grounded in an action that is perfect in itself. This is clear in relation to the action of Christ; however, no immediate influence of a perfect action would appear to be admissible in relation to our own actions. Yet if we consider that any genuine action of spirit is conceivable only as mediated by flesh, then unification of flesh with spirit must be presupposed for all broadening action and indeed as a unification that is perfected in itself. Let us stop to consider the case that appears to call forth the most opposition, namely, everything that concerns the sanctification of an individual human being. As long as there is still some progress in sanctification, we suppose that there remain actions of an individual directed to himself—that is, immanent actions. It seems to follow from this that there is no transitive action. And also no action perfect in itself. That is, if there is an action of a person from himself and on himself, and if we concede that this occurs only insofar as he has not yet reached complete unification of spirit with flesh at any point, no unification is indeed as yet present to be the source from which this action of a person on himself can proceed.

Certainly, this is how the matter appears at first glance. But if we look more closely, then we must still say: "Given that we are assuming an action of a person on himself and are supposing it to be an efficacious action, not supposing it to be a purely presentational action, it is obvious that we are supposing a twofold-edness, a subject and an object; thus we are dividing a person into an agent and that which is acted upon, into a ποιοῦν and a πάσχον.[3] Accordingly, moreover, we again have our type of action that proceeds out of itself; the aspect of a person that is ποιοῦν upon the aspect that is πάσχον." Now, however, we must also say: "If an action seen in this way is an advance in sanctification, then the ποιοῦν within it can be agent only insofar as flesh acts completely as an organ of spirit, not insofar as it opposes spirit in any way. For if the agent is not in a state of complete unity of spirit with flesh—rather, the two are still divided—no progress toward sanctification can proceed on that basis." Whether such an action of a person on himself can be accepted, we leave undecided; but insofar as it can be accepted, it must correspond to our type. Thus, this remains secure.

A second opposition is the following. When we imagine the action of Christ, we think of him as an individual human being, and as such he is not only a person, a quantitative unity, but also an individual, a qualitative unity. If we want to distinguish him as a human being from all other persons, we must certainly think of him as church teaching has expressed it—in absolute sinlessness and in such a way that the human and divine natures in him are absolutely unified. However, this does not yet exhaust the matter; this is so, for he was not the unity of divine and human in a general way, but in one person, as is characteristic of a rational being, that each one is also determined as qualitatively other, thus determined in a particular way. Along with this in turn, all the actions of Christ, considered in themselves, were something individual. But how was it if we look at the result itself? All the actions of Christ were to result in persons' sin being overcome in them and thus in unifying flesh with spirit. This result was to be the same in all persons; however, each person was to become a mentally alive single being—only in a higher grade and out of higher material—thus again a unique individual, each one different from all others. If all had become the same, then one could truly say that they have become this directly by means of the action of Christ precisely insofar as this action is something individual.

However, insofar as each Christian as a new creation is also a distinctively determined single being, we must also imagine that surely one and the same result follows for all, and that yet each person takes in the same distinctiveness and by means of this becomes again something particular. Thus the action of Christ in its point of origin was something individual; however, the result it had on persons was something universal, and only by means of this could something that was properly individual arise again in each person. Yet precisely in its going out from Christ, the action of Christ was perfected in itself; and in its effects on others, it was in the first place what went forward out of itself. So we must say that everywhere both aspects coincide and that every broadening action is something individual and perfected in itself in its starting point, and in its point of contact it is something that proceeds outward from itself and is, as such, something universal.

We have seen that in every genuine action, whatever form it may take, there are always also elements of the other forms of action. Applying this to our current topic, this means that "in every broadening action there is always also an element of presentational action and of purifying action." When we say, "That which is perfected in itself is that which underlies what goes forth from itself, and broadening action is something individual in the point from which it proceeds; so it is, considered in the point from which it proceeds, that which is perfected in itself, and this is presentational action. This is the case, for insofar as an action has not yet arrived at its object, it is not yet an efficacious action, but it still remains one that manifests itself. Thus, by means of every efficacious action, insofar as we disregard its results, a person manifests himself at the same time. Spirit can only act through organs that it has formed itself. However, spirit only acts through these organs to the degree that they are united with it, and this organ must also always present itself. It follows from this that efficacious action is always at the same time what we call revelation, an action through which spirit brings its organ into play, and this is the presentational feature in every efficacious action.

It is clear that this presentational feature should not be absent in Christ's action. This is the case, for if his sinlessness and divine nature had not been manifest in every one of his actions, we would have to give up including his action under this type, because we would not be able to recognize his constancy in them at all. However, regarding the other point, that every broadening action also includes a purifying element within itself, we cannot apply this point to Christ in the way that it can be applied regarding broadening action where he is conceived as both subject and object at the same time. Rather, Christ's broadening action can only be conceived as purifying action insofar as others were his object. On the other hand, for us the purifying feature can appear in every form of broadening action, and here what we must say is precisely that insofar as human action still also presupposes in itself an as-yet-imperfect union of flesh with spirit, we must suppose that in the organs of spirit an obstinacy toward the spirit remains that will be continually overcome through the action itself. This [means the] overcoming of obstinacy to the action, obstinacy present in the action itself, which we call "exertion," and this exertion is the feature of purifying action that is present in every broadening action. In Christ, restoring action of this type is inconceivable. This is so, for exertion cannot exist without the presupposition not of a deficiency of goodwill, but of an unequally divided goodwill in the whole agent. Thus we can find an analogy for this form of restoring action in Christ only insofar as we think of those on whom Christ acts, as already identified with him in a particular way. Christ's steadfastness toward the obstinacy that has been established in others is the analogue to this exertion.

There remains yet a third opposition to be considered. That is, all broadening action on the one hand presupposes community, and on the other hand creates community. How are we to imagine this in our original type, in the broadening action of Christ? It is completely clear how the actions of Christ went forth in order to create community; nonetheless, this is not at all the case for the other aspect, that Christ's action also presupposed community already existing. However, this can be traced back to the concept that everywhere broadening action presupposes a feeling of pleasure in the agent; this feeling is an excess of power by means of which the feeling is able to go forth out of itself. At the same time a feeling of receptivity in the recipient is also presupposed since otherwise the action would not have an object; that is, desire in the recipient for the influence of the agent is also presupposed.

Yet if that feeling, without which a broadening action could have no way to begin, is reciprocal, a true κοινωνία[4] is certainly always already presupposed. However, is it not a contradiction to say that a given action both presupposes and establishes community? The particular idea that the presupposed community and the community that is created are different from each other is impossible, for in reality both are one and the same, based on a definite relationship between spirit and flesh in which spirit has dominion. However, the solution lies in the fact that the condition of the community is original, that it is always already present where it is possible to call for a broadening action. We understand "spirit," if we take no view of what is specifically Christian, to be general human intelligence, νοῦς;[5] however, from the point of view of Christian ethics, we understand "spirit" to be πνεῦμα,[6] which itself then exists in distinction to νοῦς, with νοῦς being an aspect of flesh.

Now, if we consider this matter from a general human perspective, it is obvious that if we imagine human beings in a state where they can give themselves rules for action, community is also always already present. If we return to the presupposition of one original human being, for this person no community can exist until the division into two sexes is present. As long as we imagine this person being totally isolated, there does not yet exist a true theory of action, but only a progressive unfolding that is lacking in consciousness. This is so, for all determining mental stimulations from the outside would be lacking for that individual, who as such would exist only in distinction from the infinite in respect to our task. Stimulations would have to come to the individual from within; however, stimulation coming solely from within appears to us always as something that is only incidental. Since it is incidental, nothing at all can be definite about it. Thus it is evident that stimulation coming from without would still have to be dominant; moreover, all stimulation from without could only be of a sensorial nature and only the kind of stimulation that necessitates a response in order that sensorial life can be maintained. It follows that where there is no community, no theory of broadening action can be set forth.

Yet how does the matter stand when we consider it from a distinctively Christian point of view, when we thus imagine πνεῦμα, which has been planted in persons or is to be planted in persons in order that everything in the person—the whole person existing in the opposition between spirit and flesh in the wider sense—may be united with πνεῦμα and may be formed into πνεῦμα's organ? Now, if we return from here to the very beginning, this πνεῦμα, this divine principle, was originally in Christ alone, and thus it still appears as if community must first have been established, not that it was already present. If we nonetheless consider the Christian church as already existing, however small it might have been, then community indeed already existed, and then our proposition faces only a small difficulty such as would exist from a general human standpoint. Now, it is impossible for us to give up the analogy between our actions and those of Christ because we would completely lose the original standard for our actions. Thus we cannot avoid the question, "How was it with this analogy when, to be sure, Christ existed, but the Christian church did not yet exist?"

Here there are two points to which we must return. One is easier to take in, the other more difficult, and each provides by itself a complete solution; however, since each makes reference to the other, we cannot do without either. Concerning the point that is easier to take in, Scripture indicates that Christ was first to appear in the world in the fullness of time;[7] this expression, certainly indefinite and yet quite pregnant with meaning, fits our present requirement precisely. That is, the time was not fulfilled until the desire for the influence of spirit was so clearly expressed that as soon as spirit itself appeared in Christ, community was also already begun. Had this not happened, neither would the time have been fulfilled. Now, that this is truly the actual meaning of this expression is seen in the larger interconnection in which it is found. That is, as long as we imagine that humanity was content with obedience to a law, the letter of which is always σαρκικόν, even though Paul is completely right to call it πνευματικόν according to its origin,[8] as long as there was no desire for spirit, neither was the time fulfilled. Yet this point makes reference to the second, more difficult point. That is, the state of desire for the appearance of spirit when it has not yet appeared necessarily presupposes community between "spirit" in a general human—for desire could exist only here—and πνεῦμα, the divine principle of Christianity.

However, a community cannot be conceived of without some unity among its members, in this case without identity between "spirit" in a general human sense and "spirit" in the Christian sense. Thus it appears that we have at once touched on the so-called rational view of Christianity, according to which the πνεῦμα of Christ is nothing but spirit in the general human sense, except that it appears in a heightened form. However, we can just as well put forward the following formula: "It must be presupposed that both are identical; consequently spirit in a general human sense is nothing but what πνεῦμα is as well, but spirit is πνεῦμα at a lower level of potency." Thus when we now say that this lower potency cannot raise itself to the higher level by itself; we have brought together what appears to be rationalistic and what appears to be supernaturalistic, and we have reduced the difference between these two to nothing. This is the result that one always necessarily comes to if one follows the opposition between these two to its end. However, given this, it follows that we can say that the identity of these two positions can be proved to be contained in the idea of time fulfilled and time not fulfilled. Namely, if we ask, "What did the apostle have in mind when he said, Ὅτε δὲ ἦλθε τὸ πλήρωμα τοῦ χρόνου?"[9] we must still answer, "Obviously, he had the period of messianic expectation in view." Of what does this period actually consist? It can be expressed in terms of these two ideas: discontent at being under the law and a feeling of the law's insufficiency, together with a presentiment of a new development coming out of the previously existing state and resting on an individual, which would rise to a condition higher than that under the law.

Now, every law has its origin in νοῦς, in spirit in a general human sense. Thus, if we also say that before Christ πνεῦμα was not present as an agent, we must still say, "Under the form of desire, it was indeed present as longing," for this is the way it has been represented to us in the period of messianic expectation, and we must say that "the time being fulfilled" is nothing other than the period of expectation having its full effect for the first time. So it becomes evident that, like spirit in the human sense, spirit in the Christian sense was both present and not present; that is, present as desire, but it was impossible for it to appear without Christ, thus [present] as desire that cannot pass over into fulfillment in and of itself. Thus the supernaturalistic postulate is included herein. This is the solution to the apparent contradiction in relation to the first beginning of a truly Christian life. From this point of view the whole existence of Christ appears to us as the true beginning, the fulfillment of the desire for πνεῦμα, this being the positive pole, as it were, satisfying the negative pole that already existed. And this is something different from the founding of a community because community was already present before the appearance.

Now, in order to establish an arrangement for this form of action, we must seek to lay out the whole domain of the broadening action in a general way. As an agent πνεῦμα is absolutely simple in and of itself; thus there is nothing in πνεῦμα that would provide us an opportunity for division into parts. On the other hand, flesh in its entirety is absolutely manifold. But even flesh in and of itself cannot provide us with a principle for division: it would not be moral since it would be derived from material that is completely sensorial. Thus all that remains is to search out the way that spirit and flesh are united. One indication of this can already be found in what we have said about the relationship of νοῦς to πνεῦμα. Seen from a Christian point of view, νοῦς, reason, spirit in a general human sense—these belong together with σάρξ and provide that νοῦς is not to be taken prisoner under the obedience of faith (as Luther falsely translates it);[10] still the apostle [Paul] intends that the νοήματα, the action of spirit in a general human sense, is to be comprehended under πίστις, and the proposition that non-Christian virtues are nothing but magnificent vices can be taken in all seriousness because they relate themselves more or less to a narrow domain, as the domain of nationality, for example, and thus they belong to what is sensorial, to σάρξ, as opposed to πνεῦμα.

In spite of this, we must always still distinguish carefully between spirit in a general human sense and flesh and say, "Now if πνεῦμα is the sole agent, still νοῦς, the organism of intelligence, is much closer to πνεῦμα than is the more sensorial physical organism and what is bodily, which is bound together with it." Thus this brings us to a distinction between a more inner way and a more outer way, in which πνεῦμα is the actual agent. The more inner way is πνεῦμα becoming one with νοῦς, with the whole mental organism of human nature, thus what we call "disposition." The more outer way is the unity of πνεῦμα with ψυχή—with the organism of the different sensorial functions of human beings, however only by means of the νοῦς, thus what we call "talent" as distinguished from disposition. Now it cannot be denied that both disposition and talent lie in the same way completely within the domain of morality. This is so, for by "disposition" in a general sense, we always understand a fixed and settled direction of the will, bound naturally together with the approval of that which corresponds to this direction and disapproval of that which is opposed to it.

If we speak of "dispositions," this is already a linguistic usage that is secondary and no longer completely comprehensive of the concept; this is so, for what we seek and what we set forth as our task is unity in the direction of the will throughout, and we believe that we will not have found the proper expression for direction of the will until we have traced it back to a unity, so that even what appears as a multiplicity is only a definite manifestation of this unity. However, by talent we understand a skill that is already in service of the will and can itself no longer be regarded as will. Thus, insofar as talent is something acquired, we consider it as a skill that the will can set in motion. However, is it not also for us something original, a natural gift, independent of a manifestation of the will and preceding the will? Certainly, but this is not in contradiction to the other claim; rather, the two hang together in a precise way. Thus we cannot even say that this distinction moves us out of the moral domain. Surely, to some extent one does foster talent, for example in the domain of art, not regarding it as a matter of morality because, of course, one cannot make it a moral requirement that anyone should have talent. However, this rests on a defective perspective, namely, that the whole moral task is comprehended too much in terms of individual persons and too little in terms of the whole.

Chapter 5

Broadening Action
in the Church

INTRODUCTION

The immediate goal of this action is the broadening of Christian disposition and
the broadening of all true mental talents[1] for the sake of the disposition. This is
the true character of this action. Now, if this action is to be depicted, the next
step must be to return to the character of the community itself, that is, insofar
as we saw that the apparent contradiction between these two propositions—one
that the broadening tendency always already presupposes community, and the
other that it always creates community—may be resolved only by saying that
community must always be created anew so that it is always able to be presupposed. However, in that we begin by having this persistence of community in
view, we must first ask about the scope of community. Where will we find it? We
will find it only if we return to the origins of the Christian church and to the idea
that underlay it as its basis. Here, however, we can only begin with the fact that
precisely the disposition that is the object of the community and of broadening
existed originally only in the person of Christ, and yet that the power to broaden
it was simultaneously present in Christ. Since, indeed, this power is an infinite
power, and its infinite expansion is limited only by the capacity of those who
take the spirit that proceeds from Christ up into themselves, accordingly the
broadening of disposition that proceeds from Christ in an outward direction is

limited only by human nature itself, within which we presuppose such capacity everywhere.

Consequently we have two limiting points: on the one hand, the individual personal existence of Christ as the beginning point of the process, and on the other hand, the perfection of the whole of the human race in Christ as the endpoint. The former is the presupposition that comes before all of our prior activity; the latter is the community that can never be presupposed, but is always only to be created. This is so, for if this goal were to be reached at some point, there would no longer be broadening action, nor would there any longer be theory concerning it. However, even in our practice this individual personal existence is always something that already preexists the process.

Now, however, how does this individual personal existence come to be given to us? Its origin is conditioned by the natural process of propagation. The question as to whether even the personal appearance of Christ is bound up completely with this natural process or only in part does not concern us here. Since Christ in himself lies outside of ethics in that there can be no ethics for him, we do not have to settle this question here; rather, it remains a purely dogmatic question. However, it is certain that the broadening action that proceeds from the power of Christ imparted to us and which is manifest as the Spirit of God in the Christian community can continue only by means of and through the form of individual personal existence. So individual personal existence must, in turn, always be present. However, since individual personal existence cannot be present except by means of the natural process of propagation, this natural process must also continue. This is so, for without it the process of broadening would come to an end, not because it had been completed, but because it would be lacking the necessary organs.

Now, precisely on that account, because the appearance of individual personal existence is grounded in that natural process, a plurality of individual personal existences and some organic bond between them must be presupposed that can be applicable to every point at which a moral task persists and thus [applicable] to the theory that we seek. Yet the organic bond of those who as persons are already organs of the broadening process is the Christian church as it actually exists in the present. Thus here between the beginning point (individual personal existence) and the endpoint (the broadening of the Christian disposition through the whole human race) we have two communities. One community relates to the beginning point and seeks to produce personal existence, the marriage union; the other relates to the ending point, the organic union of those in whom there can already be an action that broadens the Christian disposition, the Christian church. . . .

ON MARRIAGE

What kind of relationship exists between the marriage union[2] and the church? If we return to the very beginning of the church, we find that at that time it

consisted not of families, nor of individuals who always formed marriage relations, but only of individuals, of an organic union of individual persons who
belonged to different households, and insofar as this was the case, accordingly
the one community appeared to be independent of the other community. However, on the other hand, we can only see this as an imperfect condition of the
Christian church, especially if we pay attention to the way the process is suc-
cessful among us in the present. This is so, for everywhere that the Christian
disposition exists, there is also a movement toward its broadening, and if this
movement cannot be without result because its basis is in what is divine communicated to the human soul, to begin with it appears natural that it also has
results here among the objects nearest to it.

Thus it would be most natural for disposition always to broaden itself, beginning from one point and moving through a whole household; in terms of its
organization, the Christian church only appears in its completeness where it
exists composed solely of Christian households. However, such an imperfect
condition in which the church is composed only of individuals would necessarily
have had to exist at one time and would have preceded the more perfect form.
Thus, on the one hand, in that we recognize the independence of the family
from the Christian church, it appears to be an association that cannot have its
starting point only in Christian disposition. However, on the other hand, if we
say, "The Christian church is only completely organized when it exists composed
only of Christian households," included therein is the idea that when the distinctive principle of Christianity enters in turn into a household, accordingly it must
be modified in a distinctive way. The whole theory of Christian ethics regarding
the establishment of households must be based on these two points.

A household consists of the marriage union together with the results that
come from this union. However, the marriage union is a fact of nature, the
natural condition of human existence on earth, directed toward the propagation
of the human race; this being the case, viewed from its moral side, it belongs
especially and essentially to the broadening process as its original form. This is
so, for it produces new unions of intelligence with earthly material in the form
of organisms, and this union forms the basis for all the other permeations of
matter by reason of what occurs subsequently. However, precisely because this
propagation of the human race is the original form of the broadening process, it
belongs just as much to that side of the process for which talent formation is the
high point as to that side for which the high point is formation of disposition;
it determines the continuing existence of civil society no less than it does that
of the church. Yet insofar as civil society existed before the church, the character
of the marriage union in civil society is earlier than its character in the church.

Now what follows from this as the first rule of Christian ethics in this connection is that where a marriage union already exists before the Christian disposition enters into it, the marriage union is not to be destroyed because one
party takes on Christian disposition and the other does not, or as Paul expresses
this principle, that if in a marriage one is believer while the other remains an

unbeliever, the believer is not to divorce the unbeliever.[3] If we ask for yet another grounding beyond the biblical one, first of all it is clear that even if a marriage happens before the entrance of Christian disposition into one of the marriage parties, nonetheless marriage has not only come to belong to a process of nature, but even in a moral way, it has also come to belong to the moral task. If that is the case, however, one party to the moral task still may not disturb another party to it. Then it is to be borne in mind, that if one party is Christian and the other is not, this is never to be seen as an absolute opposition, but rather only a distinction between one who has already become Christian and the other who has not yet become so. This is so, for the hope that the other party could also be open to the Christian disposition could never be given up, however hostile that person might appear as long as it would still remain impossible for a Christian to be overcome by evil in the fulfillment of his moral duty. To be sure, Paul still compares our rule with the other rule, that if the unbelieving party were to want to divorce, the believer is to allow it;[4] however, this is only to be understood according to the standard of what is right and proper for the marriage union as it exists in civil society.

For example, if the law determines that only men would have the right to end a marriage, the believing husband would not be allowed to break the marriage bond because of the desire of the unbelieving wife; his Christian disposition would not allow him to do so, just as it would make it impossible for him to give up hope that the other party may yet be converted. On the other hand, if the laws of the state were to treat each party equally, a completely different situation would obtain. This is so, for in that case the believing man would not be bound to dissolve the marriage because the state would leave this completely as a matter of choice, and he would not be justified in so doing because his disposition would allow him to hold fast to hope. In this case the believing party could not infringe on the right of the unbelieving party, and then it would indeed become just a matter of trust, for still one could not have absolute certainty as to whether the conversion of the unbelieving party would result from continuation of the marriage.[5]

Now if it is not justifiable for a Christian party to make a claim on the right that he has as a member of the state to dissolve a marriage even in the case of the greatest differences that are conceivable between marriage parties—namely, a complete deficiency of the Christian disposition in the other party—it follows that nothing can justify him in dissolving a marriage, and that in the Christian church marriage is absolutely unbreakable. Paul teaches this in 1 Corinthians 7:10–11 and indeed affirms it as the express command of Christ; and where Christ appears to allow for divorce, namely, where one party has violated the marriage bond,[6] he does not speak exactly about marriage among Christians as does Paul, but rather about marriage among Jews.

However, before we consider the conflict between our theory and our own church, we must first seek for a second rule, in addition to the first rule that establishes for us the true form of the marriage union. We have found above that the Christian church is first completely organized when it has appropriated for itself the whole of the marriage union as family and has fully interpenetrated it. If we consider this more closely, what follows from this is that the marriage union, insofar as it is intended for the Christian church, has as its sole intention propagating and reproducing human individuals who are capable of the higher life. However, if procreation is completely intended for the higher life, to that degree it is also true that procreation and upbringing cannot be separated at all but are one and the same process. However, then it also follows immediately that the only form that the marriage union can have in the Christian church is that of monogamy, that it can only be "marriage" in the narrower sense of the word.

Polygamy is rooted in a view of marriage that is exclusively civil. This is so, since for the state the man alone is the representative of the family, and the female sex is always subordinated to the male sex. Among primitive people this often goes so far that the condition of women is difficult to differentiate from that of slaves, and from this fact it naturally develops that as one man can have many slaves, he can also have many wives. However, the Christian church does not recognize such subordination; in the church's view all human souls stand in one and the same relationship to the divine work of redemption, for all persons receive one and the same spiritual life from one and the same source. If women are excluded from something, still they are not excluded from particular gifts of the Spirit, but only from a specific way of expressing them. Thus in Christianity the reason for polygamy is not present. Yet this is only one side of the matter. The other side is as follows. If procreation and education are identical, education is also something that is communal, and if this is the case, under the conditions of polygamy it is evident that a man comes into contradiction with himself. This is so, for if one abstracts from the idea of subordination, it is not possible for education to be the same with a number of wives. Each of these wives is different from every other wife; thus each wife would shape her portion of the communal education in a different way, and because of this the education of males would have to be led in some courses that would be essentially different from each other. Thus, except in a case of absolute stupidity, the relationship with one mother could not be the same as that with the other mothers, and so one wife would have to subordinate all the rest to herself. In this way polygamy would move itself toward monogamy.

Surely to say that monogamy is actually indebted to Christianity for its origin is to say too much, for the Germanic people practiced monogamy before Christianity was here. However, monogamy had its true moral grounding and its essential bearing first in Christianity. This is so, for when monogamy comes about in the Muhammadan religion, in which polygamy is the dominant form, it is only a product of poverty. Among the Jews it [polygamy] was not a matter of principle, but only became prevalent because polygamy was considered to be a matter of luxury and evoked the suspicion of wealth; and for the pre-Christian Germanic people, it [monogamy] did not have a moral grounding, but was based on outer circumstances, on climate, and on the character of sexual urges. Only in

Christianity is monogamy completely a matter of principle. Of course, there is no express command to this effect in Scripture. This is the case, for what is said in a couple places about a bishop—that he is to be the husband of one wife[7]—on the one hand is a dubious interpretation and on the other hand could be seen as applying only to bishops. However, the matter is as follows. In part it was that the first Christians came from those classes in which monogamy was already the dominant state; in part Scripture considers marriage more as something already established rather than a relationship that needs first to be established. Therefore a specific command on this point is not to be expected.

Yet what is lacking in Scripture is supplied in a very specific way by Christian ethics; this is the case since polygamy was pronounced to be completely unchristian at a very early date. Indirect indications on this matter are not lacking in Scripture; this is shown since monogamy is traced back to the first human pair[8] as the form of marriage originally ordained by God and likewise by comparison of the relationship between husband and wife with the relationship between Christ and the congregation. This is so, for it is evident that for the apostle there is only one church. . . .[9]

[ON DIVORCE]

Now, if it is clear that the Catholic Church is in error in ascribing greater holiness to being single than to marriage, does the Catholic Church not hold marriage to be more holy than does the Evangelical Church? The Catholic Church acknowledges only a relative separation of a marriage, one that allows for the possibility of reunion. Viewed in this way, the difference with the Evangelical Church would only be a matter of appearance, only a difference in form. However, the essential difference between the two is that the Catholic Church forbids divorced spouses from entering into a new marriage union while the other party is still living; on the other hand, the Evangelical Church allows it. And surely here the Catholic Church has the letter of Scripture on its side, the word of Christ: "Whoever divorces his wife and marries another commits adultery against her, just as a wife who divorces her husband and marries another commits adultery."[10] However, to claim that because of this the Catholic Church holds marriage to be holier than we do is still a claim that is more appearance than truth. With us it is gradually becoming the case that generally speaking the dissolution of a marriage is coming to be seen as a matter for the courts. In actuality the church has nothing to do with this process, except to seek reconciliation. If reconciliation does not occur, the divorce is carried out by the state. However, surely if afterward the church consecrates a second marriage for those who have been divorced, the church recognizes that by means of the judicial divorce, the marriage has been dissolved, and the Catholic Church does not do this.

On the other hand, however, a Roman bishop has the right in this regard, certainly not to dissolve a marriage, but still to annul it, even if he does this only rarely and even if he only makes use of this for the benefit of the nobility and of kings. In truth, this practice is much worse than our practice of allowing divorce, for by means of this practice not only do the children lose their status as being born within the bonds of marriage, but also the dissolution of the marriage is actually granted exclusively by the church, and in this way it is one of the chief of the remaining churchly abuses that have been singled out for being of the worst kind. It is therefore certain that the principles of the Catholic Church are no better than ours; if the Catholic Church does not recognize divorce that is arranged by the state in the way we do, the only ground for this is that they have a more favorable status in relation to the state than we have. Now it is evident that every dissolution of a marriage is an imperfection; nonetheless it is still also clear that marriage that is truly Christian can only be understood as something that is in the process of becoming, as is the case for every other relationship that is truly Christian. However, if that is the case, it cannot fail to happen that two spouses would be very unequal in their relationship with each other, and consciousness of the particular imperfection between them would often become so great that both spouses would have no wish that is more pressing than that they would never have married and that they could return to their previous state.

In view of this consideration, the formula of the Catholic Church expresses the matter with greater rectitude when it thus says, "Marriage could be dissolved only when a person realizes that it never should have been concluded in the first place." However, this is not superior in actuality, but only as a formula. This is so, for our church still intends precisely the same thing, and that our church expresses its formula in such an indefinite way still has value in that for us children can still be seen as born within the bonds of marriage in spite of divorce. Thus the matter is as follows: the church can never regard divorce in itself as permissible without arguing against what it recognizes as perfection, indeed, without violating a specific dictum of Christ. However, as long as the state holds that it is conducive to the common good to allow marriage to be dissolved under certain circumstances, the church cannot hinder it because marriage is not exclusively an ecclesial matter, but equally a political matter, and because the church cannot want to establish superiority over the state as the Catholic Church has presumed to do for itself. Even if the state suddenly wanted to give us the same position that the Catholic Church has in this respect, we would no doubt find ourselves in no less difficulty.

This is so, since the desire to dissolve marriage exists always and only where pure passion or other foreign motives have led to marriage being concluded: what result can we expect? No result except the forced continuation of all marriages that were nothing but appearance from the beginning and whose dissolution was continuously desired by both parties. Thus the church must first gain greater influence over the way marriage is concluded before it can claim that the time has arrived to declare that all existing marriages are indissoluble, and until that time we must see the possibility of divorce as an indication of the imperfection of the church in its appearance and hold it as very doubtful that it will ever be wholly negated by means of purism. Yet in this respect all of ecclesial life must also always strive to overcome imperfection more completely, and this is the only correct way to make divorce ever less frequent and for married life to approach ever more closely to its pure and true Christian state.

CONCERNING THE ECCLESIAL COMMUNITY IN RELATION TO THE BROADENING PROCESS

We cannot imagine the personal existence of Christ without the broadening of the divine principle going out from him to others. This is the case in the first place, for only these two characteristics taken together constitute the quality of the Redeemer: his own sinlessness and his power to communicate it to others. The former is the condition sine qua non of his being Redeemer; the latter is the positive side of his redeeming activity. Now, however, if we presuppose that the divine Spirit is implanted in several others, but without the goal of penetrating the whole human race having yet been reached, it follows that the orientation toward broadening must also have been communicated to these others. From this, however, it follows that if each individual were to have this orientation only for himself, there would be no church; this is so, for the church is an organic union of believers, which is the basis for broadening of the Christian spirit, and thus they would have to be organically bound together. If they are not bound together, our task cannot be completed.

This is so, for each individual who is to share in the Christian disposition needs the united influence of others on himself, since absolute completion is never accomplished in any one individual in this world, and accordingly each must contribute his influence to the completion of the process. Moreover, if every person influences each point only in a random way, there is no community in the narrow sense, and community instead exists only in an unconscious way. However, such a random community would itself be something imperfect; thus if nothing else were present but this imperfect community, the next task would be to build it up to be a conscious community. It follows that all persons must be organically bound together and work in an organic community: in other words, they must be church.

This is not the place to present a complete theory of the church. The theory of marriage was presented here because marriage is inclined predominantly to the portion of the task that we are now considering. Indeed, the broadening process is an essential function of the church as well, but the true innermost nature of the church still exists in the common life of believers insofar as this common life exists, not insofar as it is to be communicated to others; thus the theory of the church has its essential place in presentational action. The connection here is this: in relation to the purifying action, we have presupposed both communities, family and church; here in broadening action was the place to develop the origin of the family, but the church still remains as a presupposition, for in order to describe how the broadening process is to be carried out in it, we have to look more at its ongoing existence than at its origin; moreover, the place to develop its genesis will also be under presentational action.

Now, if the church must exist in order for there to be broadening action, how is the broadening action of the church to be carried out? We have spoken about marriage and indeed have done so directly in that marriage is commissioned by means of the broadening process, but we have not indicated how broadening action is to be structured within marriage. However, there is also no need for this. This is so, for the special form of broadening action belongs to educational technique proper, and we have nothing to do with that here. Irrespective of this, broadening action in the family will be completely described along with broadening action in the church in general, just as in the church an individual's action directed to himself is what we always postulate within the common life and is hardly conceivable otherwise since in truth it is only the church that acts in a broadening way, and the immediate subjects of these actions are thereby only organs of the church. This is also in agreement with what we must admit to be its counterpart, that everything we imagine as being completed in relation to the broadening process is eo ipso [by that very fact] church and ceases to exist for itself as something individual. Thus we must regard broadening action in the household as action of the church and must take it up into the church. However, because the church is more perfectly organized insofar as families have been taken up into it and insofar as it is an organic union of Christian households, and is less perfect insofar as it is only an organic union of individuals, we will have to distinguish two forms of the broadening action in the church: one action that is related to the perfected condition of the organization—action within the family and that proceeds from the family; and one action that is found even in the imperfect organization—action of individuals. However, we do not yet recognize other organic unions that are subordinate parts of the church; thus we cannot yet take these into consideration.

Let us ask about the content of broadening action in the church. According to our earlier development, it is directed to the formation of disposition and to formation of talent only for the sake of the formation of disposition. Yet what is it that is to be broadened in the broadening of disposition? Above we have already indicated that the distinction between disposition and talent is only relative. Thus even if talent exists as a plurality and disposition exists as a unity, insofar as one is contrasted with the other, it is still true that disposition considered in itself is only a relative unity, and it can be seen as a plurality, without passing over into the domain of talent. However, insofar as it is a unity, it is nothing other than the dominion of the Holy Spirit.

Let us remain here for a moment and ask again how this dominion is to be produced in a person in whom it is as yet nonexistent. We can only answer, "Through the influence of others in whom the Holy Spirit already has dominion." However, this influence will be empty if there is no receptivity to the influencing principle in the individual who is to be influenced. Now this first principle takes us back directly to the idea of a redeemed individual, so we must say, "Without receptivity in the human race, the appearance of the Redeemer would be for nothing." However, it is also clear that if receptivity could pass over into spontaneity of itself, the appearance of the Redeemer would be superfluous. It follows that even the transition from receptivity to spontaneity can only be thought of as a product of an influence coming from outside.

Nevertheless, here we come to an apparent contradiction when we ask how the broadening process is to come to be therewith. That is, the broadening process is based on a feeling of religious pleasure, on the consciousness of ability to influence another. But where is one to direct this power? Obviously toward the receptivity universally presupposed in the human race. But where within human receptivity? Obviously where receptivity comes forth in a definite way and accordingly has an effect on strength in a definite way. Yet how does receptivity come forth in a definite way if it has not already been influenced? Thus it appears here that strength would have to wait on receptivity and vice versa—and it appears that the one would not to be able to come forward in a definite way before it would have been called forth in a definite way by the other. In actuality this would be an insoluble contradiction if there were no other activity of the reigning divine Spirit except for broadening action. However, this is resolved immediately when we return to presentational action, in which the church has its essential place and which is the only source from which broadening action can be developed. That is, in that the dominion of the Holy Spirit manifests itself in the inner life of the church, this life appears by means of presentational action; so by these means the Spirit itself becomes apparent and perceptible and is able to awaken the receptivity of those who are outside the church so that now, for their part, they also make known that they have found the true object of their desire. Moreover, it was certainly also this way in the life of Christ: the pure presentation of his own person made him visible to those to whom he was able to direct his own broadening action.

Yet now, returning to the question of the actual content of the communication of the dominion of the Spirit, we must say, "To begin with, it is spirit in the universal human sense that is to be raised to the potency of spirit in the Christian sense and thereby to be deified." However, spirit in the universal human sense reveals itself in the soul already in two different forms that cannot be separated from one another: the capacity to form notions, and the capacity to form desire, understanding, and will. Consequently, the broadening of the disposition itself will also be such a twofold matter, and included in this is the idea that both the capacity to form notions and the capacity to form desire are organs of spirit that will only be thought and willed under the potency of the divine Spirit. However, in that we have presupposed that the very beginning could be brought about only by means of the influence of the divine Spirit proceeding from another, this influence would still have to be received. Thus first there would have to be a capacity to receive it, and both of these together would produce a change in self-consciousness so that the first thing that would happen would be that the

Spirit penetrates into feeling, into immediate self-consciousness, and the second thing is that spirit becomes spontaneous by means of the transition between the twofold character of understanding and will; this is so, for in the immediate self-consciousness in and for itself spirit remains receptive.

Now, however, the whole process is also included therein, including the intensive completion of the whole task. This is so, for if self-consciousness is nothing other than receptivity for the divine Spirit, and if the twofold character of understanding and will would be completely formed to be an organ of the Spirit, on the one hand it would be impossible that the subordinate function—what Scripture calls "flesh"—could exist in some way by itself and have dominion, and on the other hand it would be impossible that something in some way essential to the fulfillment of the whole moral task could be lacking. Thus we have the complete formula for the whole process and are now able to consider what is truly special about the church in relation to broadening and how broadening action is to be developed further in relation to the distinctions we have already set forth.

The distinction between extensive and intensive directions is surely only relative, but it still allows itself to be fixed in a definite way. The effect of extensive broadening is that more and more persons become Christian; the effect of intensive broadening is that in all those who already belong to the community of Christian disposition, the power of the Christian spirit will always become more complete. Thus it is evident that the former actually is a joining together that is always being renewed and that the latter includes in itself what follows after this joining together. The only limit the extensive direction can have is the totality of the human race itself, and thus it is infinite insofar as we imagine ourselves continuing to exist on earth with the changes brought about by death and procreation. However, how is it in this respect with the intensive direction? If we imagine here the church as the subject that is acting and those who have already been taken up into the community of disposition but still need further action toward them as the objects, we can view this matter in a twofold way. That is, we can say, "Here is an action of the church toward those who are already church in a certain sense, but in another sense they are not yet church." However, we can also say, "Here is an action of the church toward itself in that in any case all those in whom the Christian disposition has already begun belong to the Christian community." . . .

Thus the Christian community, as it on the one hand is involved in the extensive broadening of the Christian disposition, must on the other hand take up the task of bringing to religious maturity those in whom the Christian spirit has first begun to work and then to support them to the point that they gain the right to communicate their judgments as to what represents the perfection of the Christian disposition to everyone, thus [claiming] a right to participate in the general process of increase. Included therein at the same time is the idea that one who can join in speaking morally would also be seen as one in whom strength could produce increase in the community as a whole. It is evident that this task can never be completed in such a way that no inequality would remain in the Christian community; inequality will always have its own spaces and departments. However, the task is to be completed in such a way that there can be work toward ongoing increase in each individual, and no other limit will be accepted except for the limit each has in his own receptivity. Now, if we ask, "How can this be accomplished?" we must return to the twofold character in which the dominion of the Spirit is presented, and thus to this dominion in the form of determination of thought and in the form of determination of the will.

[FORMATION: CHURCH AS SCHOOL]

In general we will have to say, however, that insofar as the Christian church is involved in this action, it presents itself to us under the form of a school, and indeed in the double meaning of this expression; on the one hand, school is presented to us as a tradition of propagation and conservation, a tradition of specific teaching, and on the other hand, it is also presented to us as an institution of practice. In other words, [it is an institution of practice] insofar as, on the one hand, it is more related to the idea of science or, on the other hand, more to the idea of art. However, we are not using the expression "school" as it relates to talent formation, to the development of skills. Rather, when we say the Christian church is to be organized as a school oriented toward the increase of disposition, we only mean it is to be an institution that supports itself in that it always arouses its principle anew in each of its members and thereby permanently forms its principle in them and by means of them, and all this is still essentially included in the concept of a school.

Now how can a definite way of forming the activity of the will in an individual be aroused by means of the influence of such a school? This is only possible if we presuppose or call forth a twofoldedness in an individual, by virtue of it appertaining to us on the one hand to be objects of activity, and also on the other hand to be what is to influence them. We must say, "All the effectiveness of the church in elevating the disposition of an individual is based on the individual already belonging to the effectiveness of the Christian community through its common feeling, and at the same time through his personal feeling being an object on which the community has influence. We are able to raise this formula to a living perception if we accept in addition that a way of acting in a whole that is ongoing and remains the same is what we call "morality," as when we observe this way of acting in an individual and now say, "The church acting as a school to elevate the activity of the will is nothing but an institution of common morality that remains the same." This institution as a common life lays hold of the individual so that he cannot tear himself loose from it. In the very beginning he appears to be led by the common life, but the more the contrast blends together, the more all of his own activity is assimilated to the common activity of the will, the individual's agreement with the common morality becomes his own activity, and this is the transition from the condition in which the Christian church influences him to that in virtue of which he works together with the church.

Thus from this side the task is resolved by means of the existence of a uniform morality in the church, into which all individuals are brought ever more fully; however, this uniformity itself must also be seen as capable of improvement as long as the church is still in the process of becoming. If the expression "morality" is often related only to what is more external, that is a restriction into which we will not go here. We understand morality to be the whole of the Christian way of acting, which presents itself in the totality of Christian virtues. Moreover, this is again a point where we must refer to the section that follows on presentational action. This is so, for if we ask, "What does morality consist of materially?" this does not belong here, but rather to presentational action. Here we consider it in a purely formal way and say, "Insofar as morality reigns in the Christian church, it is a school, a structure of formation for the activity of the will of individuals."

Now, however, what is this effectiveness as the activity of individuals who together create the Christian community? Nothing other than the effectiveness of a good example. The more this is present in the church, the more quickly the developmental process in individuals makes progress; the less this is so, the more the effectiveness of the whole is restricted, the effectiveness of Christian morality as school. Thus it falls to everyone to contribute his good example so that the effectiveness of the church in this connection reaches its maximum, that is, always remains on the path of the good example. Surely, when it is often said that a person must do much for the sake of a good example, which he would not otherwise do, this is completely reprehensible. Such an action would be untrue, thus neither could it ever further morality; it could never be a good example. Therefore, a person can only be a good example when what he does materially is what he would do whether or not it was being counted as an example. The good example is nothing other than the dominion of Christian morality itself. Of course, against this one could say from the other side, now it would be certain that the expression "good example" has been purified, but this would also be completely empty. This is so, for if what I were to do as a good example were what I would already do anyway for the sake of my own morality, by means of this formula nothing would be added to my action.

However, there is to be nothing material added to the action. If, as we are already agreed, each of the three forms of action can be reduced to any of the others, so all broadening action can be seen as included in presentational action. This is completely true. However, there is still something that is added in broadening action, surely nothing external, but in the action itself the fact that a person will define his action as done in accord with Christian morality is also a moral element in the broadening process of the whole; there is a raising of consciousness about one's own action so that it is seen to be part of the broadening process in the whole. And in this sense a person can claim that he is giving a good example: he has the consciousness that, to the degree to which his disposition is in accord with Christian morality, it includes within itself at the same time an increase or a decrease of broadening action in the community.

Now if we want to make a general overview of the other side in precisely the same way—the broadening of the disposition, under the form of the capacity for forming notions—we must go back even farther than we did with the previous point. That is to say, it is equally clear in itself that, viewed from all sides, an altered way of acting must come to be as soon as the Christian spirit enters into an individual human life, notwithstanding that the change will be greater if to this point the individual has been under the domination of sensorial nature, less if the individual is found to be already under the dominion of reason. However, if one says, "The entry of the Christian spirit into a human life also effects a complete change in the formation of thought," this is not immediately clear in and of itself. This difference has its basis in the predominance that most persons give to what is practical over what is theoretical. Nonetheless, however, there is still just such an alteration on this side as on the other, and we must seek to attain clearer insight about this matter. No one will deny this in a general way because the parallel between the two functions in human beings is too clear; however, it must also be made clear in particular. The process of thought and the way determination of our will develops always point back to each other. As we can say, "There is a way of acting that is purely materialistic and atomistic," we can also say, "There is a way of thinking that is purely sensorial and material." This means that we can bring all of this together in the formula: with the entry of the Christian Spirit, there would have to arise an altered perspective on everything that fills up the process of human thought.

When, in a completely general way, a new direction of the will comes about, everything that is the object of Christian knowledge must come to have a different value. As a result, however, objects of cognition also come to be classified differently; thus concepts have completely different ramifications, and consequently there is a completely new form of thought formation. This new form of thought formation, in turn, cannot exist without an altered formation of language; this is true since thought and language must always be traced back to each other. This is so, for all of history teaches that the development of this aspect of Christian disposition always comes to be recognized by means of the formation of its own distinctive language. However, in the whole scope of the word, *language* is a deposition of a distinctive system of concepts in which is included a distinctive system of judgments, and it thus is completely the same in the domain of thought as what we have called "morality" in the domain of the determination of the will; language is the common way of thinking, just as morality is the common way of acting. Thus the proposition "The church considered in terms of the intensive side of the broadening process of the disposition is school" means that on the side of the capacity for thought and for forming notions, "The church is an institution for regular support of a distinctive language by means of which each individual must build his way of thought, but which is itself also capable of improvement as long as the church is still in the process of becoming."

Now if language develops in a person before he can take Christian disposition into himself in a living way, there must be a reconstruction of language and thought in him. This is so, for before this ensues, what is distinctively Christian in language is nonexistent in the individual, that is, in terms of content; and the church cannot do anything other than to assimilate the individual into the content of the church's language in order to elevate Christian disposition as a way of thought in him. Yet this process of the appropriation of language, which can in no way be acquired by study, is completely the same as what happens on the side of the capacity for desire. The negation of Christian content in language for one in whom the Christian disposition is not yet present is his own personal action. Now, if we consider the entry of the divine Spirit into this person, the entry of the Christian disposition, the Spirit is the analogue to the way of thought in the whole Christian church; as the individual recognizes this way of thought, it is also in him, but only from the side of his communal consciousness, and then to begin it must always become personal in him before he can cease to be purely receptive in the church and begin to be productive in it.

Yet within this becoming personal there is precisely a true living appropriation of the Christian way of thought so that from this point forward the individual can be productive in Christian thought formation. However, as long as the opposition between personal consciousness and communal consciousness remains in an individual, the possibility exists that Christian language as the manifestation of Christian disposition can become impure once again; therefore precisely for this reason school is necessary as a permanent institution, to prevent such impurity and to implant the Christian way of thought in individuals, and therefore increase can always and only result from this school and naturally only from those who have been taught in this school.

Just as on the one hand we must here refrain from discussing the content of this efficacious action of the church, so on the other hand we will not even allow ourselves to develop its form further, for this would lead us into a technical domain that belongs to practical theology. The church seen as school builds two great systems—on the practical side, morality; on the theoretical side, language. However, how these systems are to be appropriately constituted is an undertaking that no longer belongs to the actual domain of ethics. This is especially clear on the theoretical side. This is so, for as we find a twofold character almost everywhere in the church—a popular institution and a scientific institution, and each organized in a definite way—so that no one doubts that establishing the principles for this belongs to practical theology. However, here we are still obliged in the first place to determine the activity of individuals in both of these institutions that belong to the theoretical side. Now just as the efficacious action of individuals on the practical side was summed up in the formula of the good example, we would have to say that on the theoretical side efficacious action of individuals would be summed up in the formula of instruction. Instruction always proceeds from individuals.

This is so, for even granting that individuals are organs of the whole in a completely defined way, in teaching what is personal in them always remains predominant. Even a cursory look at worship life in our Evangelical Church will convince us of that. Evangelical worship life includes a liturgical component, from which the personal is completely excluded, and this is no less the case regarding instruction. Every element of liturgy is nothing other than tradition in a particular form, nothing but pure presentation. By comparison, the other component, the sermon, belongs also to the domain of presentation, yet it also belongs no less to the church as school. Although the sermon is actual presentation, it must include instruction for the purpose of presentation; in order to be clear, it makes contact with abnormal notions and corrects them. Yet therefore personal existence to a great extent comes at once to the fore. Now just as instruction must stand out in this fully organized form, it must also stand out everywhere from the sermon down to the completely formless art of religious speech that happens in intimate conversation; this is so, for a Christian may not overlook any opportunity to work as an organ of the whole in all directions, offering instruction. However, further moral direction about this may not be given.

We must merely hold fast to the analogy that already happens between purifying and broadening actions and to the principle that all instruction may only be a communal search for the truth, governed by means of the different relationships in which individuals stand to each other and by means of the authority that is due to each individual according to the maturity of his mental development, according to the perfection of his consciousness, and the diversity of his experience. This thus means that instruction in all forms is traced back to the rule of free communication, set forth above. Thus it is also evident that both sides, the more practical and the more theoretical, always remain side by side here, and every Christian, as a member of the whole, always has vocation in relation to both sides at the same time, the one in a more definite form in the organization of the whole, and the other in a more indefinite form. It is not conceivable that the one side could stand in the way of the other; rather, each always joins itself together with the other. This is so, for there is no domain of life where speech does not exist continually joined together with action, and speech has no place except by virtue of the constitution of society, thus no place except the domain of morality.

Chapter 6

Broadening Action
in the State

Within this moral process of broadening, the cultivation of talent is what comes first, yet the chief feature exists in such a way that reference to persons' disposition is always presupposed; this [cultivation of talent], as we have seen, is already present before the Christian principle appears. Thus the true question will not be, "How is the whole process to be construed on the basis of the Christian principle?" but rather, "How is the process transformed by means of the Christian principle?"

We are also already in agreement that we understand "talent formation" to be the development of the organism for the sake of spirit. The ἅγιον πνεῦμα first takes possession of νοῦς, the κοινὸς λόγος, which exists in us only in the twofold form of the capacity to form notions and the capacity for desire. The capacity to form notions and the capacity for desire are made manifest in and penetrate into all the rest of the way human life is organized, into the psychic and physical, and accordingly this is the circle into which we now enter. Yet we must go still further and say, "The relation of human nature to the whole of nature, of which it is a part, is this: that the intelligence in humans is the subject, whose power is not to be limited to individual persons, but is to pass over to outer nature." Thus we are to bind together both talent formation and formation of nature for the preservation and continuation of the human race on the whole earth, and we consider them to be one and the same process. This can be made clear by two points.

In the first place, we must proceed from the fact that everything in nature can be traced back to the idea of life, and that everything falls under the relative opposition between individual life and life in general. Yet in the second place, every talent is a particular function of individual life relating to a particular side of life in general. Since talent can only gain mastery over a particular side of life in general by means of practice, we must posit both an ongoing activity of the capacity distinctive to humans and a bearing of outer nature in an ongoing way that corresponds to that activity. However, in that this bearing of nature has as its purpose the formation of nature for the sake of humans, it must always reveal itself also in particular structures of the formation of nature. This formula can easily be applied to everything that can be said to be practical in some way; the application appears to be difficult only insofar as we see cognition as a matter of talent. However, even cognition always has the world or nature as its object, and thus here again we have the same thing—on the one hand, practice and the growth of talent, and on the other hand, the further development of nature so that it is known in a complete way by the human spirit. Yet if both of these are always determinative of each other and never separated from the other, then talent formation and nature formation are one and the same process. What could allow us to separate the two is only that we cannot always aim the formation of talent and the further development of nature to the same point. Yet this matter does not interest us here at all, where we consider what is moral only in a completely general way.

The other standpoint is that of the intelligence. Intelligence stands in contrast to the whole of nature and desires to become one with it. Thus every efficacious action of intelligence desires to permeate the whole of nature in an absolute way and must spread itself from each original point outwardly in all directions, in accord with the law of continuity. Moreover, even here when we have the goal of the process in view, we have no reason at all to make a separation. In every activity of spirit, a person's organism that is directly connected to something external to him has always already become identical with that aspect of external nature that corresponds to it, as is made manifest by all operations of the senses. This is the case, since, for example, we cannot see until light comes together with the eye; and when they come together, we can no longer say that the organ belongs exclusively to the active subject. Hence, from the perspective of ethics, the formation of a person, meaning the formation of the totality of his talent, and the formation of nature—these are one and the same process for persons.

We can also make this just as clear from a point that is far removed from here. If we were to divide the two [formation of a person and formation of his talent] and would want to consider the totality of talent as something existing purely for itself, talent would always exist only in individuals, and personal existence and its constitution would be the true center of attention and goal of the ethical process.

However, this cannot be the case because intelligence is one and the same thing in all individuals.[1] Thus we must say, "The development of all personal existence collectively, seen as one, is the goal, not the development of an individual." Yet if that is so, it is also the case that the development of external nature cannot be separated from the development of collective personal existence, because it is nature that establishes and joins together with personal existence, so that we will still always be returned again to the unity of talent formation and nature formation, if we do not want to remain with a perspective that is amoral.

However, in this one proposition—that from our perspective we must see the development of human talent itself and the formation of nature for the sake of humanity by means of talent formation as one and the same process—the question about the scope of our task is completely answered. Our task is infinite in every point.

If we consider our broadening process under the general formula of all broadening action, we see that the process proceeds from moral consciousness motivated by pleasure, thus from the consciousness of the moral life as a power whose object is given in no way except immediately together with its receptivity for the object's influence. This is so, for pleasure only arises in this way because power without an object could produce no consciousness of activity, nor could it produce consciousness of pleasure or of a lack of pleasure but only of indifference; and power which has an object, but no receptivity for the object, can call forth no consciousness, except consciousness of a lack of pleasure. Now, however, this pleasure is not sensorial, but it is pleasure that is truly moral, belonging to the higher level of feeling, and is based on consciousness of the original identity of spirit and nature that is to manifest itself in spirit taking possession of nature. By means of this we see that intelligence is a thoroughly driving, moving thing; therefore this pleasure refers only to intelligence. Surely the view that is sharply opposed to this is often set forth; the whole process of talent and nature formation has its origin in sensorial lack of pleasure, namely, in the sensorial and distressing feeling of need and boredom; but this derivation is based on none other than a materialistic principle, and it is therefore completely amoral.

Now, we have already mentioned that it would also be amoral if we wanted to see the constitution of personal existence as the goal of our broadening process. Yet since we say that the broadening process would have its genesis in the feeling of pleasure that still would always have its place only in the individual, in personal existence, it appears that we would have to say that personal existence would be the beginning point, the principle of the process. However, we must also deny this. This is so since an individual is a result of the process and cannot be its beginning point. An individual is always a result of a sexual union, and the process of propagation itself is merely the physical side of the broadening process. However, if we also wanted to set this matter aside, we must not overlook the fact that individual persons do not take part in the broadening process until they have reached a certain level of development. Now if one can only attain this level by previously being the object of the process, no individual can be the beginning point of the process, for then we would be speaking of the first humans. And this topic is and remains beyond the scope of a scientific presentation.

Now, however, if an individual is just as little the final goal as he is the very beginning of the process, then he can only be a transition point in the process, in the sense that the further continuation of the process consists in the self-generated moral activity of each individual in every moment. Thus if we have determined the material scope of the whole process such that its material side is not completed until the totality of talent reaches a complete development and nature is completely formed for the sake of intelligence, then in terms of form we will have to define it as follows: "The formation of all talent and the formation of nature for the sake of spirit, both posited as one, is essentially the communal act of all the individuals who belong to the human race." This is based above all on the fact that each individual who takes part in the process is at the same time a result of this very process, so that, accordingly, some of the talent and nature forming activity of others must be posited as influencing an individual so that the process can begin in him. Or in other words, "Based on the fact that the self-activity of every individual is determined by that of others, accordingly the actual self-activity of an individual and the self-activity of all those through whom his activity is determined is a result that is communal." However, this is related only to the dependence of an individual on the succession of determinations and is only one side of the matter.

Yet there is also a communal character that coexists in a way that is just as definite. This is so, for spirit—which exists in contrast to the whole of nature—exercises its influence by means of an organism that is personal. Now, however, we cannot say a priori that nature as absolute object would be divided in this connection and would stand in contrast to spirit only as all its individual members were brought together, but intelligence in each individual would always only stand in contrast to a particular part of nature. Rather, spirit exhibits itself at each such living point as being contrasted to the whole of nature. One who wanted to be suspicious of this could say, "According to what you claim about the direction of spirit toward activity, of which we are speaking, the impulse for formation would have to be infinite in each individual." Yet now we still see that for each person the impulse for formation is originally limited to what is closest at hand, and it widens only gradually. At the beginning there is always a very great part of nature about which an individual is indifferent, and just for this reason the individual restricts himself to the development of certain talents and forgoes the development of others. However, that would actually be no cause for suspicion; rather, it is nothing more than what we have already said, namely, that talent formation and nature formation are determined by each other.

Human formation of nature is limited by talent formation, and talent formation is limited by the way in which it has created a place for itself in nature—nature, which comes to it already structured. This gives the appearance that each person sets a limited task for himself. However, it will not be denied that talent formation expands, so what we claim will also be admitted: the impulse for formation is infinite. Now, how is it with the claim that each person is able to give up certain talents in order to develop others in himself? An absolute giving up of certain talents never takes place; rather, it is only the case that a person develops some talents more fully, others less so, and there is no kind of talent that is not developed at all, even if some develop only to a very limited degree.

And how is it with the other claim, that a person would remain indifferent toward a greater part of nature? If we go back and consider history, we must surely admit that in the beginning persons had interest only in what was in their immediate environment. However, it has already become clear now that when a person is at a higher level of formation, he remains indifferent toward no part of nature, and this will become ever more evident to the degree that all communications are becoming more realized as the process of nature formation thus increases. Hence, the more one makes this suspicion clear, the more one must always return again to the claim that the task at each point is the whole and one that is infinite. And from this the absolutely communal character of all that coexists follows of itself: in this process no individual can isolate himself along with his activity. This is so, for each individual has one and the same object as do all other persons. It also follows that what happens in one part of nature is never a personal work, but always a work that is communal in character.

However, although an act is one that is completely communal even in relation to all that coexists with it, still the process continues only under the conditions for the appearance of human life and under the conditions for efficacious action by spirit, in the form of personal existence; the process cannot be rightly understood at any point except as being under this form of communal character in the form of personal existence, just as this comes together with the claim that personal existence is neither the beginning nor the endpoint, but a transition point through which the process passes. However, the fact that no one can isolate himself in his process of nature formation belongs together with the fact that no one can fix any result of the process in his own personal existence in an absolute way for just this reason, whether at this point it is a matter of talent formation or of nature formation. For since all results are at the same time objects, the idea of absolutely communal character must lie just as much in the results as in the activity itself.

These are the general principles that we must set forth here as if they were in a servant role, for we cannot say that they would be dependent on a religious point of view. We would have to set forth these principles in order to represent the object correctly in its distinctive nature. Now, to begin, we will consider what will happen to the object when the Christian principle enters and takes possession of its forms.

The principles of individuality[2] and communication[3] are immediately given along with what we have been discussing up until now. For if the process of formation is one that is absolutely communal, it is indeed the case that everything an individual uses is an organ of the whole, yet in such a way that an individual may not be disturbed in using these organs, and this is the basis of individuality. The results that each individual has produced are necessarily formed by one for all, and this is the basis of communication. Moreover, viewed from this side, the absolutely communal character of the whole process of formation is realized on the basis of these two forms.

Now, if we consider the whole from the viewpoint of community as it actually exists, the following two limits are set before us in this regard: on the one hand, even in relation to this part of the moral task, no individual can be isolated; and on the other hand, the absolutely communal character of the whole with all cannot be perfectly realized in any moment. Thus the question arises as to whether between these two endpoints only an indeterminate [community]—on the one hand fragmentary, and on the other hand chaotic growth of the formation process—is to be posited, or whether between the two there is definiteness to the community. History and experience provide us with definiteness since we do not see sheer increase of the formation process coming out of the community from individual families; rather, what appears to us in this regard is that even persons who are part of the same ethnic community are sometimes relatively united with each other and sometimes relatively separated from each other.

In spite of this, many have believed that the fragmentary and chaotic growth must be preferred, and indeed do so directly out of a religious standpoint; they have claimed that political unity is only a necessary evil and the actual goal is an absolutely communal character of such a kind that all partial unities would come to an end. There is an important distinction here that is not to be overlooked: a distinction between an association of persons to form a people and an association of persons to form a state. This is so, for in relation to the latter, philosophical ethics has also claimed the state as such to be a necessary evil and the goal of every association that forms a state to be to make itself superfluous. However, the association of persons to form a people has never been seen in this way, whereas some, on the basis of a religious point of view, have also wanted to negate this association.

Now, how does this matter stand according to the spirit of Christianity? Among all the forms of religious ethics, it is only Christian ethics that has put forward the proposition concerning the negation of national differences, to be sure less often in truly scientific theory than in popular presentation; however, we must still ignore this distinction completely for the time being. What is the basis for this proposition? Obviously the basis is that absolute community is actually postulated in the inner sphere, which we have treated, and that we cannot see the reign of God on earth as perfected until it has been spread as one over the whole human race. Now as from this higher perspective, however, talent is subordinate to disposition, and since national differences can only be seen as having their place in the domain of talent, both talent formation in general and also differences within talent formation must be considered as subordinate to the formation of disposition. This is a true Christian proposition, and the unity of the reign of God cannot be construed at all without it. This proposition will be realized everywhere in the domain of the church, for both the Eastern and Western churches have spread themselves over a plurality of peoples without the unity of the church being hindered by national differences.

However, if we ask whether it is right to say, "Both in the process of talent formation and nature formation, national differences must completely disappear so that nothing comes forward except this form of absolutely communal character," we must deny this; indeed, we do so directly from a Christian point of view, because different types of national formation are indeed included in the organization of the church's service itself and for its whole broadening process. If, because the church is one in the different nations, one therefore had reason to press for morality, language, and everything else that belongs here to be identical, somehow there would have been preparation for this postulate, and a transition to it would be present. However, this is not at all the case. Surely, the Catholic Church has sought to have one and the same language for its worship, but still it has had no choice but to concede the right of the different languages to exist, and it has not even sought to make morality identical, much less has it been able to bring it about. Thus, since even within the church the permanence of national differences is recognized, the church must recognize differences all the more where the talent and nature formation process, upon which the differences still rest, is the main concern. . . .

[TRANSFORMATION OF THE STATE BY THE CHRISTIAN PRINCIPLE]

Now, however, at this point the question arises for us, "In this connection is religious ethics only to sanction what can already be demonstrated to be natural, or is religious ethics also to transform it?" In the latter case we would have to say, "Indeed, everyone is able to have civil virtue without the divine Spirit, yet under the influence of the divine Spirit, they become something different." In the first case we would have to say, "Christianity changes nothing in the whole idea of civil virtue." However, this question leads us immediately to another that we entertained in the general introduction: "Can religious ethics include something other than what natural ethics includes, and of what does this other consist?" We will have to say again, "Strictly speaking, it cannot be claimed that Christian ethics can give instructions other than what natural ethics gives; but no more can it be claimed that the morality that arises from religious principle could be different than morality that is based on another principle." This is so, for the former idea would establish a contradiction between the claims of Christianity and those of general human reason; however, the latter idea would completely separate the realm of piety from that of morality. Thus if we assume that the civil virtue of a Christian is in no way different from that of any other person, we separate piety completely from civil virtue; yet if we suppose a difference, then we also establish a contradiction. How are we to find a way out of this dilemma?

Perhaps we will find the key to this in the biblical passage where Paul says that it is necessary to subject oneself to the authorities, not only for the sake of avoiding punishment, but also for the sake of conscience.[4] At first glance it surely appears that we have not found the distinction that we have in mind; this is so, for reason will also say, "Being subject—thus the practice of the whole civil virtue—purely out of fear of punishment is no virtue at all, and civil society is the more imperfect as the more punishment is needed." However, for the sake of conscience—is that not something different for the Christian, or when based altogether on religious principle, and something different when it is based only on civil principle? Certainly. That is, the purely civil conscience is merely the agreement of individuals' orientation of will with that of the whole, and conscientiousness exists when no orientation of will comes to realization without this agreement.

Now, in this connection there is no consideration of absolutely communal character; rather, the conscience of the individual aims exclusively at the self-consciousness of the whole to which the individual belongs, thus to the greater personal existence formed by a people. Hence we also quite frequently find that in areas outside of Christianity, and generally where ethics is less connected with what is religious (we have the whole of classical antiquity as an example of this), as soon as one intends civil virtue for absolutely communal character, it becomes unjust. Now this could never happen with religious conscience because religious conscience has no choice but to relate the existence of an individual people to the universal relationship among all persons, and because religious conscience is essentially the consciousness of the agreement of the one's own will with what is divine and thus must necessarily relate everything to the divine will. Therefore in relation to civil virtue, it [conscience] is indeed always consciousness of the way that I direct my own will toward the communal will, but yet never without being conscious that the communal will can also appear as divine will.

Thus it is clear, moreover, that civil virtue that would be considered an injustice from a cosmopolitan point of view could not exist since divine foreordination can never be directed toward the existence of only one people; rather, in an essential way it always aims at the existence of all peoples together. However, if the religious point of view—not speaking here at all about the Christian perspective—cannot ordain a patriotism that makes the fatherland into a selfish moral person, and if the point of view that is strictly political does not steel itself against such patriotism, then a difference in conscience is also unmistakable. Now, does the Christian principle bring something new to this matter? The Christian can only intend the whole sphere of the talent- and nature-forming processes for the broadening of the reign of God according to the Christian idea. However, the church as it exists in any given moment is always also only a limited whole since the greater part of the human race is still outside of it. How then does conscience that aims at the whole of Christianity relate itself to conscience that aims at the whole of the human race? The one is to pass over into the other; the whole of the broadening process is directed toward this end. Thus there can be no way of acting in relation to those in whom the good of redemption is not yet established, except a way that stands together with the expectation that they also will share in this good.

Now, moreover, when we say, "For a Christian the main point is formation of disposition; talent formation is only what is subordinate," it also follows that a Christian intends all of civil virtue only for the sake of this broadening of the reign of God and allows nothing to be ordered on the basis of his relation to the state that could hinder the broadening of the reign of God. The Christian says, "There can be no civil virtue that creates hostility between one portion of the human race and another." Now, however, this is valid not only in relation to what the Christian church is in comparison with what it has not yet become, but also in relation to the intensive increase that is the task of the Christian church everywhere. Also therefore conscience can never be satisfied with civil virtue that does not at the same time intend all talent and nature formation for an increase of Christian disposition. In this way we clearly see that the civil virtue of a Christian is different from that of all others not in terms of its matter, but in terms of its form, because it always brings together both broadening of talent and broadening of Christian disposition.

However, we also may not overlook the distinction between the more extensive and more intensive sides of our process of talent and nature formation. The character of communality and all that follows from it can be applied just as well to one side as it can to the other. Yet we only want to accentuate what follows.

Clearly the preservation of human life belongs to the extensive side of the broadening process, because without the former, the latter would cease at every point. Repeatedly some have distinguished the preservation of human life from the preservation of the community and thereby have become entangled in great difficulty. However, from our point of view, this way of situating the two in relation to each other is completely inadmissible; this is the case since for us the self-preservation of the individual is also an interest of the community; for us, each individual cares for himself only as part of the whole community's task; and so for us, these difficulties disappear. For one who only practices the obligation to self-preservation as an organ of the whole, there can be no conflict between this obligation and the obligation to preserve the common being, nor can such a person ever be in a situation of doing something immoral for the sake of self-preservation because in that case the individual would cease to be an organ of the whole in the moral process and would cease to serve the whole by means of his self-preservation. Difficulties can only arise when self-preservation is conceived as a sensorial drive of the individual, and this drive is seen as irresistible. Otherwise self-preservation and its relation to the other parts of the task will always be governed in a definite way whenever the whole talent and nature-formation process is still included in the civil unity, and what extends beyond the scope of the state is also ordered by means of morality and custom.

The further formation of individuals as such also belongs to the broadening process of the whole, but to the intensive process that, accordingly, must also be able to be traced back to the common will. Included herein is the idea that no unconditional exercise of free will can occur in the process of the continuing development of individuals; rather, even here each individual is subordinate to law and morality. The activity of the whole, which the individual is to represent, will only be represented in this case when the individual freely subordinates himself to the whole; this means that the individual must receive his freedom with consideration for the proper formation and the artistic purpose and effectiveness of the whole; in everything that the individual does in this regard, he must be able to be seen as an organ of the whole if his whole development is to be truly free and moral. If we consider the different ways of structuring this process among different peoples, we find that the freedom of the individual is present to greatly differing degrees. Where a caste system dominates, freedom is nonexistent. Considered in and for itself, the caste system certainly appears to be a bad way to calculate what is advantageous for the whole; this is so, for nature does not keep to what is the given basis of birth in a definite way and often disperses the highest gifts directly to those whose ancestors have for a long time been involved with the most unimportant matters, and surely we have no choice but to see the caste system as an extremely imperfect state. However, in spite of this, an individual is bound to this system where it exists. Neither can it be denied that there are some differences in the processes of living nature itself. Nature produces life both where what is individual[5] in general comes to the fore, and in other cases where it remains in the background; where an institution exists such as the caste system, it can only develop where what is individual in personal existence recedes to the greatest degree, and such settled levels can only disappear to the extent that what is individual builds itself in a more living manner.

[MECHANIZATION IN LABOR]

The last matter to be considered is the different content of the individual[6] elements of the whole process. We have taken as our starting point the fact that the formation of human nature and the formation of outer nature for humanity must be seen as one and the same process. Moreover, this is completely correct as long as we have in view only the relationship of spirit to nature. Now, however, important differences still arise here that are not to be overlooked. That is, one can think of an activity for which the formation of nature is entirely predominant and talent formation recedes into the background, and this kind of action is what we call "mechanical," κατ᾽ ἐξοχήν,[7] the domain of mechanism in the broadest sense of the word. One can also think of activity that is the opposite of this, in which talent formation predominates and nature formation recedes; this is scientific activity, speculative activity in the broadest sense of the word.

Now, we want first to consider these two extremes. If in a mechanical activity, talent formation is completely negated, this activity itself is no longer moral, for then the connection with the disposition is completely broken. No person is to be involved in such an activity. That is, suppose we imagine any kind of wholly mechanical process of nature formation that, however, still has something of theory in it, so that talent formation is not totally negated, for in this case talent still has its own space for reflection and space to choose what is better. However, if even this space is also no longer present at all, then an individual person becomes nothing more than a replacement for a machine, and that is something that is utterly unfree, whereby mental activity is absolutely negated. And the more the mechanical process places itself at this level, which is especially promoted by the division of labor, the more necessary it is then for actual machines to take the place of human activity. It is also evident that under such conditions intensive advancement of humanity will no longer be possible at all; that is, the additional activity fills up all time [that otherwise would be] for intensive advancement. Instead, the formation process for persons is absolutely ended as soon as they enter into this situation.

The rules for the advance of this process that can be developed from here are on the one hand not universal, and on the other hand quite complicated. However, we can sum up the rules in this way: "In society two aspects must exist in an equal relationship and always keep in step with each other: on the one hand, division of labor, and on the other, introduction of machines, sheer mechanical power in the place of the power of living persons, if the process is not to become immoral." Now here is one of the points where religious ethics is able to set forth something more definite than philosophical ethics is generally able to do—at least more definite than it could have before Christianity set it forth—even if one is not actually permitted to say this. That is, if we look at the distinction between free persons and slaves, this has its true ground only in a slave's taking the place of a machine, as Aristotle rightly defines slaves as ὄργανον ζῷον.[8] Now, even if persons are not slaves de jure, they are slaves de facto the more they are immersed in what is mechanistic, for thereby they always lose more of the possibility for free mental life. Now, that such a difference is not to exist [should not exist] was not taught by the philosophical ethics of the ancients; it was much more the case that they always found it to be very good and advantageous. However, a Christian point of view has never been able to validate this distinction, and we must always insist on its being overcome, for one who is capable of communion with Christ—and according to the Christian view this is all people—must be a free being and participate in mental life, not be a living machine. Slavery is contrary to the broadening process because it negates individuals in relation to that process.

DIFFERENT COMMUNITIES MUST WORK TOGETHER

The smallest community that stands in contrast to individuals is the family.[9] It is in the family that determinations are first made about an individual's career and way of life. In this connection parents are to act as organs of the absolute community, yet they are still to act with consciousness that they and their children belong to the same natural whole, within which each household is a person and has its place appointed to it. Parents are to accept their household's placement in the whole, approving of it in a free and moral way; they are always to allow the greater whole to codetermine its placement, knowing that on their own they cannot have complete knowledge of the needs of the whole. On the other hand, the greater whole is always to take the judgment of the household into account as it makes its determination. Thus it is all a matter of the communication between the two being fully organized, and the form in which this working together is arranged is the organization of what is called civil freedom. Civil freedom must be altered when either of the two parties can no longer keep a good conscience for itself, for along with this progress is always lost.

The different groupings within civil society and their relation to it are to be defined essentially in just this way; thus at once we can pass over to the domain where the forms cannot be defined in this way; therefore in the same way we can skip over the area where the forms cannot be so completely determined. This is so since it is impossible for the whole of humanity to work together in such a definite way with an individual state as a state can work together with its various corporate bodies, families, and individuals. For a long time and perhaps still in the present the dominant view has been that there could be no claim to subordinate states for the human race as a whole, rather that the morality of a state would be to seek its own advantage, and that the final goal of the formation process proceeding from it would be to establish its own distinct personal existence. However, that would bring about a complete separation of politics from morality and thus would be in contradiction with Christianity. This is so, for if the whole process of nature formation is intended for the disposition, and if the disposition were not included in such a way that a Christian or any kind of Christian totality could not hold itself responsible to the whole of the human race, it also follows that no Christian state would be able to consider [all of] humanity, rather than itself, as the goal of its process of nature formation, nor would it be able to see itself as only an organ of this process.

Every Christian and every Christian totality must view the duty to broaden and heighten the Christian disposition as a duty to the whole of humanity. Surely the state as such has nothing directly to do with broadening of Christian disposition; instead, its activity is relatively self-contained within the realm of talent and nature formation. However, this self-containment is still only to be construed in such a way that there are no hindrances to the universal effort of the divine Spirit to broaden itself over the whole human race. Consequently the state must grant its subjects full freedom to fulfill their duties in this regard, and since this is only possible without restrictions to morality and with preservation of good conscience when it is completely universal and there is peaceful exchange among all peoples, the state may only order and pursue its process of nature formation as a living organ of the absolute community and for its sake. Thus the general law is also valid here, with the provision that every state must simply carry the law within itself and cannot expect it to be determined in a definite way by the absolute community because it is not at all possible for the absolute community to act in definite ways. Yet in this connection an effort to seek a middle term is natural; it also occurs that, as a result of the growing dominion of the true Christian consciousness, states seek to establish and secure peaceful exchange among themselves, to be sure no longer merely from a self-interested point of view—for on this basis it had already made favorable treaties for free exchange—yet simply out of love for the absolute community. And where this result comes about, it is the highest high of political life and the most lordly triumph of the Christian spirit, for nothing more powerful than the self-interest of the state can ever oppose Christianity.

Thus a people can only act with a good conscience when that group pursues its formation process as an organ of the whole human race. A people is never able to understand the opinion of the absolute community in a definite way; however, in spite of this it can still act purely in the interest of the latter. Now, however, could it not also work this way within a people? Is it not possible for significant groupings within a people, for the families and even the individuals as well, to act purely in the interest of a people and base their whole process of formation upon the people, without being able to understand the opinion of the whole in a definite way? Within a people the common need and common will are made public by means of law; yet how does a people come to a definite relation with all of humanity, and how does it learn about the need of humanity as a whole? A people learns about the general need only by means of a free exchange of peoples with each other, and this becomes definite only by means of a people's indwelling, living effort aimed at spreading the divine Spirit over the whole of humanity and at bringing the formation process to its maximum; but could it not happen in just this way within a people? Could the form of law not also fall away in this case?

Within the family the most significant distinction is that between those who are mature and those who are immature. The latter are surely in need of direction; yet is it not possible that the immature could be such that parents could presuppose with certainty that they have the ability to apprehend correctly what is in the interest of the whole and be motivated purely by this interest? Certainly this is the case. Neither can we deny that the state can have no other goal than that its citizens become mature. This means being able to rightly recognize the common need by means of free exchange with each other, and by means of the divine Spirit through whom love of the fatherland and the universal human interest come together, to have all the impulses that the state must presuppose if it is to have the trust of the people. Yet in spite of this we cannot say that the state could become superfluous at some point or that it must have as its only intention making itself superfluous.

To be sure, the rewards and punishments of the law are no longer needed where the divine Spirit is the agent; however, there will always have to be government that gives the kind of laws that make known what is to be done and how goods are to be distributed, doing so on the basis of the only point of view from which the whole can be seen in a complete way. This is so, for just as little can good government cease to exist—government that allows for the free exchange of all with each other as a way of ascertaining the common needs of all, even making this the responsibility of all—and just as little can they believe that a correct orientation can be achieved without citizens' love of the fatherland and without having a living and certain knowledge of the fatherland, so it is just as certain that a living moral exchange of citizens always exists only in always forming the government anew, that is, truly establishing it. . . .

PART TWO
PRESENTATIONAL ACTION

Chapter 7

Introduction [to Presentational Action]

In the "General Introduction" we have explained that it is proper for religious ethics to derive its different forms of action from the most internal alterations of self-consciousness. In the same place we have also demonstrated that the affections of self-consciousness are related to the opposition between spirit and flesh, taking the forms of pleasure and lack of pleasure. It is also the case that both portions of our presentation that we have just completed are based on this opposition. However, we have also already said that these two forms do not exhaust the whole realm of action. We have instead said that in a certain sense purifying and broadening actions can only indicate the way toward attaining the true goal, the complete dominion of spirit over flesh, and do not indicate this goal itself. Further, we have also said that, accordingly, based on this standpoint there must be a goal that is higher still, and this is precisely the expression of the perfected dominion of the spirit in everything that can in any way be recognized as a combining of spirit with flesh. This is so, for it is impossible for this expression itself to be included within the opposition between pleasure and lack of pleasure, since lack of pleasure in a very decisive way presupposes a need, and pleasure always simply presupposes an expression of power that at some other point would correspond to sheer receptivity.

From this consideration it follows that we could only call the determination of self-consciousness, which lies at the foundation, to be "blessedness," even if only in a relative sense of the word. Now, if we want to see presentational action as originating out of the relative internal blessedness of persons, it indeed seems that it can be initiated only after the whole restoring and broadening process is completed, thus that it can only come into being after this present life is over. Yet we on the other hand have already had to admit as well that, necessarily, any individual action of one or the other of these processes always already presupposes the determination of self-consciousness that we have in view here. If something is yet to be restored, the state [condition] that has been overcome in a relative way must already be present in some manner. Now, the only thing to be restored is the power of spirit over flesh. Thus it is precisely this power of spirit over flesh that must already be present in some sense: the self-consciousness that we are here calling "blessedness," which is neither pleasure nor lack of pleasure, must also be present.

Moreover, it is precisely the same for the other case as well. If a morally active being is to be conscious of having the power to bring another being under the dominion of spirit, another who is capable of being brought under the mighty influence of spirit but is not yet under this influence, it is always true that this can happen only insofar as the other is already under the sway of the spirit. This is the case because spirit can be active only by means of organic expressions, only by means of the whole physical nature of persons, so that a being who wants to influence another must know that his own physical nature is already under the sway of spirit. In and of itself such a condition cannot be either pleasure or lack of pleasure but must be simply analogous to blessedness, which thus not only follows after restoring and broadening action but also precedes both.

Now, however, we will not be able to say that the blessedness that precedes the actions we have considered up until now, and the other blessedness that comes to be only after the completion of these actions—that both would be one and the same in every respect. This is so, for if the blessedness that purifying and broadening actions bring about were absolutely the same as the blessedness on which they depend, the self-consciousness would either not have to represent this state of blessedness at all, or all purifying and broadening actions would have to amount to nothing, for the existence of that state and its coming to completion could indeed not have produced any effect at that point on what should actually have been conditioned by means of them. Thus we will have to concede this in any case. Yet in what will this difference consist? Obviously not in the fact that one state of blessedness would be less indifferent to the opposition between pleasure and lack of pleasure than the other, for if this were so, they would no longer be identical in terms of concept. On the contrary, when we say, "Something must be added to the one so that it can become the other," it follows that what is added can only be an increase in intensity, and that between the one and the other is a span within which each point indeed has the same character, yet each point is also increased incrementally bit by bit. Obviously, this can only be an incremental increase in consciousness itself; thus this means that we receive an increase of consciousness itself. The character of this consciousness remains the same.

However, we can conceive of an increase of consciousness itself only if we imagine it being contrasted to awareness of a lack of consciousness; this is so, for an increase in consciousness always presupposes a disappearing lack of consciousness, just as consciousness itself always appears to us as arising only out of a lack of consciousness, and we know how to think about the maximum and perfection of consciousness only in terms of an absolute overcoming of a lack of consciousness. Thus our formula is as follows: "Between blessedness that precedes an efficacious action and blessedness that follows after the completion of that action, each point—when compared with the point that follows it—still includes within itself a lack of consciousness." And in order to give content to this formula, we assume two instances in which one point follows after another, in the one case in such a way that the progress from one point to another is conditioned by a purifying action, in the other case in such a way that progress from one to the other is conditioned by a broadening action.

Thus, let us suppose an instance of self-consciousness in the form of blessedness, which yet enters into a purifying action; this means that in this instance of consciousness under the form of blessedness, there was still a lack of consciousness, namely, lack of consciousness of a possible retrograde motion, by which a purifying action would become necessary; this is a lack of consciousness of a kernel lacking pleasure that still lay within this state of blessedness. Now if the purifying action is completed, this lack of consciousness would be brought into consciousness; lack of pleasure would have entered in, but in turn it would also have been overcome in a moral sense, and the blessedness that would now exist would be consciousness of the lack of pleasure that has been overcome, just as the previous lack of consciousness concerned the possibility of a lack of pleasure, so that consciousness thus would have come to be where previously there had been lack of consciousness.

It is just the same on the other side. Suppose an instance of self-consciousness in the form of blessedness, which yet enters into a broadening action; this means that in this instance of self-consciousness under the form of blessedness, there was an instance of self-consciousness, determined as pleasure, that would have opened up; for without this no broadening action is conceivable. Thus, this self-consciousness as blessedness would have been, in itself, at rest and unconscious of the summons to broaden the dominion of spirit. Now, however, suppose that the process of broadening action has been completed: self-consciousness would have been able to assume the form of blessedness in turn only if consciousness taken up under the dominion of spirit would have been coposited; previously it would have been outside the dominion of spirit, but without any consciousness of such dominion having been formed. Thus once more a lack of consciousness is brought to consciousness; hence blessedness has received an intensive increase. Surely it also appears that blessedness would also have broadened extensively, but this consideration does not belong here.

Now, this will be important in order to indicate more clearly the character of the action that proceeds from self-consciousness and takes the form of blessedness. That is, it follows from what has been said that the increment by means of which each later moment of blessedness distinguishes itself from earlier moments can only come to be by means of a purifying or broadening action that has occurred in between the two. This implies that when self-consciousness as blessedness becomes an impulse, when an action proceeds from it—insofar as it is nothing but self-consciousness that takes the form of blessedness—this can in no way be the ground of the increment that differentiates the later moment of blessedness from that which comes earlier.

However, this purely negative determination is so very exclusive that it actually appears to bring to nothing actions that proceed from self-consciousness that takes the form of blessedness. This is so, for an action that has no efficacy outside itself, that produces a change neither externally nor internally, an action completely without effect, without result, is very difficult to imagine. Moreover, this is indeed the case not only where it is a matter of making its content visible, but most especially where it is a question of persuading someone of the action's necessity or that it is an essential component of the moral task as a whole. Persuading someone of the action's necessity is difficult because we always imagine that each action, insofar as it is to be a conscious one, always has as its ground the idea of a result, whether it is in the form of a purpose or in the form of an instinct. This is so, for insofar as it is an actual living action and not merely a transmission of some movement, it appears that it can be thought of only in terms of one of these two forms [purpose or instinct]. Persuading someone that it is an essential component of the moral task is difficult because we usually would not consider an action that continues to have no result as belonging to the whole of the moral task. This is so, for what place are we to allocate for this kind of action? It could be anywhere; for this reason, however, it also appears it could be nowhere, and where this is the case with one portion, how then is the whole moral task to avoid dissolving into this nothingness?

Both of these results appear so unfavorable to us that we must, accordingly, now consider them more closely. Concerning the first result, about which we have said that we could not exhibit such an action, we have said this only insofar as the action is precisely a conscious one. Now, however, we can say that each moment of self-consciousness in the form of blessedness which passes over into a purifying or broadening action is relatively without consciousness. Thus actions that have this character denote precisely the side of consciousness in virtue of which and after which something different would still have to follow; consequently it would only be the very indication that self-consciousness in the form of blessedness would simply be a preceding element of the process. As concerns the second result, however, of which we have said such an action does not appear to be a distinct part of the total moral task, we must say again, "Insofar as we consider such a determination of self-consciousness to be a moment that follows after, it includes within itself the completion of purifying and broadening actions, and each moment coming out of an action that precedes it generally has its place insofar as either process can be seen as completed by that moment of consciousness."

Thus, if we imagine these processes as actually completed—and this underlies the expression "eternal life"—no further action whatsoever can be conceived except one that has no function in relation to the result, precisely because no further result is to be expected. Instead, only the sign and expression of the completed process and the sign and expression of the result achieved are to be expected. So this result then proceeds as a positive conclusion, and between the determination of self-consciousness itself in the form of blessedness and the action that proceeds from this determination, there can be no other distinction except that between self-consciousness in itself and the manifestation of self-consciousness. This is the case because there is no efficacious action contained within it and no result to be produced by it, and there remains nothing else to do but return to the distinction between inner and outer and to say, "What is present along with the action that manifests the determination of self-consciousness in the form of blessedness is nothing but the pure outward expression of it." This alone indicates the true meaning of the title that we have already given to this part of our task: "presentational action."

So if we bring all the foregoing together, we must say that presentational action as compared with purifying and broadening actions appears to have no efficacy at all in that it produces no change of moral condition in either the subject or the object. We can also express it in this way: there is actually no "moving out" from the given moment, as is always the case with an efficacious action; rather, in this respect it is a "remaining within itself." It is a "moving out from itself" only in respect to the determination of self-consciousness in itself; this is so, for it is a movement outward of the determination of self-consciousness rather than an inner self-consciousness alone.

Now, however, what is then the basis for self-consciousness in the form of blessedness moving outward, if nonetheless by means of it no change in moral condition is to be produced? There would be no answer to this question if presentational action were not also conditioned by the idea of community. This is so, for if an individual person were completely by himself and isolated, not only from other persons as such but also in each of his own moments purely of itself, there would be no ground even to be able to think about inner self-consciousness becoming outward. However, an individual can in no way be conceived without community; consequently communication of the individual's state in the moment is always assigned to him. This communication is twofold. That is, insofar as we consider an individual in himself as a being who exists under the conditions of time, times exist as communication from one moment to another. However, to the extent that we consider an individual as an example of the species, to that extent we thus think of personal feeling and communal feeling in the individual's self-consciousness as identical, and then communication is from one individual being to another. And taking the two together encompasses the whole realm of community as it exists for human beings.

Thus we can say, "Insofar as all presentational action is nothing but the coming into appearance of an inner state, it sprouts into community." Surely presentational action also proceeds from community; thus it always presupposes community already existing, so that we come to the same circle that we have already construed in another place. However, these two are also easily united again, namely, in the fact that community on the one hand, and presentational action on the other—both are equally original. That is, an individual person could not be a being that exists under the form of time if there were not for that person a becoming outward of what is inner. In just this way, an individual person could not be an individuation of the species without an outward expression of what is inner. This is the case, for only under this condition can human nature be dispersed among a totality of individual beings. Spirit is one and the same in all individuals and, considered in itself, it does not include the concept of strictly personal existence in itself at all, whether we consider it as κοινὸς λόγος[1] or as ἅγιον πνεῦμα.[2] Thus, if there is to be personal existence, it must be made of some other substratum. As such, however, nothing is conceivable except the whole system of psychical and physical organization, which spirit appropriates for itself.

Hence, if there must be a connection between this system and spirit, there must also be that without which this connection could not be conceived: the becoming outward of what is inner. Now, moreover, suppose the whole interconnection between a determination of self-consciousness in this form and the way that it becomes impulse for an action that proceeds from it rests, accordingly, on this impersonal identity of spirit; thus it is obvious that presentational action is also divided into two different areas, insofar as it is related to those determinations of self-consciousness for which intelligence in the general human sense is central, or insofar as it relates to those determinations of self-consciousness in which spirit in the Christian sense is central. These two realms can exist in this context only as they were in the forms of purifying and broadening actions.

The outward movement of an inner determination of self-consciousness, presentational action, rests upon community and produces community. We have expressed that by means of the formula, "Both are equally original," a formula that we immediately transform into an actual conception when we say, "Presentational action is community itself coming into appearance; thus presentational action is also the means by which community can first become an object of consciousness." It is clear that this is equally valid for both spheres. However, if presentational action is community itself coming into appearance, insofar as this is true, its principle can be none other than love, that is to say, the love of one for another, both of whom, by means of the identity of spirit, are equal. This equality cannot be better described than by the expression "brotherly love." Moreover, for this reason the love that is the principle of presentational action is brotherly love.

Now in the outer sphere this is obviously universal love of human beings. However, what is it in the distinctively Christian sphere? Are we to say that its objects would be only those who are identical with us by means of the divine Spirit, insofar as it is in them and in us? It appears that this is analogous to the outer sphere. However, then presentational action would have nothing to do with communication by the church in an outward direction, and this could not be combined with Christian consciousness. This is so, for saying "Presentational action in the Christian church is done only for itself" does not exhaust the meaning of the term in any way. It would also be true that one cannot combine with this idea the fact that all three forms of action [purifying, broadening, presenting] can never be absolutely separated in reality. Thus we must also include all persons as such in the brotherly love of Christians; yet we must not refer back to spirit in the universal human sense; rather, we say, "No one can be conscious of the divine Spirit except insofar as one is conscious at the same time that the whole human race belongs to this Spirit; the distinction among individuals is only temporal, which is to say that some already have the πνεῦμα ἅγιον, and others do not yet have it." And Christian brotherly love is entirely universal: some are included as already partaking of the divine Spirit, and others are included to whom the Spirit is to be communicated. Thus in the one case presentational action addresses itself to those who already have an experience of the divine Spirit, and in the other case to those who have the receptivity that is presupposed.

Now presupposing this, accordingly, we will have the following foundation. As certainly as the divine Spirit is present in an individual, just as certainly is there also a community between this individual and all other persons, which yet can only be gradually realized over time. This community refers to the same relationship of human nature in all persons to the divine Spirit, and the only thing that is to happen is the coming into appearance of that self-consciousness in which the dominion of the divine Spirit over flesh is established in an absolute way. Obviously, however, the difference between those in whom the divine Spirit is already present and those in whom it is not yet present is not to be overlooked. So such presentational action is, accordingly, in a more perfect degree for the one group than it is for the other. For those in the one group, it is necessarily an awakening and expansion of its self-consciousness in the form of blessedness. For those in the other group, it is only a vision of blessedness that is offered to them, one so real that it has the possibility of exciting the receptivity for the divine Spirit, since within the appearance of the Christian self-consciousness that same divine Spirit is offered.

And if we contrast the one with the other as sharply as possible, we see how the one includes within itself a relationship to the founding of a community, and the other includes within itself a relationship to a community that is already present. Hence the one shows us an element of broadening action within that of presentational action; the other shows us presentational action purely in and of itself; however, presentational action is equally able to attach to another form of action—only under the presupposition that a regression is possible because of the temporal passage to which the Christian church is subject—and thus to this degree the element of purifying action is also established.

Chapter 8

The Inner Sphere,
or the Church

In what has just been discussed, we now have the first elements for construing what the Christian church is. It was not possible to give this construal earlier; this is the case, for the necessity of an institution such as the church allows itself to be looked into based on the necessity and natural character of presentational action. If the higher consciousness could be completely exhausted by the forms of pleasure and lack of pleasure, no other actions could be imagined in addition except for broadening and purifying actions. Now surely included in the idea of these two actions is the fact that each has influence on the other, but still such influence is not constant; as influence it has no continuity and rather arises always only where an opportunity presents itself; from this point of view influence is accordingly always dissolved again when the opportunity is met. An outward occasion is required if purifying or broadening actions are to have influence on each other, and when influence is realized, the summons to action stops, and consequently community stops as well.

On the other hand, the higher self-consciousness in the form of blessedness, inasmuch as it does not at all stand under the opposition between pleasure and lack of pleasure, is the true and basic feeling for a Christian, a feeling that there is some power of spirit over flesh. Moreover, since it is dependent on no outward occasion and yet must essentially also become an impulse, this then means that presentational action is independent of outward occasions and is present only by means of the basic character of a human being as a whole, insofar as persons are twofold: spirit and flesh. However, that this determination of self-consciousness does not rest, but also wants to appear and does appear, can again only be conceived of based on the two elements set forth above, to which we have traced back this determination, and which actually postulates community as a continuum. It is given in our original self-consciousness that we can only connect together individual moments of existence as what is in one moment becomes an object for another moment. This is only possible by means of a coming forth into appearance, so that the identity of personal feeling and communal feeling is only genuine insofar as we are in community with others and can exchange our respective self-consciousness; this means that all presentation is nothing but the continual realization of human nature itself.

Now, however, for this reason the conception of community also has its distinctive place here. Thus in the Christian realm, community rests purely in the fact that the divine Spirit is one and the same in all and for all and in the fact that all individuals are only its instruments, and therefore that each individual would also bear the divine Spirit completely in himself only insofar as the consciousness that all others are likewise instruments of the divine Spirit has come into self-consciousness in him. However, this happens only insofar as a person takes the self-consciousness of others into his own, which in turn can happen only insofar as the self-consciousness of each one passes over into appearance. And this inner necessity for the continual joining of self-consciousnesseses separated by personal existence is the essence of brotherly love and conditions both presentational action and the continuity of community.

However, just as brotherly love is the basis of religious community, of the church, so also all members of this community are also as such essentially equal to each other, and indeed this has a twofold ground. That is, the ἅγιον πνεῦμα is essentially divine, that is, never passive, but always active, consequently never affected or modified. However, precisely for this reason the Spirit also does not belong to personal existence, but the Spirit is an agent that is identical in all. Accordingly, the essential equality of all members of the church is grounded in the Spirit. Now, however, if in addition all persons as equally individual possessions of the divine Spirit are equal to each other, they must still be unequal as organs of the Spirit, in that the process of appropriation in some is more advanced than it is in others. Nonetheless even this inequality vanishes, and this is the second ground upon which the essential equality of all members of the church rests: [equality] through the absolute superiority of Christ over all and through the fact that church members' relation to Christ is dominant over all other relationships. However, this in turn presupposes the divine in Christ; this is so, for one who only wants to assign to Christ some other dignity cannot even place him as absolutely supreme over all others; thus one must also in turn give equal validity to the inequality of individuals with each other. It is important to be aware that what is essential about this dogma, which cannot be treated without severe difficulties, is immediately recognizable as a basic condition also where it is a matter of how the original determination of Christian self-consciousness developed in its practical application.

Now, however, here we must also bear in mind once again that this construction of the Christian church out of consciousness of the essential equality of all Christians can be briefly defined in the following formula: the Spirit wants the consciousness of the Spirit's being the possession of all others to be in every other individual at the same time, and the Spirit wants consciousness that each individual is an organ of the Spirit to be passed on from each individual to all others. This is so, for the entire task of presentational action rests upon this mutual "taking up of this consciousness into oneself," so that this construction of the Christian church is already distinctively Protestant.

This is the case, for the Catholic Church takes an original inequality into its construction: the contrast between priests and laypeople. All priestly churches are built upon a principle of inequality because they neither recognize the contrast that exists between the Redeemer and the redeemed, nor recognize equality in the divine communication as it is formulated in Christianity by the idea of the Holy Spirit. Indeed, the Jewish church was also a priestly church, but it still had along with this a somewhat different story. It forms a transition from a genuinely priestly church to Christianity. For it, priestly dignity rested on the Mosaic law and consisted only of authority over certain functions, but it was entirely excluded from any claims to a special divine communication. Priestly dignity did indeed also exist in the form of a high-priestly oracle, but this was in no way an inner divine communication, only an outward one, that is, as far as we know, only a communication based on the form of casting lots. The special inner divine communication recognized in the law, namely, the prophetic communication, was completely independent of the priestly office, and by means of the prophetic office a transition was possible from Judaism as a priestly church to Christianity, in which a priestly office as something distinct did not exist at all. The religious dignity of the giving of the law was overcome, and religious communication went from being something special to being something general.

Now, however, how did this old principle come yet again into the Catholic Church? We can only answer this question historically, and along with this we must surely always acknowledge that all historical presentation is always at the same time an interpretation, and to this extent it is also subjective. However, from our position we can only say that the special priestly character of the Catholic Church was something that crept in only later; this was completely foreign to the original constitution of the church. The apostles had no priestly office. Rather, their only superiority lay in the fact that on account of their personal intimacy with Christ, they were the source of Christian tradition, as concerns both its teaching and its institutions. Where is the first Christian church exhibited to us? In the Acts of the Apostles. However, here it is never the apostles alone who establish the church, but a great mass of individuals, even including women, and of all of them together it was said that they were all together of one mind in prayer and in praise of God, thus engaged in presentational action, where ὁμοθυμαδόν[1] indicates that in no way were some purely receptive, others purely active, but that brotherly equality was what was essential both as to matter and as to form.[2]

The Catholic Church tells another story; it presupposes a history depending on a tradition that cannot be proved, that the distinction between priests and laity was instituted by Christ himself. Now Christ is the one whose relationship to all others is the basis for the absolute equality of those others among themselves. Thus insofar as the Catholic Church traces inequality back to Christ, it indeed saves the Christian principle and remains a Christian church. However, suppose that its presupposition were also true: Christ still cannot have established inequality in such a way that the original equality would have been negated thereby. Thus the original equality must always be properly preserved, insofar as it grounds all having the same relation to Christ and establishes the fact that the distinction among believers can always be only a relative one.

Now, in order to see this rightly, we must show that the germ of this distinction is also in the Protestant church. That is, there is a similar difference for us, but for us it is not accorded the same worth. In our general formula concerning the construction of the church, which is based on the consciousness of the absolute equality of all believers as compared with Christ, a twofoldedness is also established—a communication of oneself to others, and a taking up for oneself of the Christian life and existence of others, in their relationship to the divine Spirit—accordingly, a twofoldedness between spontaneity and receptivity. However, we say that both of these are necessary for each person. If the Catholic Church denies this, there would be no affinity at all between it and us. However, it does not deny this. This is the case, for the Catholic Church does not deny that priests on their part are also receptive and that laity can also participate in spontaneity; indeed, this is very much in the background in the church's public appearance, but it still is not totally negated in that the church still takes up family life into its construction, even if not as the highest form, and it sees family as something that is not purely civil.

In other respects regarding this point about taking up the family into the formation of the church, I refer to what was said about it in the section on efficacious action, but here I reduce it in brief to the points that are particularly relevant to our current consideration. That is, the family as such exists prior to the church, but in turn the church also exists before the family becomes Christian. This is so, for the construction of the church from individual beings is the earlier event, even if it is also the one that is less fully formed. Thus, we will have to distinguish and discuss what presentational action in the church would be without a definite relationship to the family as an organic element of the church, and then what presentational action in the church would be if it were essentially based just on the church. Yet first it is necessary to discuss the general character of presentational action in terms of its content insofar as its character effects the relationship to the church, so that we first have what is universal, the original unity to which the subordinated oppositions can be related.

We have already said in the "General Introduction" that all presentational action taken as a whole is essentially what we call "worship."[3] It surely appears as if very little would be given by means of this formula because the word itself is inexact and accordingly only points to an indeterminant notion that is currently used in common life. How can we perform service to God? If here we look at the content of the term, broadening action looks like service to God more than presentational action does. Yet even in other spheres of life we know and use the word "service" in just such a way that it signifies the natural expression of a relationship between one who is set lower and one who is higher; thus it indicates not a "demonstration of service" but a "testimony of service," and what is included in this notion is just that one is presented as an organ of the other. Thus worship is the totality of all actions through which we present ourselves as organs of God, by means of the divine Spirit. Efficacious action is naturally excluded from this because efficacious action is that by which we produce something as organs of God, not actions by means of which we present ourselves as organs.

Surely we have already asserted that each form of action includes the others within itself, and so even the explanation that has been given is not to rule out the fact that presentational action *per accidens* [by accident] always also includes efficacious action within itself. This is the case, for each pure presentation also enhances the habit of observing oneself based on the point from which one presents oneself, and just so also increases the ease with which one can comply with the demands that arise from this point of view. However, still in this way efficacious action is only dependent on presentational action, but efficacious action is not made out to be of the essence of the latter.

However, by what means does it happen that we present ourselves as organs of God in such an essential way? We cannot answer this question without at the same time making our way into a whole series of contrasts that would really describe the whole. However, a general answer is still easily drawn out of what has already been said. That is, only in comparison with the absolute inwardness of self-consciousness in and for itself is presentational action a "going out of itself," but not in comparison with efficacious action, because the idea of an effect does not underlie presentational action. In addition, presentational action can also exist only on the presupposition of community. However, from this it follows, without any kind of result being expected, that there can be results for the actor himself, and also for others: for the actor himself insofar as he is thought of in another moment; for others insofar as every other person exists in the same community in each moment. Thus, in both cases the nature of presentational action consists in an outer expression of what is inner, so that this can be recognized for what it is. However, the inner factor that is to be presented is, in our particular area, the state of the free dominion of spirit over flesh, the consciousness of blessedness, the untroubled state hovering in the middle between pleasure and lack of pleasure.

However, the narrower question, how what is inner becomes something outer, also takes us back again to something that in relation to our distinctive area appears to us as something that happens naturally. Namely, entirely without reference to the divine Spirit, the same task is already set by means of the κοινὸς λόγος; thus presentational action is demanded before the existence of any Christian church, the object of which is to reveal the dominion of intelligence in sensorial nature. Now, Christian presentational action as such has no other means of presentation than those that are available to the rational person as such; and since spirit itself is rational, it can also become something outer only in accord with what belongs to its nature in the realm of appearance, accordingly by means of the sensorial nature of persons. The means of presentation must lie in persons' sensorial nature, but only in such a way that we must presuppose them as organs already formed for general human intelligence. From this, one could want to conclude that the only individuals who are already morally formed could enter the Christian church; however, this would contradict all of Christian practice as well as our Christian feeling.

On the one hand, redemption will not wait for the perfect moral formation of persons; otherwise even the time when Christ appeared would indeed not have been the fullness of time. On the other hand, there would be no human state [condition] in which persons would not already be prepared to receive Christianity. Thus, that presupposition would be patently false. However, even here this is not meant so much in terms of morality, but much more in terms of general intelligence. There is nothing in the outward appearance of persons that would not already be built up to a certain degree by means of human life itself as an organ for intelligence, quite apart from the contrast between what is moral and what is immoral; this is the case since both are equally expressions of human intelligence. The gestalt of a person is expressive by its very nature, and above all physiognomy is an expression of intelligence.

However, the richest means for a presentation of intelligence is language, which we do not see as ethical in the narrow sense of the word. A person takes possession of language only gradually, and before one has become capable of it to a certain degree, one cannot participate in presentational action. Here this presupposition is only meant in the wider sense of the word, and what we want to say is only this: The means of presentation in themselves are not a product of the divine Spirit in the narrower sense; rather, they are present already by means of general human intelligence taken up as an organic totality. And the divine Spirit can only appropriate them for the Spirit's self by means that will not at all negate the distinction between the special inner sphere of distinctively Christian presentation and that of human beings in general.

Yet in order to consider this more exactly, we want to seek to present the whole scope of the task in a more real way. Insofar as the division that we have made is correct, we will be able to say, "All actions that proceed from the divine

Spirit and are not efficacious—such actions are presentational and indeed presentational in our special domain." At first this may not seem to be a fruitful formula, but it gains the advantage for us that now we can still consider presentational action as it is connected with efficacious action.[4] The latter we have divided into one that is truly broadening from inside and in an outward direction, and another that increases toward the inside. If we compare these two, we can say, "All actions that broaden only in an outward direction, without an increase inwardly in relation to the specific level that the dominion of spirit has reached, are not efficacious, but presentational." Initially, we can best become clear about this in a domain that is not immediately religious. That is, all actions that expand the dominion of humanity over nature in an outward direction are presentations of the level to which this dominion is already present. All actions that only preserve a given condition as it is have less a broadening than a protective character, and yet they have much more of a presentational character. Thus, in all efficacious action there is an aspect that is subordinated to the presentational domain.

This comes most to the fore in the preserving functions of the extensive process. However, we also find this in the process that is intensive since all increases of the dominion of the Spirit in the domain of human nature proceed from the original efficacious action of Christ. In Christ and in his influence upon the human race, there is no possibility of increase; rather, here the whole process is only an extensive one. It is his eternally established dominion over the human race that spreads itself farther and farther. In this connection the intensive process itself has a presentational character; this is the case, for it is always only the constant influence of Christ that produces increase, and the increase is nothing but the exponent of the efficacious activity of Christ. This is surely nothing new for us since it is only an application of the general proposition that in actuality all of the different forms of action cannot be separated from each other. However, we have recalled this and brought it to the fore in a special way in order to indicate that presentational action does not create its own domain exclusively for itself; instead, at the same time it includes in itself the whole scope of efficacious action.

The biblical directive also expresses this when it extends presentational action even to the most insignificant aspect of the nature-forming process, in order to express it with the greatest generality. This is so, for Paul said, "If you eat or if you drink or whatever you do, do everything to the glory of God."[5] To act to the glory of God is, however, nothing other than to act in such a way that one presents oneself as being an organ of God. Thus the apostle wants the character of presentational action to stamp itself absolutely in all actions, even in the most sensorial material, which is made to be an object of the broadening process.

Now if we proceed on the basis of the concept of worship, we will be able to say, "For us presentational action is divided into two different domains, which yet are also not absolutely separated, but only relatively contrasted." That is, there is one domain in which presentational action stands out in a special way, where it forms its own distinctive circle, and this is worship in the narrower sense. There is also another domain that mostly brings presentational action into appearance, and that is also one in which presentational action is coposited in what belongs mostly to efficacious action, and this is worship in the wider sense, which is spread over the whole of life. The divine Spirit must take possession of the whole spiritual organism in human beings and in the twofoldedness of their capacity to form notions and to form desire—or however one wants to name this relative opposition that exists in persons, for how it is named does not matter at all here. Every use of this function belongs in a certain way to efficacious action since even as practice it is always expanding over the course of time, a fortification and strengthening of a condition that already exists.

However, it always also expresses this condition, and insofar as it is pure expression, it belongs to presentational action. If the action is chiefly a broadening one, it goes back to a modification of self-consciousness viewed as pleasure; if it is chiefly a purifying one, it goes back to a modification of self-consciousness viewed as lack of pleasure. However, both modifications always spring up first from an overall consciousness of the higher spiritual life, and thus it must always consist in a relation to self-consciousness determined by indifference that is neither pleasure nor lack of pleasure. And the less broadening or purifying power is present in an action, the more it appears as presentational action, without, however, ever ceasing to be at the same time broadening or purifying action.

Now, this on the one hand expands our domain; yet on the other hand it also appears to create entanglements, and so we must still seek to preserve its fixed boundaries as compared with the other domains. Thus here we must return again to the most important point, to the relationship between presentational action and efficacious action, as it proceeds, for both kinds of action come from the forms of self-consciousness that underlie it. We have already seen earlier that the self-consciousness that underlies presentational action can be established in two different ways: as preceding modified self-consciousness that underlies efficacious action and as following the same. If we regard these two different forms in which self-consciousness viewed as blessedness can be established as being a pure endpoint, we have something that cannot be given to us in experience, thus something from which no moral rule can be derived. This is so, for no moral rule is to be derived from that for which there is no use in practice.

Thus we have to imagine it as a point in between and in such a way that the twofold character that we just discussed is not lost. At that very point, however, we must also imagine efficacious action as, on the one hand, that which is to be relatively a first beginning, and on the other hand, that which is relatively completed; thus presentational action could enter into the pauses within efficacious action. That is the sort of thing we must imagine; we must imagine time as a continuum and action in time as a row of discrete quantities, between which a transition is possible. Now in relation to efficacious action, presentational action fills in the pauses in the former and forms a transition from one moment of efficacious action to another in two respects: in respect to the beginning and in respect to the completion. And if we consider the way we have already portrayed the area of worship in the narrower sense in a provisional way, with presentational action appearing mostly as a law unto itself, it is self-evident that here everything is based on pauses being made within efficacious action, pauses into which presentational action enters; this is so, for otherwise there could in no way be a union of persons for the purpose of presentational action.

However, how is it for worship in the broader sense? Presentational action distinguishes itself from efficacious action not in terms of content, but only in terms of intention. When we gain any new insight into what we are to do, a new action also starts with it that can be a purifying action or even a broadening action. All practice begins with a minimum of readiness that gradually increases. As long as this readiness is increasing, the action has the character of efficacious action; and when it reaches a certain level, then practices related to this way of acting occur that no longer have the character of training, because there is nothing more to be done that is essential for readiness. Now, insofar as a person intends these practices for the realm of outward formation, they still remain efficacious actions; however, if they are intended for one's own state, as pure practices they too are only presentations because they want to produce no further change. Yet then, from this point onward efficacious action comes to an end as well, and presentational action takes its place. And so a drop away from efficacious action into presentational action always occurs here for us. This refers to what is yet beyond all experience, that we must imagine the completed condition of humanity as that in which efficacious action no longer takes place at all; rather, there is only pure presentation of that which is and always remains the same, a pure becoming outward of what is inner.

However, if we ask, "How are the two domains of worship actually distinguished from each other in terms of their content?" we would have to say, "In those actions which are to constitute worship in the narrower sense, the character of efficacious action must step back in an almost absolute way." Thus, this means that the relationship to the whole process of nature formation within it must step back. However, it follows from this that both talent and outward nature must be presupposed as already equally formed within this domain, thus precisely what we have designated as art, so that we would have to say, "Worship in the narrower sense is always presentational action in the domain of art in the widest sense of the word. Worship in the broad sense, however, is that action which appears to us as efficacious action in its becoming and only appears to us as presentational action when it has been completed." Thus, the whole process of nature formation must always be seen in this kind of action; it is presentational action only in the domain of active life. This means that the moral totality of efficacious action in its two branches, insofar as it is seen as completed in terms of its form, is at the same time presentational action in this sense.

And this view is perfectly confirmed for us when we compare it with what we meet in life itself as the result of the moral process. This is so, for how has the church constituted its worship? In no other way than that worship is always put together out of different artistic elements, and we can never deny that a cultured people can have a more complete worship than a coarse people can, and that worship must be developed more completely to the same degree that the realm of art improves. However, this also corresponds precisely with the general feeling that true worship, insofar as it occurs in pauses within efficacious action, is something completely empty if there is not a corresponding intention that is regularly ongoing to continue presentational action in all of active life, to express in all of active life that it is to be a presentation of the rule of spirit over flesh. This is the case, for to the degree that this is lacking, worship becomes opus operatum,[6] a result of superstition. On the other hand, if someone were to say that he would want to be satisfied with worship in the broader sense, thus with presentational action that is included in efficacious action, and not allow for efficacious action to be interrupted by such pauses as actual worship requires, we would ask him to bear in mind that he would thereby put himself in no position to increase his efficacious action—which still matters to him above all—so that the longer it goes on, the more it could be efficacious action that is worship in the broader sense.

This is so, for efficacious action can only cease to be training, can only be increased to become pure performance, if self-consciousness is given room to develop itself in actual presentational action. One who wants to reduce all of life to work, in laborious exertion that cuts off all free practice, makes all of effective life, in turn, into an opus operatum in relation to moral content, because life only exists for him without the idea of perfection that underlies life, because one has life only in its nonbeing, in its becoming. Hence only both areas taken together and in immediate connection with each other encompass the idea of presentational action; neither may be separated from the other at any time, and both must always be recognized as equally original. It has been held this way in the Christian church since the beginning. At the same time, in its origin the church has followed the pattern of granting worship its own time, its own existence; however, the church has also always urged that the whole active life be transformed into worship; it has accordingly always taken pains that the highest religious point of view from which life can be considered would not be neglected.

WORSHIP IN THE NARROWER SENSE

Here we come to the domain of practical theology, which has the task of putting worship in the narrower sense in order. Practical theology presupposes worship's ethical grounding and principally treats matters of technique. In this place we pass over technique and fix our eyes on the task of providing the ethical grounding for worship.

As we have seen, presentational action in the distinctively Christian domain cannot produce its own means of presentation since they are already given to the Christian domain along with general human presentation. These means of presentation form the domain of art, and all worship in the narrower sense is composed of elements of art. Now, however, if we regard that domain as established in such a way that other means of presentation cannot come forward, still the question is whether everything that is art may be taken up into the domain of worship. Obviously this question still belongs to our discipline because the immediate product of the Christian Spirit's first impulse is to find means of presentation; thus we are obliged to show the direction in which the Spirit must thereby reach out, or whether for the Spirit everything that is an organic part of the domain of presentation would be equally valid.

Here history points us toward an important distinction. For if we compare Christian worship with non-Christian worship, we find much in the latter that is excluded from the former, and if we compare Protestant and Catholic worship, we also come upon great differences at least as compared with each other. . . . Now, are all these differences morally grounded or are they simply incidental? In Christian worship as it was originally organized, everything that included sensorial display was cleared out, as was everything that belonged to sensorial presentation and the activity of persons themselves. Regarding the first point, outward display, we find in the Catholic Church a great approximation to Jewish and heathen worship.

Regarding the latter point, the sensorial self-presentation of persons, as present in mime activities and found in heathenism and Judaism, is always completely excluded from Christianity. Why? Is a definite boundary set in this regard for Christianity, or can it still take up these elements to some extent again? It is less for the sake of these individual elements themselves than for the sake of the general consideration that we pose this question. That is, therewith we must return to the fact that in the Christian view even intelligence in the general human sense in its relative opposition to the divine Spirit is also placed on the side of flesh. This also enters in here. The ἅγιον πνεῦμα is the true life-principle in our domain; thus, as long as it has not become completely one with human intelligence, there remains nothing to do but to include intelligence in the psychic organization of which the Spirit is to take hold. Then, however, intelligence in its two forms, as capacity to form notions and to form desire, is the first organ for the ἅγιον πνεῦμα and accordingly also that in which the basic characteristics for presentation must lie. Now surely there is no other way for presentation to be manifest except by means of sensorial nature; however, since what is corporeal is a bit more withdrawn from impulse in the Christian domain than it is in the outer domain, it is obvious that in our domain what is corporeal can pass over into presentation much less than it can in the outer sphere.

Here we cannot imagine in the least that an expression of spirit coming to appearance in what is corporeal is to be an element of presentation in and of itself; we can only accept it as something incidental, not as part of the task. Therefore, to be sure, the withdrawal of what is corporeal is essential to Christian worship, yet it is just as distinctive for Christianity as is consciousness of the ἅγιον πνεῦμα and consciousness of the difference between the ἅγιον πνεῦμα and the κοινὸς λόγος. And on this basis it also appears that we can immediately derive what we can view as the main difference between Protestant worship and Catholic worship: What lies closest to the Spirit in the corporeal domain is the whole system of language; the immediate expression of what is spiritual. What is mimetic is much more easily an expression of what is emotional, which is never to be presented here, because in the Spirit's dominion over flesh, the Spirit can always only appear as self-activity. Thus, this of itself is already an indication of a great predominance given to all those means of presentation that are related to language, thus above all the arts of speech. However, insofar as language itself is always already in a certain sense singing, which it becomes to an ever higher degree the more that excitement increases, we have here an immediate point of contact for music with the arts of speech as a means of presentation in worship; yet all plastic and graphic arts, which have more to do with form, withdraw more in Christian worship.

This relationship is expressed in a much more definite manner in the Protestant church than it is in the Catholic Church. We must consider this in such a way that we track it back to the analogy with that from which we have proceeded. Christianity cannot form its own means of presentation; it can only take them out of the domain in which the human spirit has already proved their value for presentation over a long period of time. However, Christianity entered not merely into human life in general, but even into a given religious life, into Jewish and heathen religious life; thus it could only select from general means of presentation insofar as they already belonged immediately to religious presentation. And as soon as we imagine this, we must naturally find in turn a variance in the way Christian character stands out as contrasted with other religious presentation; in this regard the Protestant church has structured Christian worship more in contrast with Jewish and heathen worship, but the Catholic Church has done so more in analogy with both of them. Since each church appears to be as one-sided as the other, we must simply say that the Protestant church structured worship in a somewhat stricter way, but also in that respect a somewhat more humble way; by contrast the Catholic Church has done it in a somewhat more lax way, but also in that respect in a more arrogant way.

That is, the Protestant church was concerned that some corruption or other could actually creep into what is Christian, along with Jewish and heathen means of presentation, and it sought to protect itself against what the church's use of these means naturally discovers in turn about the relation of what is sensorial or what is corporeal with them. However, the Catholic Church is based on arrogance, as if the church were past such danger, and along with this there is immediately a lascivious striving for the sensorial effects of presentation. If it were conceivable that Christianity could have arisen without opposition to other forms of religion, perhaps it would have come to a construction of its means of presentation that could have held more to the middle. However, that is why striving for this middle is the only correct effort. In the Protestant church there are in different regions and even in the difference between the two evangelical confessions—yet the confessional differences actually have nothing to do with this—differences in the construction of worship in this respect. That is, in the Reformed church, the contrast with what is Catholic is the strongest; in the Lutheran church, drawing near to what is Catholic is the strongest.

However, because of that we cannot say that from the beginning there should have been more striving for the middle in the Lutheran church, but it was moderation, a certain caution, that led to not taking away from the people all at once too much that was familiar and in which they found an expression of holiness. It now appears, therefore, that where there has been work to overcome the opposition between the two parties with such results, the decision to give up efforts toward the middle has been correct; however, the decision about which spiritual means of presentation and which sensorial means may be maintained is to be made with great caution and sensitive investigation.

Another question concerns not the material of worship, but the form of worship. We have taken the starting point that presentational action, in that it is equally original with community, is based on the principle of brotherly love, on the principle of equality of all Christians as belonging together because the identical Spirit dwells within them, and as equally dependent upon Christ. Thus, now this equality in presentational action is always to be expressed. However, we do not find this to be the case; instead, Christian worship is construed in such a way that some individuals who are present are predominantly active, and others predominantly receptive. The basis for this has already been given in that we have observed that each individual has a twofold task, on the one hand to communicate himself to others, on the other hand to take up the existence of others in his own self. This is so, since where there is such a twofold task, absolute balance between the two aspects cannot exist in a given moment, but balance can always only be produced by means of an exchange of partial subordination, and therein lies the basis for the fact that equality exists subordinated to some inequality.

And now if we consider the structure of Christian worship, we find a great number of gradations in which inequality emerges, from the closest approach to the original equality to the closest analogy to priestly religion; yet we can bring all of these gradations again under the relative opposition between what is Catholic and what is Protestant. We want to take as our starting point the principle of equality and see how the matter is construed for us from this point. In every individual moment of presentation, some must always be active, others receptive; and each whole presentation that appears exists in a sequence of different moments since worship in the narrower sense, as we have seen, is a system made of different artistic elements and artistic forms. Thus the minimum of inequality is in a construction where already in one and the same complete act the relationship reverses itself; so each person is active in some moments and in some other moments is receptive, but a constant inequality would not be established at all.

The worship of the Quakers most closely corresponds to this construction. This is so, since for them every course of worship is to consist in an exchange in which some give and then also receive again, but a constant difference does not exist at all. This form is so near the limit that sometimes it happens that worship does not occur at all, and indeed, furthermore, precisely because no constant inequality at all is organized, it naturally remains completely incidental as to whether in some moments the assembly finds just the person in whom there is a preponderance of pleasure and readiness for spontaneous presentation. However, the opposite extreme is where there is a completely constant difference, so that some are absolutely only communicating and others absolutely only receiving, where no exchange occurs either in the difference of persons or in the difference of moments. This extreme is represented in the mass, for here the priest alone is active, and all others are purely receptive and take up what is given, and in the whole course of worship, there occurs no change of this relationship. Such worship presents just as sharp an extreme as any other. This is so, for it can easily happen that those who are designated to take up what is given take up nothing at all any longer; thus no real relation between the two parts exists anymore. For if the mass is held in a foreign language and even its symbolism is not understood by everyone, indeed a certain general relationship can well be present, but as such the action itself coming into appearance can produce no living result, and there can be no thought of a truly mutual relationship between those who are self-active and those who are to take up what is given.

Thus both of these forms stand at a boundary, so that in both of them, each in an opposing way, the domain of worship disappears. Hence we can immediately conclude from this that what lies between these two extremes is a Christian form, with the proviso that each is obliged to continually increase the distance between one's own position and the closest extreme. Now, what more we would be able to adduce from these two points would belong to the realm of technique since in itself the difference between what is Evangelical and what is Catholic is exhausted in what has been said about their moral grounding. So what additionally is still recognized to be different in appearance and cannot be traced back to moral grounding is not to be understood in terms of the distinctive inner relationship that the two churches have with each other, but out of differences between peoples among whom one or the other forms of worship has become dominant.

Now, however, within this inequality, how is each person to determine his own place, or how is a person's place to be determined for him in a way that is truly moral? Where a specific form prevails in which those who are particularly active in worship make up a special class, one could want to trace this question back to the more general issue of choice and determination of vocation. However, in every case this would still provide only a very insufficient answer. This is so, for the kinds of vocations in the civil realm rest on the division of forms of work and the transmission of what is common to individuals. However, this analogy is not to be applied here at all. This is so, for division and transmission can never be seen here as something original; this is already taught by the most cursory look at the earliest condition of the church. Rather, here everyone is capable of being productive of presentation in some moments, and receptive in other moments. It would also be a debasement of this whole function if one wanted to trace it back to an analogy with the process of nature formation. Thus, in order to achieve a general solution to this task, we must consider the matter itself once more from another side.

As we have set up and explained presentational action, differentiating between worship in the narrower sense and presentational action in life, we have bound two elements together; we must discuss the relationship of the two elements still more closely. Our general explanation was that presentational action is nothing but the becoming outward of what is inner, the expression of feeling in an organic act. Our particular explanation, with which we have construed the narrower domain of worship, was that true worship is always put together out of artistic elements. Thus, now we come to a question that here we can only assume from another domain: How does the whole domain of art relate to the primary elements of the general explanation, that presentational action is expression? Psychology and aesthetics must actually give the answer, and here in a brief way we can take from them only as much as is indispensably necessary. Now everything that is a natural expression of feeling, of a definite inner stimulation, which passes over into the realm of art and which is simply elementary in the realm of art in the narrower sense, is also in terms of its original nature such an expression.

The two elements are interwoven with each other. That is, if we imagine the most original expression of stimulation, it consists of demeanor and tone. However, these are also elements of art: demeanor is the element of mimesis, tone the element of music. If we consider the plastic arts, which we could ignore here since they recede into the background in worship, it is certainly not so clear. However, everyone is still immediately aware that every inner construal of a picture is always the necessary reflex of an impression of a certain strength. So the inner construal rests on the impression that we have of a person, on the basis of which we later reproduce a picture of him. However, other parts of this domain rest originally on the fact that nature is a symbol of spirit, which belongs to our basic consciousness of the correlation and parallelism between corporeality and intelligence, and in this way even pictures that originally seem strange can be symbols of spirit, even if they are only symbols expressing inner states, expressing stimulations of spirit. However, art first arises out of the linking together and attachment of these individual elements.

The pure artistic element, considered as original expression, is always involuntary and to a great extent unconscious; but the composition, the actual art, is always completely conscious and can, in the first place, achieve a certain level of self-confidence only by means of completely developed consciousness. On this basis a relative opposition is formed for us between a form of presentational action that lies more on the side of what is involuntary and unconscious, and one that lies more on the side of what is conscious, and the task arises of dividing the two within the whole domain. With the fulfillment of this task, however, the practice itself is already anticipated, for it always precedes theory in these matters, and we are not to ignore it, but we are to justify it. That is, practice divides worship in the narrower sense into more public and more private forms, or into churchly and household forms. However, to the latter belong all quiet and solitary moments, when an individual naturally presents only to himself.

Now, if we view the solitary moments as an extreme on the one side, and a festival, the maximum of churchly worship, as the extreme on the other side, the relative opposition for us divides of itself into these two realms. This is so, for it is in the latter [festival] that presentation as an artistic whole has its place; in the former [solitary moments], unintentional expression of pious stimulation has its place. The more the occasion for worship lies in the shared life of individuals or in household life, the more it has a common character; and the more it is purely subjective, the more it is originally worship of a solitary person. That this is completely natural is immediately clear on the basis of the correspondence that is manifest here. Nonetheless, however, we must consider the matter yet more closely. Differences in the strength of self-consciousness are what is most originally involuntary. No one can say, "Now I am going to produce a strong feeling in myself." One can seek to do this, but one can have no assurance of success because there can be no method at all that can provide such assurance. Rather, it will only succeed when a proper presentiment of success present in the soul already underlies the very desire for success.

Likewise no one can say, "I will extinguish and exterminate a strong feeling in myself." To be sure, we are able to temper such feelings, but even tempering them is only possible by means of another element of life, thus introducing another activity. Consequently, first something else must enter between the two; a sheer act of will is not sufficient. Thus the actual determination of self-consciousness is what is involuntary, and here what is involuntary is the originating factor; consequently, the involuntary expression of self-consciousness is original. Truly, in individual lives nothing but this can occur, and the intention to put oneself into a strong religious stimulation at a specific time is, for individuals considered in themselves, something empty. However, this is surely the case only for individuals considered purely in themselves, so that, to be sure, our claim is not to be taken absolutely, precisely because no person can be thought of as absolutely isolated and without any connection to the whole.

WORSHIP IN THE BROADER SENSE

Worship in the broader sense exists in the presentation of the dominion of spirit in the Christian sense over flesh in what we have called the Christian virtues, insofar as they are not training, but pure performance. However, we must also remember here that in reality the different forms of action are always contained within one another; thus also that no broadening or purifying action can exist without this presentation of the dominion of the spirit occurring within it. That is, presentation of the dominion of spirit emerges thereby, completely apart from the actual purpose of the action, in the ease of its performance as presentation of the level of the spirit's domination over flesh. Consequently, the main definition, which we have taken as our starting point, only appears to be negative: worship is all actions insofar as they exclude broadening or purification as their true purpose. However, we must seek to change this definition into something positive because otherwise we will achieve nothing constructive.

If we return to the way we have distinguished the impulses of these actions from each other, it appears that the exclusion of the impulses out of which broadening and purifying arise is understandable in and of itself and is automatic. The impulse to broadening action is feeling in the form of pleasure, while consciousness of an excess of power binds itself together with consciousness of an object that is receptive to its influence. In purifying action the feeling of lack of pleasure is the impulse, while memory of an earlier more perfect condition binds itself together with a feeling of need. Now if we have to do here with self-consciousness insofar as neither pleasure nor lack of pleasure predominates in it [worship], but also as it [worship] relates itself to individuals not just insofar as they are members of individual religious communities, but also insofar as they stand precisely within the totality of life—then we must also seek for something by means of which this feeling, which appears to rest so completely in itself, can increase to become an impulse. Here we must remain with the opposition between spirit and flesh.

Presentation itself can only be an activity in which the relationship between spirit and flesh is revealed; this relationship is the ground of the self-consciousness that is to be presented. Thus, in like manner this action would require an occasion to present this consciousness, an occasion beyond the consciousness that lies at its ground, and consequently the action appears as a reaction to the occasion. If we hold fast to this, it follows that the action, insofar as it is predominantly presentational, relates itself as a reaction to what we indicate by means of the expression "affect," thus to that which is the "setting into motion of self-consciousness." In the wider sense of the word, affect must precede an emotional condition, to which presentational action expresses a reaction.

We can make this clear in the most definite way if we return to the symbolic idea of eternal life, in which it is posited that all broadening and purifying action is entirely completed, so that only presentational action remains. However, if we ask, "What kind of action is this presentational action that is thought of and described as the fulfillment of eternal life?" we find that it presents itself to us only as worship in the narrower sense, as the community of the sanctified involved in worship of God; this is so, for even presentational action in the broader sense can no longer find any place here because a complete separation is supposed between the blessed and those who are not yet blessed; thus there can no longer be any thought of what could be produced by an emotional condition in the blessed. Hence it appears that virtue, with which we are concerned here, rests on the presupposition of an emotional condition by which self-consciousness is stimulated in a definite way, and here is just the place to look at this more closely.

We want to consider this first in terms of some individual examples so that we can grasp the idea correctly and can then bring it to a complete construction much more easily. However, in order to do this it is best to return to some of the original philosophical terminology. Greek philosophy, especially from Aristotle onward, makes an essential distinction between σωφοσύνη[7] and ἐγκράτεια.[8] The latter of these virtues presupposes desire, an emotional condition; by contrast, the former virtue is actually to present an incapacity for the emotional condition of desire. When a person has a feeling of sensual inclination, but is able to subordinate it to a moral inclination, that is ἐγκράτεια. This applies to every kind of pleasure and every kind of lack of pleasure. However, σώφρων is that in which nothing appears that would be immediately disturbing or which would not have its immediate origin in something higher, which would not have its basis immediately in νοῦς. Yet how can σωφοσύνη be recognized? Only by means of comparison. With one-person states, stimulated self-consciousness occurs in which ἐγκράτεια manifests itself; but with σώφρων, stimulated self-consciousness does not occur; rather, the subordination of flesh to spirit stands fast in an a priori way. When a person is visibly stimulated to bitterness but controls himself, then he has ἐγκρατὴς θυμοῦ.[9] However, a person who remains in a state of pure contemplation without becoming stimulated to an affect is σώφρων.

Yet above all this presupposes that one can make the comparison, and then, that something is present out of which stimulation can proceed; thus a state in which what is complete and what is incomplete are present together. In our concept of eternal life, there is no such mixing; thus there our σωφοσύνη would be present in all because we think of all persons as being perfected, yet this σωφοσύνη would not come into appearance in anyone, but would remain something that is purely inner in everyone, because no comparisons could be drawn since all persons are equally perfect. Now, however, if we suppose some individuals who, on some occasion, bring others into an emotional condition, but remain completely without affect, so that not even the slightest beginning of a movement proceeding out of sensuality is visible, and also not the slightest beginning of an opposition between sensuality and spirit, two situations are possible. Either the individual's sensuality has a natural lack of excitability, he is ἀπαθής[10] by nature, or his sensuality is completely subordinated to spirit, thus his ἀπάθεια[11] is not natural; instead, it is a result of the dominion of spirit in him that is so perfected that no independent movement of sensuality is possible.

Distinguishing between these two presupposes a comparison of different states in the same person. If I had known the same person earlier in states in which he had stepped forward not as σώφρων, but as ἐγκρατής, but now I see him without affect, in spite of the fact that there is occasion for it to be stimulated—then I would have to suppose that the dominion of spirit in him has increased. However, if I had found him unstimulated in the same way, when spirit had not as yet gained dominion, I would have to suppose that his ἀπάθεια is a natural one, and then it would be a natural imperfection. Thus the presentational action with which we are now concerned exists, on the one hand, only in the domain of the continual temporal development of persons, and on the other hand, only where those who are morally more perfect and those who are morally more imperfect are mixed together, thus where every person is in circumstances where an occasion for sensual excitement can always arise.

Now, combining this with what we said earlier, we must stand fast and say, "Outside the domain of true presentation, worship in the narrower sense, there can be no predominantly presentational action, except insofar as it is related to the domain of impression and reactions to impressions, yet without at all intending an outer result, for an action having this intention would fail to be a purifying or broadening action." In accord with the principle that the different forms of action cannot be separated in actuality, we must surely say, "Presentational action in the broad sense, Christian virtues as pure performance, must always have a result, yet the result does not lie in its intention, but it is a συμβεβηκός,[12] existing *per accidens*, and the idea of the action is always only pure presentation."

Now, can we bring the Christian virtues in this sense under a general formula that comprehends their particular unity in such a way that we will be able to divide them again later? We must see the matter this way: "In order for such an action to occur, there would have to be the inner presupposition of a certain level of dominion of spirit over flesh, that is, a level sufficient for this instance. This is so, for otherwise only a purifying or a broadening action could occur, which still does not lie in the idea of this presentation." Beyond this, however, there is also presupposed an outer occasion, which, if the former inner level of dominion of spirit over flesh were not present, would call forth something else, brought about by what would have been the current deficiency in the dominion of spirit. However, from this it follows immediately that the more the dominion of spirit is manifest in an action as exertion, that much less is the action presentational in our sense; this is so, since exertion appears to the same degree that the dominion of spirit still needs an increase. Thus the dominion of spirit must have the character of ease, and now our formula is, "The action about which we are speaking is the presentation of the dominion of spirit without exertion. However, this is what, elsewhere, it has been customary for us to call 'the beautiful' or 'the graceful' in a moral respect, and precisely this, the morally beautiful or graceful in a distinctively Christian form, is the essential character of this presentational action."

Let us consider the matter from yet another side. Up to this point the expressions that we have used are not those of Christian speech; they are not native to Scripture, thus neither does what is distinctively Christian stand out in these expressions. However, let us imagine some person in the kind of situation where an emotional state would arise in him if his sensorial nature were not already subordinated to the divine Spirit to a certain level; how would this be indicated in Christian language, in Scripture? We would have to say, as temptation, for that is essentially the same concept—a stimulation of a person from outside by means of which something could be developed in him that would manifest a deficiency of the dominion of spirit over flesh and by means of which the dominion of flesh would later be strengthened. Thus, where a person has to undergo temptations, presentational action of which we are speaking is already no longer there, but in this case his action must, at the same time, have a purifying purpose, and therefore it must also pass over into a purifying action. And likewise from the other side, it must also be a broadening action, that is, an influence on that from which the temptation proceeds. Undergoing a temptation always involves exertion as well, and it is evident from all sides that our presentational action is conceivable only to the degree that exertion no longer exists and there is ease in the performance of virtue.

However, this leads us to yet another consideration. That is, the fact that a person is never to believe that he will be raised above all temptation appears appropriate to Christian character and can also be developed out of Christian character in a particular way; this is so, for only Christ arrives at this moral perfection. Christ is the only one who has been tempted in all ways, but is without sin; that is, Christ is the only one for whom everything which is temptation for us never becomes temptation at any level for him.[13] This is so, for just as little as we can imagine that he would undergo temptation can we imagine that first he would have to overcome temptation, because that would always have to presuppose an imperfection, a capacity for sin, in him.[14] However, precisely because this rests upon the distinctive character of Christ, in which the good was not something that was becoming but something that was original, here we must always set ourselves in contrast to Christ, and accordingly it appears as if we must say, "Only Christ was capable of our presentational action, because he alone with his absolute perfection was put under the conditions that we have presupposed as necessary for this presentational action." We, on the other hand, are never absolutely perfected; thus we are always subjected to temptation so that we must exist as being incapable of pure performance of virtue.

In spite of this, however, we cannot allow this rubric to remain empty in relation to us; it is likewise the case that everyone's feeling says to oneself that we must always make a distinction between an action that is predominantly expressive of being perfected, and an action that is predominantly expressive of perfection already attained. To be sure, the absolute fulfillment of the idea of presentational action in this domain is also only to be found in the life of Christ, so that in him everything was pure presentation. However, in a relative way we must also ascribe this action to every Christian as a person who is gradually expanding and being perfected even though he never reaches the perfection of Christ; the more perfect the Christian has already become, the greater the domain where he can present and express the growing perfection. Thus, here we abstract from the fact that a Christian never reaches the absolute ease of the dominion of spirit over flesh and is always at least still subject to a minimum of temptation in order to consider presentational action from our point of view, just as we abstract here from all results that we kept in view in a definite way when we spoke of Christian virtue in broadening action.

Chapter 9

The Outer or
General Social Sphere

Now there remains still for us the last area, namely, the consideration of presentational action in the common life of humanity insofar as it precedes the Christian community and accordingly is also older than it and relatively independent of it. This is so, for as in our consideration of broadening action, we divided formation of disposition from formation of talent, or divided churchly community from civil community, so we must also make an analogous division here. Strictly as such, however, civil community has its place completely in broadening action; in contrast, presentational action as such has its place in the social life of persons insofar as social life is precisely not what is truly industrious, but predominantly what is contemplative and enjoyable. Thus, here we must return to human intelligence, as it exists apart from the distinctively Christian principle, to spirit in the general human sense.

[COMMUNAL FORMATION OF PERSONS AND NATURE]

Now, if we wanted to see what was analogous to the higher self-consciousness in the Christian domain as it hovers between pleasure and lack of pleasure, it is presented to us entirely of itself when we see how social life in the communal formation of persons and nature on the one hand produces in self-consciousness a feeling of pleasure, and on the other hand produces a feeling of lack of pleasure, in accord with the sufficiency or insufficiency indicated in a given moment. This is so: since humanity's self-consciousness of its higher nature underlies both forms [pleasure and lack of pleasure], what is essential to humanity must pass over into presentational action, just as this is pointed out in the most definite way in all social relationships. Now when we spoke of worship in the narrower sense, we had already come to the place—precisely the place, considered in the general human development—in which art in the narrow sense is produced, and we have seen that this place must also provide the means for presentation. Each person takes part in some way, only with different measures of self-activity and receptivity, in what constitutes the life of art in the domain of a specific human society.

However, if this artistic life were totally lacking, then the condition at hand is one we call "coarseness," which however can never be ongoing: to the degree that the society becomes formed and mature, it also develops within itself a common domain of art. Now, this domain stands in contrast to the domain of worship in the narrower sense, identical with it by means of the identity of means of presentation, differentiated from it by means of the difference in what is presented. In the one domain it is the distinctively Christian life that is presented; in the other domain is the presentation of general human life, modified by the particular character of an interdependent community.

The general principle that all presentation presupposes community and creates and preserves community does not need to be recalled here, nor the fact that we must also accept that in this domain there are limiting points to community. That is, one limiting point is the absolute community of all with all, that surely is realized in no moment; however, still along with it what is always given is that no individual is excluded a priori from community; rather, each is immediately taken up in it, if the outward possibility for this is at hand and he is sufficiently advanced so that he can understand presentation. And then, the other limiting point is the primitive community, the community of nature: we find that humanity has always already transcended this because there is no condition in which a family could occur completely closed up from us in its individuality. And between these two limiting points, there are other communities, which are determined by means of relations of location and above all are separated by means of language. We have already anticipated all of this, and it can be presupposed in what has come before.

Now, however, can divisions also be made here, analogous to those that we have found in the actual religious domain? Of course. However, the limits cannot be drawn here in such a definite way as in the domain where we can judge everything more according to the same standard and can have fewer reasons to make divisions. And this cannot be otherwise. This is so, for in the religious domain the relation of the individual to the whole is dominant; in contrast, in general social life this relation is less important, and the relationship of one individual to another dominates. Therefore, here everything must be more mixed together, general human presentation in the narrower sense and in the wider sense: [1] the more conscious and organized, thus more in the character of a festival; and [2] the more arbitrary and immediate, thus emerging in more of a free form. In addition to that comes the following: We can well distinguish Christian worship as religious artistic presentation in what is grand from the manifestation of art in social life; however, in the presentation of the inner distinctiveness of an individual and presentation of the moral material on which he stands in terms of the relation of one individual to another, there are no means at all by which to separate worship in the wider sense from general human presentation since there are truly no means at all for that purpose. This is so, for the virtues named as Christian must also have dominion over relationships of one individual to another as a whole.

Thus, outside of this particular domain, we will still have to consider precisely how the virtues that we have pointed out as manifestations of what is Christian modify the relationships of persons in the general human domain that is outside of what is distinctively Christian, and how these relationships take up the character of these virtues in themselves. This is so, for it can only happen in this way because it is inconceivable that morally speaking there could be one self-presentation in one domain and a different one in another domain. Surely it happens often enough that conflicts arise between the claims of Christian ethics and what is permitted by general morality in social life. However, if such a conflict could be thought of as insoluble, a double conscience would have to be presupposed. Thus, where a double conscience exists, the task of resolving this conflict also exists, and we must seek the requisite principles for this task.

It is not necessary to give evidence of the existence of conflict, above all else in relation to the social relationships of individuals, since the existence of conflict can be recognized everywhere from each point of presentational action. Thus, if we consider the idea of purity, we find that a completely different standard for judgment is laid out in life as compared with the one we have put forward. And it is just this way in relation to patience and humility, for not seldom does social morality demand an assertiveness, which is dismissed by Christian humility as inappropriate; not seldom does social morality demand that one not suffer a wrong; in contrast to this, Christian patience calls for one to observe a completely different way of conducting oneself. Thus, conflict is present, yet how shall it be settled? We must return to that upon which the whole division of presentational action into two domains rests, the domain in which the Christian principle in the narrow sense is what is presented, and the domain in which the general human intelligence is what is presented—the domain in which Christianity is found to be already existing everywhere, the general social community of persons.

Yet how is Christianity to relate to what was in existence earlier than it was itself? If we look at the time of the emergence of Christianity, we see that conflict occurred there as well. The social life that Christianity found already existing was built upon heathen principles, and these principles were valid not only in terms of what was religious, but they also structured the morality of societal life in the most definite way, as, for example, the way that impurity was duly sanctioned in both domains. Thus, here the individual, because he is Christian, runs into conflict, and often there was nothing for him to do except either give up the rigorous nature of the Christian principle or be completely excluded from society. However, neither of these alternatives can be named "good" on the basis of the Christian principle since Christianity always demands both that an individual always remain true to Christianity and that he should seek to interject Christianity into public life.

Taken by itself, this does not yet exhaust the matter. For if we ask, "Are these two one and the same act—one in which an individual who has accepted Christianity takes up the Christian principle into himself, and the other in which he judges all cases in life on the basis of the Christian principle and rightly ascribes to it?" We must deny this since properly ascribing to a principle is a matter of practice, a readiness that is only acquired gradually. Thus, Christians in the earliest period surely did much that they only later recognized to be contrary to the Christian principle. Moreover, this admission that we must make regarding the development of individual feeling—this admission we find just as deeply rooted in the development of communal feeling, and thus it is often the case that the latter development even stretches over a whole series of generations.

It will not be difficult to prove this in a specific case. That is, no one will claim that dueling could be justified in a Christian way. Dueling is an action that is not self-contained, and in terms of its results it is the completely unintended outbreak of an aroused personal existence; hence the condition that produces it is completely contrary to Christian patience and gentleness. In spite of this, we still find dueling always present in Christendom; what is more, we find Christians justifying it. Accordingly, this means that we find a false submission to the Christian principle, which can always be traced back to a rigorous application of the Christian principle being somewhat relaxed owing to the influence of a communal feeling that is dominant in the society. Yet this situation always creates an inner contradiction in which no one can want to remain, and we have in this case the same situation that occurred so often for Christians in the earliest period, that there was nothing for the individual to do but to choose one of two options: either giving up the rigorous nature of the Christian principle, or excluding himself from his own society.

Yet is this a situation that we are able to praise and must see as ongoing? Certainly not, for it belongs to the moral task to overcome all such apparent moral contradictions. Wherein does the basis for this situation lie? It is based on the fact that the communal feeling in which Christianity found society already existing was not yet rightly penetrated by the Christian principle. However, what then is a Christian individual to do if he comes into the situation of having to choose between the two extremes of this dilemma? Christian ethics decides, "He is to remain true to the Christian principle even if he would have to allow himself to be excluded from a society in which the non-Christian element still exists; he is to preserve the rigorous nature of the Christian principle and proceed on the basis of the conviction that by doing so he will draw the company of people to his side sooner or later, and the communal feeling will be purified." A person who does the opposite of this declares that Christian feeling is too weak in him, as compared with another feeling, and that he is not in a place to be able to act as a Christian in all circumstances. He makes a confession in the presence of the totality that he needs a purifying action to be directed to himself so that Christian feeling can attain to the level of strength that he recognizes but that he has not yet been able to attain.

Thus we are able to recognize no other principle but this principle of rigor. Yet it must also be appropriately limited, not as if it would require a restriction, but only that it needs to be correctly understood, for it cannot be denied that many misunderstandings exist. That is, it is frequently completely overlooked that the presentational virtues are never to rest on natural apathy. And along with this, then, there comes at the same time another misunderstanding that is the antithesis of the previous one. That is, it is the same thing whether there is a deficiency of receptivity in me or whether no opportunity is given me to produce the state in which the presentational virtue can be expressed. Thus if one says, "In order to be certain of achieving this state, one must seek to remove all opportunities by which the state that is in doubt can be created." By means of this, presentational virtue will not be achieved, but it will be negated, for what happens along with this is essentially the same as what natural apathy produces.

For example, if we consider purity in relation to sexual desire, accordingly it is not to rest on natural apathy. Taking pleasure in physical beauty is not to be non-existent; rather, it is to be received, the only restriction being that lust is not to result from it. Now if one says, in order that lust not result, the sexes would have to be kept completely separate up until marriage, this means the complete negation of the virtue of purity for this period of time. Thus, if under the pretext of making the Christian principle valid, a structuring of social relationship is postulated that produces the same effects as natural apathy, this is a misunderstanding of the Christian principle. This misunderstanding is the basis, for example, of the Moravian discipline, according to which the sexes are separated as much as possible, and with this discipline the virtue of purity cannot arise; it can only be hindered because this discipline makes the appearance of this virtue impossible.

The same thing results when we consider purity in relation to any other sensorial pleasure. For if one says that one would have to refrain from everything that excites sensorial pleasure, purity would have no opportunity to indicate its presence since feeling would be uprooted and natural apathy would be produced. Thus, the greater portion of conflicts in this domain arise from false demands being made in the name of the Christian principle, just as all of ancient asceticism did nothing but proceed on this basis in order to produce apathy. The twofold morality that is in itself absolutely objectionable rests on ancient asceticism: a special morality for those who choose the ascetic life, and another morality for everyone else.

Or if we consider the matter in relation to forbearance, Christian ethics obviously says, "One who wrongs his neighbor is an object of true Christian pity, and one must direct a purifying action toward him." Yet precisely for that reason the feeling that results from being wronged is not allowed to produce any reaction at all, except to produce knowledge of the state in which the wrongdoer finds himself. And where this is the case, Christian gentleness is present. Thus, all the wronged Christian can do is to bring the one who has wronged him to a correct knowledge of his immoral state, or if there are circumstances that do not allow him to do this, then he must leave the matter to others, and it is nothing to him at all. If anything at all were grounded in the feeling that opposes the wrong committed, it would also need to be expressed in exactly the form in which it is given, that is, as communal feeling. If the community rebukes one who, as a Christian, acts against a wrongdoer, it does so in virtue of the communal spirit. Thus the community would also have to will the action opposing the wrong as communal feeling, and also the community actually does will it from one side in that it says, "We cannot judge what the individual holds to be correct, but as a member of our community, he is not to act in this way."

However, what would follow from this? This: that if the action opposing the wrong is to be willed as communal feeling, the reaction must also emerge in communal form, not as the action of an individual. Yet the feeling requires that the reaction be the direct action of an individual; thus the feeling is in contradiction with itself. If the communal feeling as such is to react and do so in a moral way, it can only react in definite forms. Now, in the civil community this happens where society looks after the individuals who have been wronged and is concerned that no wrong remain without an expression of public displeasure. However, this requires that the wrong can be comprehended within civil relations in a definite way. But it is said that there are wrongs that cannot be comprehended. Of course there are such wrongs, and then even the state cannot punish them. However, these wrongs will still be comprehended within social relations in general, or will be comprehended in some other relationships that are not civil in nature, be they as large or as small as they will. Now, if such a society recognizes something as punishable, good; then the reaction may proceed from it, and it may create the forms in which public displeasure against those who have committed a wrong can be expressed. However, if the society requires that the individual who has suffered the wrong avenge himself, that is wrong through and through. Thus, in this case the conflict is easily and precisely resolved.

A person who wants to act as a Christian must seek to create forms for the expression of public displeasure while he lets vengeance go. This is so, for it is certainly necessary that when something happens that habitually wrongs others, a presentation of general displeasure against the injustice is required, and this must be the basis for purifying action. However, purifying action must also proceed from communal feeling and be something communal, and the continuation of a system of personal revenge will be a direct hindrance to this. Meanwhile, if exaggerated demands are also put forward here, as they are in other domains, for example, those that claim one would have to get involved in every possible way of safeguarding against conflicts; this in turn is false because restraint on natural human relations arises from this and contradicts the Christian principle that aims precisely at penetrating all human relationships. Thus the general formula for all this is as follows: "The Christian as an individual must strive to manifest the presentational Christian virtues everywhere in all his social relationships with all individuals and always to work at the same time so that the communal feeling in each totality to which he belongs is ever more in agreement with the claims of the Christian principle."

This is true for the communal feeling in every totality to which he belongs: since the communal feeling is obviously such that as social circumstances are improved to a certain level, each individual belongs within a number of communities. This follows already from what we have said in the section on broadening action in relation to civil community. It is a necessary task to divide the general call for the formation of nature among persons so that a number of particular kinds of vocations arise and human community can first truly develop in this respect when the opposition between magistrates and subjects has emerged and when diverse smaller communities are brought together into one. Thus, indeed, we have a variety of communities for each individual. Each individual belongs to a community by virtue of his vocation, to another by virtue of the particular place that he has in the opposition between magistrate and subject, and another that he forms with all those who live in the same place with him, thus as a member of a local community: [these communities] constitute organic components of a greater whole.

Each of these different communities has its own particular principle; each has its own particular communal feeling, and in each something is found that still contradicts the Christian principle. Therefore the comparison of all these differences remains a standing task, and the individual must seek to have an effect on them in accord with the formula that we have set forth. Thus, on the one hand, the individual's conscience must always express the imperfection of each community, and on the other hand, the individual must bear the Christian principle in himself, in order to increasingly assimilate everything to it. . . .

[THE INNER CONSTITUTION
OF SOCIAL PRESENTATION]

Now let us go on to consider the qualitative aspect, the inner constitution of social presentation as this is a matter of moral principles. The first thing upon which this depends is what has already been set forth above: everything that belongs to the realm of social presentation is only permissible insofar as its impulse has its starting point not in sensuality, but in spirit. On the one hand, this rule is completely general: all human actions are moral only insofar as their impulse proceeds from spirit in a general human sense. On the other hand, if it is still to be a rule pertaining to Christian ethics, this can happen in two ways. One way is for us to be satisfied with saying, "Because the realm of social presentation existed prior to Christian presentation, we must acknowledge this realm in a general way, and our duty can only be to seek for instructions regarding this realm within particular limits." However, the other way is for us to immediately reduce what is considered to be a general ethical rule—presupposing the dominion of intelligence in a general human sense—to spirit in the Christian sense and claim that the impulse to social presentation must also have πνεῦμα ἅγιον as its starting point. The question is, "Which of these two is correct?"

Here we must return to the analogy with efficacious action, which always already existed as a necessary task before Christianity made its appearance. Here we could even say, on the one hand, "The whole process of nature formation is the general moral task of all persons, independent of every particular religious form, and thus also independent of the Christian form, and we recognize this with our Christian disposition." However, while we certainly claim that there are no special instructions to which the Christian is to submit in this regard, still together with this we do not deny that the totality of action in this domain would be modified in a particular way by means of the Christian spirit. However, on the other hand, we could also say, "The Christian spirit itself postulates this domain." This is the case in that the very Spirit of God is to prepare human nature to be a temple and an instrument; since human nature exists in a necessary interconnection with the whole of earthly nature, the Spirit of God's formative influence must also extend to the whole of earthly nature. However, it is clear from this that there will be no special instructions to which the Christian is to submit; yet it is also clear that for the Christian everything will be presented from a different point of view.

We will also be able to proceed here in the same way. Christianity has always found social presentation already preexisting it and has recognized the whole domain as existing naturally. Thus, however, the further formation of this domain has always gone its own way without being predominantly determined by Christianity. This is so, for only what is also a result of general moral instruction can be admitted in the formation process of this domain. Now we would have to make a complete revolution in this domain if its resulting from general moral instruction were to cease at any point, and we have no reason at all to do this. However, even if Christianity cannot put forth special instructions, there is still a middle way between sheer recognition and a particular material modification, that is, a way in which the point of view from which action proceeds is different insofar as in Christianity the ἅγιον πνεῦμα appropriates the κοινὸς λόγος. Now, however, to the degree that this point of view has already entered into the conception of the purpose of all actions that are included in this domain, one can always also say that the impulse for this action must also have its starting point in the Christian spirit. Thus, if according to the general apostolic rule nothing has power except faith that is active by means of love, and if as a result this rule expresses a general formula for every impulse that has its starting point in the Christian spirit, the Christian can also recognize only social presentation that corresponds to this rule.

Now, in order to see what more can be developed based on this account, we must ask, "What then is excluded from this domain of action if the Christian spirit provides its impetus?" The Christian spirit requires social presentation because social presentation is necessary for religious presentation and for efficacious action. All presentation, however, proceeds from a particular determination of self-consciousness that hovers between pleasure and a lack of pleasure, and precisely for this reason it also frees up a transition to either one. It is one thing to free up a transition to pleasure and the lack of it; it is another thing, however, to intentionally call forth one or the other. Thus, whenever social presentation aims at arousing pleasure, it already steps beyond its limit. That is, pleasure becomes an impetus to efficacious action. Now since in this domain of social presentation, intelligence is to manifest itself in its unity with the sensorial nature of persons, pleasure is not to attach only to one side of the relative opposition between intelligence and sensorial nature. Rather, it can just as well be sensorial as intelligent. However, whenever what is sensorial becomes an impetus, desire arises, and desire then obliterates the very character of presentational action. Accordingly, we must say that the agreement between social presentation and the standpoint of the Christian is limited by the fact that in social presentation nothing may happen from which desire would have to develop.

For example, it belongs to the customs of all peoples that eating and drinking are taken up into the domain of social presentation. Moreover, eating and drinking also belong essentially to this domain in that humanity has a natural need that can be satisfied only by having dominion over nature and thus by coming to know the stages by which that dominion over nature can grow. Now, if we accumulate objects from different parts of the world for a meal, this activity also belongs to social presentation insofar as we come to know the point at which the cultivation of natural resources stands. Moreover, one is also not to turn away from what is good tasting, rather being good tasting is a necessary feature, for what is bad tasting can in no way satisfy human need. It is true that sensorial desire is developed from the sensation of good-tasting food, from which one is not to turn away. Yet the moral character of this presentation is lost thereby, for desire's arising lies not in the matter itself, but in the immoral condition of the individual, in the fact that dominion of the spirit is not yet great enough in him. That is, every instance of sensorial sensation at the sensory level always has an objective aspect to it, insofar as something external is recognized on the basis of it, and that cognition can never be something nonmoral. This is also true for sensations of taste. They too have their objective aspect, which within it includes a feature of intellect: cognition. Moreover, to this degree the moral feature exists in these sensations of taste, and the more they incline toward connoisseurship, the more they must be kept pure and preserved from all desire. This is so, for what is purely objective immediately destroys desire, and only a deficiency of the dominion of the intellect in general and a deficiency of ability to objectify sensorial sensations can bring about the development of desire based on the necessary feature of sensorial good pleasure. Thus, here again we have a domain wherein a formation that is immoral can emerge from a formation that is in itself pure. However, this is always only a subjective matter for individuals, and each has his own distinctive measure in this regard.

However, just as social presentation may never aim to awaken pleasure, it also may not produce lack of pleasure. The latter rule surely appears to be opposed to the former in terms of form and seems to be empty in terms of content, precisely because social presentation never intends lack of pleasure, but always inclines itself more easily toward the opposite side. However, here we are not only talking about purposes, but also about natural results, since we must say, "It is an abuse of all the elements of social presentation when lack of pleasure is called forth; therefore precisely because it has this result, it is recognized as an abuse, therefore as something immoral." Overall in social presentation the lightness of life in general is to be revealed. However, there is an activity involved in this revelation that has its own natural limit, and if this limit is exceeded, it becomes an effort and calls forth lack of pleasure. In efficacious action there is to be effort, and the lack of pleasure that results from it is overcome, but it is not so in social presentation; in this case all effort can only be a sign that the presentation is impure. As a result of this, we are returned again to the quantitative aspect; however, both the qualitative and the quantitative aspects always form an opposition that is only relative. If it is always the case in actuality that the qualitative element, as we have identified it—if it is always only love that is active in social presentation, none of the degenerations we have described will result. This is so, for one who is led only by love can neither awaken desire nor lead others astray into exertion in social presentation, because both are opposed to love. And by means of each individual caring for all others, each individual is also cared for. Thus, if it is only love that is the common principle that all persons take as their starting point, then social presentation is safeguarded against all impurities.

Chapter 10

Social Presentation
in the Narrow Sense

At times social presentation appears more as art, at times more as play.[1] Some even conceive of all art under the category of play, that is, insofar as they define "play" as the general expression for all activity contrasted with work. Others, on the other hand, subsume all play under art, that is, insofar as for them "art" is the expression for all that is perfected in this domain. Nevertheless, we recognize the true nature of the relative opposition between art and play. Art as performance always supports theory, so that everything that belongs to the domain of art has the capacity for theory. On the other hand, play is activity-in-motion that is free, determinable in the moment, and the polar opposite of work. Also already included in this typical distinction is the idea that what is called art in the narrower sense of the word as viewed historically is generally something that can be made into a particular vocation. However, what appears in social life as play is regarded eo ipso as nonmoral, even if it can be pursued as an occupation only in the wider sense of the word.

ART IN THE NARROW SENSE

What we call art, as contrasted with free play, is also always a part of the process of nature formation, an activity of a definite human aptitude that can be brought to perfection only in and with art. In this way, for example, the speech arts are also the process for developing the capacity for speech, and indeed predominantly on the musical side, that is, on the side where speech is most immediately presentation. Thus if all human aptitudes are to reach their highest development, then art is also required, without which it can only meet the outward sensorial need, not the moral need, and without which the whole process of nature formation cannot attain an ethical level, but only an animal level. However, although all human aptitudes are to come to their highest level of development, still not all aptitudes are suitable or able in the same way to be the basis for a special vocation. No one can hold it to be immoral for a person to be a painter, for example, or a sculptor. However, is a tightrope walker an artist? Obviously the human body is a part of nature that is to be developed no less than is any other part of nature, but to make the development of the body into a special vocation is immoral.

A person who keeps the universal human task clearly in mind and has taken up a vocation is suited to contribute to the resolution of that vocation at every point; such a person may point out to us all the art involved in watercolor painting and never wound our moral feeling. However, if a person has no other vocation except that of watercolor painter, he neither has nor gives the smallest certainty of fulfilling the universal human vocation. Thus measuring the morality of a particular vocation depends on the measure in which it is in accord with the universal human vocation.

Still, what is excluded in this way is already excluded by means of rational ethics and thus also to be sure by means of the nature of Christianity. Now, however, does Christian ethics have to sanction everything else? Considered in and of itself, everything else that we have taken up (above) into the domain of Christian ethics proper must also be able to be an element of social presentation. Now we have indeed assigned the different forms of art to quite different places, but we still have excluded none absolutely. We have, for example, taken up miming as one of the natural ways of presentation through movement that is an aspect of speech in worship. Now, however, does it follow that it would also have to take a special and distinctive place in the domain of social presentation? If religious speech, like any other form of speech, to be sure, needs to be accompanied by miming, does it follow from this that that pantomime—miming emerging purely by itself and completely replacing speech—would also have to be given a place? Obviously, that would be too much inclusion. However, we may no more say that miming is to be excluded in and of itself. That anyone could make this into an actual vocation would surely appear to us as doubtful; this is so, for it is an activity that only involves the body. It can be brought to completion only by means of a great number of individual observations and practices, all of which concern only the outward form.

However, for this reason we still could not claim in a completely universal way that a Christian could not be a dancer. Thus we see that we need yet another principle in order to come to a decision about this matter. Christianity entered into society at a time when it was already developed so that all the different artistic domains had already emerged, including those about which Christianity may have had doubts. How had these artistic domains been formed? Obviously, along with the development of the nation, but also in such a way that the character of the non-Christian religion was always carried with it. Now what is national is always something that is not objectionable in and of itself. However, concerning non-Christian religions, it appears that the only rule that can be valid is the one the apostle gives: "I know that idols are nothing, so sacrifice to idols is also nothing."[2] That is, what the apostle says here about the way heathen religions affect a meal is valid for all works of art. If a Christian at the time of the apostles was at a family celebration where everything was still carried out in the old ways because the majority of the participants remained heathen, and some poetic works were recited in which there was mention of heathen gods, the Christian would not have to leave, but would take everything in merely as poetry.

The same thing can be applied to our situation. That is, viewed from one side, the whole of our modern culture is chock-full of what is old. Our own national antiquity had been in ruins for a long time and only later was again taken up into the domain of presentation. Thus when use was made of Greek mythology in many different ways, was that utterly unchristian? Obviously it is less so insofar as the presentation is removed from the truly religious domain. However, the more such poetry came to be a direct expression of inner disposition, the more an indifference toward Christianity would have to be presupposed therewith; this is so, for heathen presentation is not suitable to express Christian disposition. Thus, if a poet is able to believe that, in relation to the higher life, his own disposition is best expressed by means of the medium of heathen representations, this also means that the domain of Christian means of presentation is foreign to him, and that must stain the matter.

Let us consider this in another domain. Should a painter or may a painter still reproduce forms that are now recognized to be mythological? One who says an unqualified "No," one who wants to say that every painter among us who reproduces mythological forms can have no true Christian life in him, would commit sin. Surely presentation is not to be tolerated where purity and chastity are lacking—the general virtues in all presentation; however, if heathen subjects are presented in a pure and chaste way, this can happen with a sense that is perfectly Christian. This is so, for then the means of presentation have only symbolic importance, and only if they lack purity and chastity do we need to return to the notion that the artist would have used Christian means of presentation if he had had more Christian feeling. Now, however, to the degree that our culture is not chock-full with antiquity—for our actual popular culture has never been permeated with it—to that degree we would have to say, "In the domain of purely popular presentation, it would not be unchristian but only awkward and inappropriate to use heathen elements that are as yet understandable only to those who are cultured."

Regarding the art of poetry, however, this is valid in a special way since for us poetry is grounded in the classical ancients, so that throughout our history we find both kinds of poetry side by side, one kind that is based on what is popular, and another kind that is based on the imitation of the ancients. In a particular time period, the more the two kinds take up elements from each other, the more there is unity in that time period and the more complete its productions are. Now, if for the ancients drama was the most completely developed form of art, is it in and of itself a form that is distinctive to them? Surely not; to a much greater degree it is based in the essence of human nature itself, being the most immediate representation of everything that persons have done and do; wherever there is historical poetry, all the elements pertaining to drama are present. Surely, when Christianity entered into ancient society, the dramatic arts were already in decline, and therefore Chrysostom and others were completely correct to agitate against those who visited the theater, but in general still only insofar as the Christians of that time remained in an inner sense so near heathenism that for them to see it would easily be an immediate temptation.

Thus, they say much too much who conclude, "Because the ancient teachers of the church agitated against the theater, Christianity refuses to give its sanction to dramatic poetry and its presentation." In the first place, this is so since a person who speaks against the theater still in no way speaks eo ipso against dramatic poetry; and then there were also dramatic treatments of Christian subjects in the church from earliest times since the whole legend of the church rests to some extent on a dramatic presentation it sanctioned. Now, however, if one makes dramatic presentation into his vocation, how is this to be judged? We have said that it would be doubtful whether one could be a tightrope walker or a dancer as a profession; does this also apply to a dramatic artist? This is not the case, at least not on the same grounds, for the dramatic artist has to do with intellectual subjects, as he can only bring his art to perfection through the keenest and most exact observation of persons and the constant study of a kind of poetry that has excellent intellectual content. However, one asks, what is an actor? Is he different from what the ancients said about slaves? Is he not the ὄργανον ζῷον[3] of the poet? And not only of one poet, but also of many different poets? Thus would he not have to give up all of his own character? However, this is entirely empty.

This is so, for anyone who studies history must do the same thing that the actor does; since in general there is surely no better means of coming to self-knowledge than by placing oneself in the most exact way into the development of a life that is foreign to one: we all find within ourselves all the germs of all forms of passion. Thus if an actor has a character that is exclusively good, he will

surely not lose that good character by means of study and presentation if, moreover, he brings only the correct grounding to the process. However, the matter
stands this way. An actor exists in a twofold relationship to the author and to
the public. If the author wants the actor to present outwardly in a precise and
exact way what is within the author and the way it is inner in him, this is not
possible. This is so, for since the author always creates characters only in terms
of the plot, they are always only indefinite with him. However, in order for the
actual character to stand out, each author gives him a definite life, and the plot
is only a portion of this. The author who composes a drama or even the person
who reads a drama necessarily pictures the character. However, the characters are
essentially so indefinite that it is impossible for them to be defined by everyone
in one and the same way since the same role is always conceived in completely
different ways by different actors.

Thus if the task is not grasped in this way, nothing can result except for
the actor's considering only the details that are related to outward presentation,
and then his vocation must certainly appear to be very dubious. However, this
attaches itself only to our contemporary form of theater. If we consider the
ancients, this relationship does not exist at all. The author rehearsed the actors
himself; everything else was only a representation of a past time that was usually
intended for the audience itself, so there was nothing impossible in the actor's
task, nor could there be any attention at all to the small details of form, facial
expressions, and such because of the use of masks. In this way there have been
good conditions in modern comic theater, especially among the Italians, in that
a comedy provided only the main ideas; thus the actor continuously improvised
on the ideas of the author and consequently was an artist in a very special sense.
However, among us the relationship is the most disadvantageous that one can
imagine. The ancient tragedians were never only actors; their art did not require
them to have a special vocation. On the other hand, we have persons who are
actors as a profession, and their art is based on practicing in a mirror ahead of
time. Comic actors of the Italian sort were correct to make their art into a vocation for it was worth the effort. Our actors must of necessity make their activity
into a proper vocation, and yet it is not worth the effort.

PLAY AS IT IS RELATIVELY
OPPOSED TO ART

The terminology that has been dominant for a long time subsumes the concept
of "art" under the concept of "play" in order to set art in opposition to efficacious
action, which is comprehended under the concept of the "serious." However,
all play, when it is thought of in its perfection, must still also be subsumed
under the concept of art. Accordingly, how are these two concepts to be distinguished? The difference lies in the fact that in the domain of art there is always a

distinction between the activity and the actual work of art, even if this does not happen in the same way in all artistic domains. On the other hand, in play the activity is the work itself, and there is nothing between what is objective (when it becomes a work of art) and what is subjective (the activity).

Here, also, two points of origin are to be distinguished: one that comes out of public life and one out of private life. In ancient times we find that play in public life was completely dominant; competitive[4] play was a constitutive element of the public life of a people, and schools of this time were places in which youth already participated most fully in public life as well. Among us, where a people's public life has receded so completely, this form of play is at a minimum; at present what we call play is found solely in private society, which is joined to household life. Does this perhaps rest on the difference between Christian character and non-Christian character? Is play in the form of the public life of a people perhaps no longer Christian at all? Historically speaking, much may be said about this matter; this is so, for from very early—and surely just at the time that it began to shape life in a new way—Christianity turned predominantly to peoples who lived in a climate that made it difficult to have a public life. And not only is this so, but we also find that under more favorable natural conditions, a people's public life itself is pushed into the background in the strongest way in Christian times, even in those countries where in earlier times it had been present most powerfully. However, I still do not believe that anything can be proved on the basis of this connection. We have said that Christianity would surely always call for a state to be created where one was not to be found and that it does not favor any particular form of state. At this point, to be sure, an antagonistic kind of reasoning begins to develop; however, it rests solely on a prejudgment, and we Evangelicals may not hold back from immediately contradicting it in its most basic elements. This is so, for its opinion actually goes to the idea that Christianity has by its very nature an inclination toward monarchy, but that Protestantism inclines toward republicanism or at least is antimonarchy and is consequently non-Christian. Who can fail to see in this reasoning the political influence of public and secret Catholicism! However, we contradict this by saying that we are also good subjects, and that in spite of this we feel ourselves obliged as Christians to claim that even republicans in the strongest sense of the word can be Christians just as well as the best monarchists.

Now, if differences in the public lives of peoples do not depend immediately and exclusively on differences in the form of the state, still this is not at all to deny all connection between the two. That is, if different forms of the state are considered in their individuality—and insofar as this happens, we may look at the inclination to an open life in which play has its place, not as a residue or as an indication of unchristian elements—then we must say that resuming the ancients' form of play could only be looked at as a residue of heathenism insofar as it was joined together with heathen religion. However, it is obvious that play must be structured and judged in a completely different way depending on whether it belongs to the public life of a people or to private society. That is, in the latter case the first and original element of social intercourse is discourse. However, in the public life of a people where a great number of persons are together, discourse cannot be the most basic element. This is so, for if this were the case the whole would be broken up immediately into a number of small circles. Therefore, nothing remains here except art and play, and the matter has constituted itself in this way from the beginning.

Now, however, it is obvious that the whole mass of people is only in a state of receptivity when we are talking about art proper. This is so, for if the graphic arts were displayed or a drama were staged or there were some form of poetry recital in public, in these cases the mass of people could always only receive, and in that case the public character could only be the joint establishment of the same state of mind in all those present. It is only in the case of music, as it is manifest as religious presentation, whereby the whole congregation can be productive, and also by means of the general social form of this art, that general activity can be produced. To this musical presentation, however, mimic presentation is joined in public life in a completely natural way, so it is as if yet another form of art is always invited, that is, the mimicry of dance, which then provides a transition to play insofar as this presentation is a physical accomplishment, and the whole domain of competitive gymnastics is opened to the public life of a people along with it. The different forms of art depend on the character of a people and on climate, so that we will have to say at once, "Everything that belongs to this domain is already justified on the presupposition of moral purity and chastity, wherever there is a public life of a people." However, we will not easily be able to find something different that, when it intends to take the place of this kind of play, does not at once break apart the public character, the unity of the great mass of people in social presentation, and change it into a mere aggregate of circles of private sociality. Surely this seems to be the case wherever play is not as perfectly organized as it was in antiquity and already seems to be so with gymnastic play; however, although the masses are also divided in this, it is not yet necessarily the case that the unity is lost; instead, one can imagine the alternation between spontaneity and receptivity as a constant flow. On the other hand, if we imagine a great mass of people broken up into, for example, card-playing groups, unity and communal character are completely lost.

Notes

Preface and Acknowledgments

1. Brian A. Gerrish, *Grace and Reason: A Study in the Theology of Luther* (Oxford: Oxford University Press, 1962; Midway repr., Chicago: University of Chicago Press, 1979).
2. James M. Brandt, *All Things New: Reform of Church and Society in Schleiermacher's Christian Ethics* (Louisville, KY: Westminster John Knox Press, 2001).

Translator's Introduction

1. In 1989 John Shelley published his fine translation of *Friedrich Schleiermacher: Introduction to Christian Ethics* (Nashville: Abingdon Press). This makes available to English readers the 1826–27 version of the introductory materials to Schleiermacher's lectures on Christian ethics. It is a translation of *Schleiermacher: Christliche Sittenlehre. Einleitung*, ed. Hermann Peiter (Stuttgart: Kohlhammer, 1983). Our English translation presents Ludwig Jonas's edition of the *Christliche Sittenlehre*, based on Schleiermacher's lectures of 1822–23 (Berlin: G. Reimer, 1843). Schleiermacher himself had commissioned Jonas to prepare the Ethics materials for publication. Jonas chose the 1822–23 course of lectures because he had five student transcriptions from that year as well as notes from Schleiermacher's own hand on the purifying action. He used all these materials to create his text. Jonas also inserts long footnotes which include comparative materials from other years and four lengthy appendixes of lecture material from other years. This translation provides about one-third of the main corpus of the Jonas edition.
2. Friedrich Schleiermacher, *On Religion: Speeches to Its Cultured Despisers*, trans. Richard Crouter (Cambridge: Cambridge University Press, 1988), 103, 92, 115.
3. Richard Crouter, *Friedrich Schleiermacher between Enlightenment and Romanticism* (Cambridge: Cambridge University Press, 2007), 7.
4. Dawn DeVries and B. A. Gerrish, "Providence and Grace: Schleiermacher on Justification and Election," in *The Cambridge Companion to Friedrich Schleiermacher*, ed. Jacqueline Mariña (Cambridge: Cambridge University Press, 2005), 198.
5. Ibid.
6. John Shelley, "Translator's Introduction," in Shelley, *Schleiermacher: Introduction to Christian Ethics* (1826–27), 18.
7. See below, "Introduction" in "Division II: Broadening Action."

8. Immanuel Kant, *The Critique of Practical Reason*, trans. Lewis White Beck (Indianapolis: Bobbs-Merrill Educational Publishing Co., 1956).

9. Claude Welch, *Protestant Thought in the Nineteenth Century*, 2 vols. (New Haven and London: Yale University Press, 1972–85), 1:47.

10. See below, "General Introduction."

11. Thandeka, *The Embodied Self: Friedrich Schleiermacher's Solution to Kant's Problem of the Empirical Self* (Albany: State University of New York Press, 1995), 25.

12. Ibid., 27.

13. Friedrich Schleiermacher, *Friedrich Schleiermachers Dialektik*, ed. Rudolf Odebrecht (Leipzig: J. C. Hinrichs Verlag, 1942), esp. 12–28 and 42–44. See also Hans-Joachim Birkner, *Schleiermachers christliche Sittenlehre im Zusammenhang seiner Philosophisch-Theologischen Systems*, Theologische Bibliothek Töpelmann (Berlin: Töpelmann Verlag, 1964), 31–33.

14. Schleiermacher, *Dialektik*, 174–83, 187–208; also Birkner, *Schleiermachers christliche Sittenlehre*, 33.

15. Martin Redeker, *Schleiermacher: Life and Thought* (Philadelphia: Fortress Press, 1973), 166.

16. *Entwürfe zu einem System der Sittenlehre*, vol. 2 of *Friedrich Ernst Daniel Schleiermacher Werke: Auswahl in vier Bänden*, ed. Otto Braun and Johannes Bauer, 2nd ed. (Leipzig: Feliz Miner, 1927–28), 531–40. Hereafter referred to as *Philosophical Ethics*.

17. Friedrich Schleiermacher, "Über den Begriff des höchsten Gutes," in *Sämmtliche Werke*, div. 3, vol. 2, ed. Ludwig Jonas (Berlin: G. Reimer, 1843), 466.

18. Friedrich Schleiermacher, *Brief Outline on the Study of Theology*, trans. Terrence N. Tice (1811; Richmond: John Knox Press, 1970). Hereafter referred to as *Brief Outline*.

19. See below, "General Introduction"; and Brandt, *All Things New*, 6–8, 46–51.

20. See below, "General Introduction."

21. *Brief Outline*, 80.

22. See below, "General Introduction."

23. Birkner, *Schleiermachers christliche Sittenlehre*, 113, citing Wolfgang Trillhaas, *Ethik* (Berlin: Töpelmann, 1959), 192.

24. Brandt, *All Things New*, 53.

25. See John Thiel's argument in *Imagination and Authority: Theological Authorship in the Modern Tradition* (Minneapolis: Fortress Press, 1991) that the valorization of authorial imagination and creativity as having authoritative weight is what distinguishes modern theology from earlier forms. From this perspective, Schleiermacher is the founder of modern theology.

26. Thandeka, *The Embodied Self*.

27. William Schweiker, "Consciousness and the Good: Schleiermacher and Contemporary Theological Ethics," *Theology Today* 56, no. 2 (July 1999): 193.

28. Garrett Green, "The Relevance of Schleiermacher's Ethics Today," in *Friedrich Schleiermacher's "Toward a Theory of Sociable Conduct" and Essays on Its Intellectual-Cultural Context*, ed. Ruth Drucilla Richardson (Lewiston, NY: The Edwin Mellen Press, 1995), 74.

29. Brandt, *All Things New*, esp. 70–78.

30. Schweiker, "Consciousness and the Good," 196.

31. Ibid., 193.

32. Ibid., 190.

33. Ibid., 193.

34. See below, "Introduction" in "Part II: Presentational Action."

35. H. Richard Niebuhr, *Christ and Culture* (New York: Harper & Row, 1951), 190–227. For a fuller discussion of the *Christian Ethics* and the transformative type, see Brandt, *All Things New*, 109–30.

36. In the context of twenty-first-century religious pluralism after Christendom, Schleiermacher's expectation that Christianity would expand and ultimately include all persons appears naive and oppressive. In relation to other religions, it should be remembered that in his own context, Schleiermacher was unusual among theologians of his time in affirming the positive religious good in other religions (at least Judaism and Islam) and not rejecting them out of hand as idolatrous.

37. See below, "The Inner Sphere or the Church" in "Part II: Presentational Action."

38. See below, "Division II: Broadening Action in the State."

39. See below, "Different Communities Must Work Together" under "Broadening Action in the State" in Division II.

40. In this connection note Joerg Rieger's incisive critique of Schleiermacher's position on colonization, in *Christ and Empire: From Paul to Postcolonial Times* (Minneapolis: Fortress Press, 2007). Rieger acknowledges Schleiermacher's rejection of the use of force in the expansion of Western civilization. He also identifies ways in which Schleiermacher's theology and ethics buttress the colonial process, assuming the superiority of Western culture. Schleiermacher's emphasis on the reign of God as the absolute community of all with all may provide a resource for overcoming the imperialism he supports in significant ways.

1. General Introduction

1. The title and topic of this work is *Christliche Sittenlehre*, rendered here as Christian ethics. Translating *Sittenlehre* as "ethics" is the better English translation even though it misses the important denotation of the German term that the topic is doctrine or teaching (*Lehre*) of the Christian life. *Sitte* ordinarily refers to "customs" or "mores," but this is not the sense of the term here.

2. In contexts such as this I have chosen to use masculine pronouns when translating a reference to a human person. I strongly endorse inclusive language in reference to human persons in the 21st-century context. However, I have found that the attempt to use inclusive language for persons in a translation that remains true to the sense and syntax of Schleiermacher's German results in English constructions that are awkward and confusing. In addition, the use of masculine pronouns when necessary is in keeping with the practice of English usage contemporary to Schleiermacher.

3. The German *wissenschaftlich* is rendered here as "scientific." *Wissenschaft* is science in the broadest sense, encompassing all academic disciplines. For Schleiermacher, *Wissenschaft* comprises physics (the study of the natural world) and ethics (disciplines dealing with all realms of human historical life).

4. *Lehre* means both "teaching" and "doctrine."

5. The term here is *Glaubenslehre*, literally, "faith doctrine." This is the title Schleiermacher gives to his magnum opus (ET: *The Christian Faith*, ed. H.R. Mackintosh and J.S. Stewart. Edinburgh: T. & T. Clark, 1928); the title indicates that dogmatics is teaching about the faith, a second-order reality that is one step removed from faith. The parallel between *Sittenlehre* and *Glaubenslehre* indicates that these two are coordinate disciplines and together make up the whole of doctrinal theology. I have chosen to translate *Glaubenslehre* as "dogmatics" instead of "faith doctrine" because the former term has the weight of tradition behind it and has a common, public meaning that "faith doctrine" lacks.

6. The Greek term indicates what is "technical"; for Schleiermacher this means the actions that embody and manifest inner forms of Christian feeling. *Kunstlehre* is the German term here—in English we speak of the arts of ministry. For Schleiermacher all practical theology is a form of *Kunstlehre*.

7. The German *thetische*, a technical term in use at Schleiermacher's time, means "thematic."

8. The German root is *gelten*, which can mean "be valid" or "have currency."

9. Not just "knowledge," but "rules or ordinances passed over to the church."

10. Latin: "There are as many opinions as there are heads" (Terence, ca. 190–159 BCE).

11. "Ethics is also dogmatics."

12. *Heiligung* also has the more technical theological meaning of "sanctification."

13. The Greek word for "impulse."

14. The reference here is to Kant, particularly his second *Critique, The Critique of Practical Reason*.

15. The German here is *geistig*, which derives from *Geist* or spirit. *Geist* has primary reference to functions of the intelligence, mental activity. It can also be rendered as "spiritual," but this can be misleading in English where "spiritual" has religious connotations. Here it is a reference to "human spirit" in a general way.

2. Purifying or Restoring Action in the Christian Congregation

1. "Originating action" translates the German *Protonomie*, a rare term used occasionally by Schleiermacher.

2. *Geistig* is usually rendered as "mental," and *Geist* in persons, though rendered as "spirit," has primary reference to intelligence. Thus while I translate *geistig* as "spiritual" in this context, the term's broader connotation must be borne in mind.

3. Schleiermacher refers here to the French rule of Prussia under Napoleon (1806–13). During this period Schleiermacher was active as part of the reform movement led by Baron Karl Freiherr vom Stein that sought to overthrow the yoke of Napoleon and to reform Prussia along republican lines.

4. See below, 137–83 on "Presentational Action."

5. *Historisch* has the sense here of having actually occurred in a specific history.

6. *Öffentlichkeit*, which has the basic meaning of "being public," is here translated as "public character." At some points below *Öffentlichkeit* is translated as "public expression" where this seems to be a more appropriate way to render it in English in a particular context.

3. Purifying Action in Which the Civil Element Is Co-constitutive

1. *Hauswesen* is translated as "domestic life."

2. *Pathematical*, with its root in the Greek πάθος, παθηματικός, denotes a form of suffering that arises from a weakness of the will.

3. The German *Obrigkeit* has the primary meaning of "authority." It is translated here as "magistrate" (a secondary meaning) because the clear reference is to persons who hold authority.

4. Rom. 12:21.

5. The German is "*das handeln des Staates als Obrigkeit.*" We usually render *Obrigkeit* as "magistrate" or "authority"; here the point is the state's status as self-governing, without a concrete expression of government above or beyond itself.

6.   Warfare in early nineteenth-century Europe was conducted largely by means of opposing armies facing each other and moving directly at each other as a whole or in phalanxes. "Outposts" were sometimes used, especially for providing supply and communication and accompanying protection. Conducting raids, pursuing battles in the area of these outposts ("outpost war," German: *Vorpostenkrieg*) is condemned by Schleiermacher as unchristian.

4. Introduction [to Broadening Action]

1.   John 15:16.
2.   Gal. 5:17, "desires/lusts" are to be overcome.
3.   "Doing" and "suffering."
4.   "Community" or "fellowship."
5.   "Mind" or "intelligence."
6.   "Spirit," for Schleiermacher here in a distinctively Christian sense.
7.   Gal. 4:4.
8.   Rom. 7:14.
9.   Gal. 4:4, "When the fullness of time had come."
10.   2 Cor. 10:6.

5. Broadening Action in the Church

1.   The German is *Geistesgaben*, which means "talent" or "gift," especially of the mind or spirit. In other places Schleiermacher uses the German word *Talent*.
2.   *Geschlechtsgemeinschaft* is here translated as "marriage" or "marriage union." The German term literally means "sexual community."
3.   See 1 Cor. 7:12–14.
4.   See 1 Cor. 7:15.
5.   See 1 Cor. 7:16.
6.   Matt. 5:32.
7.   See 1 Tim. 3:2; Titus 1:6.
8.   Matt. 19:3–9; Mark 10:2–12.
9.   Eph. 5:22–32.
10.   Mark 10:11–12.

6. Broadening Action in the State

1.   For Schleiermacher, "intelligence," the capacity for understanding, is common to all persons. This is not to say that all persons have the same knowledge or intelligence, but that the basic capacity for understanding is the same in all. More importantly, in this context, is Schleiermacher's claim that intelligence is a collective or communal capacity which has moral significance in terms of its development in the human race as a whole.
2.   The German is *Eigenthums*.
3.   The German is *Verkehrs*.
4.   Rom. 13:5.
5.   The German here is *individuelle*, which in Schleiermacher has the sense of being "distinct" or "distinctive."
6.   The German adjective here is *einzelnen*, which has the sense of individual as pertaining to a particular person or other unitary identity.
7.   "Par excellence."

8. "A living machine/tool"; cf. ὄργανον ἔμψυχον (living tool) in Aristotle, *Nicomachean Ethics* 8.11; *Politics* 1.4.
9. This material is from the lectures of 1826–27, included in the Jonas edition as a footnote.

7. Introduction [to Presentational Action]

1. The Greek is "common reason" which Schleiermacher believes is present in all persons.
2. Greek is the "Holy Spirit."

8. The Inner Sphere or the Church

1. "With one mind, by common assent," as in Acts 15:25.
2. Acts 2:42–47.
3. The German word translated as worship is *Gottesdienst*, which means "service of God." In what follows, Schleiermacher explores the meaning of service of God.
4. The efficacious action that Schleiermacher has in mind here is broadening action; purifying action is not under consideration at this point.
5. See 1 Cor. 10:31.
6. "By the operating of the operation," that is, the sacraments have power in themselves, a position articulated by Augustine in opposition to the Donatist movement.
7. Usually translated as "sound judgment."
8. Usually translated as "self-control."
9. "Control of one's anger."
10. "Apathetic, lacking interest."
11. "Apathy, lack of interest."
12. "Side effect."
13. See Heb. 4:15.
14. Schleiermacher's interpretation of Christ's sinlessness and the possibility of his temptation is at odds with some New Testament passages (e.g., Mark 1:12–13; Matt. 4:1–11; Luke 4:1–13; and Heb. 5:6–8). The position articulated here is consistent with the Christology in *The Christian Faith*, §§ 93–99. For Schleiermacher, Christ's sinlessness, his perfect God-consciousness, precludes the possibility of genuine temptation. See Jacqueline Mariña, "Christology and Anthropology in Friedrich Schleiermacher" in *The Cambridge Companion to Friedrich Schleiermacher*, ed. Jacqueline Mariña (Cambridge: Cambridge University Press, 2005), 151–70, and Catherine L. Kelsey, *Thinking about Christ with Schleiermacher* (Louisville, KY: Westminster John Knox Press, 2003).

10. Social Presentation in the Narrow Sense

1. This material comes from the lectures of 1824–25 dealing with general social presentation.
2. See 1 Cor. 8:4; 10:19.
3. "Living machine/tool"; cf. ὄργανον ἔμψυχον (living tool) in Aristotle, *Nicomachean Ethics* 8.11; *Politics* 1.4.
4. The German is *agonistische Spiel*, from the Greek ἀγών, "assembly" or "contest." The reference is to a wide variety of competitive contests in the ancient world, from athletic to literary.

Index

absolute community, 17
academy, as human community, 8
action
  broadening. *See* broadening action
  efficacious. *See* efficacious action
  forms of, defining ethics, 10–11
  impulse toward, 43–44
  including all other forms of, 102
  internal and external, 30
  nonefficacious, 47–48
  opposing determinations of, 60–61
  presentational. *See* presentational
    action
  restorative. *See* restorative action
  restoring (or purifying). *See* restoring
    action
activity
  presupposing a deficiency, 38–39
  without result, 42–43
  two formulas for, 47
affect, preceding an emotional condition,
  163–64
affect theology, 13
annulment, 112–13
apologetics, 21
art, 45–46. *See also individual genres*
  life of, within human society, 168
  relation of, to play, 177, 181–83
  relation of, to worship, 157, 158,
    161
  required for highest human
    development, 178
artistic expression, 3–4, 12
asceticism, 171–72

Barth, Karl, 14
Bildung, ethics of, 15
Birkner, Hans-Joachim, 14

blessedness, 11, 140–45
  absolute, 38–42, 44, 45
  as becoming, 40–41
  as impulse, 40
  as true and basic feeling for a
    Christian, 147–48
Bonhoeffer, Dietrich, 14
Brief Outline on the Study of Theology
  (Schleiermacher), 9–10
broadening, extensive and intensive, 117
broadening action, 11, 12, 15, 44, 47–48,
  56
  always transitive, 100
  beginning and ending points of, 108
  direction of, 116
  as essential action of the church,
    114–15
  explaining the saving action of Christ,
    99–100
  including purifying element, 102
  individual nature of, 102
  individual's participation in, 59
  presupposing and creating community,
    103–4
broadening process
  individuals taking part in, at certain
    point of development, 125–26
  proceeding from moral consciousness
    motivated by pleasure, 125
brotherly love, 16–17, 145

Categorical Imperative, 6
Catholic Church
  contrasting priests and laypeople,
    149–50
  on divorce and annulment, 112
  excluding from participation
    individuals with impurities, 58–59